Dear Jiten

Amplify Your Orgasm

A Practical Guide
for Women and Men
on How to Have More Orgasm

I wish you an amazing sexual
exploration and path of amplified
orgasm. I wish that all your
sexual desires, fantasies and longings
are fulfilled and that you get to

By Michael Charming

experience whole-body and transcendental
orgasms.
With lot of love & regards

28.11.2028.

Amplify Your Orgasm: A Practical Guide for Women and Men on How to Have More Orgasm

First printed in the United Kingdom, 2019

Published by Conscious Dreams Publishing
www.consciousdreamspublishing.com

Edited by Sharon Elber

ISBN: 978-1-912551-83-5

DEDICATION

This book is dedicated to:

All the lovers in the world who desire…
   deeper relationships, nourishing sex, and amplified orgasm.

All the people who desire…
   authentic human connection and to live to their highest potential self.

Every single being who desires…
   to uncover the mysteries of self to discover love, peace, and serenity.

And, as always, *Dad, Mom, Brother, Sister-in-law*, and *Well-wishers*…
   Thank you, hugs, and love.

EPIGRAPH

My Orgasm Love

It is so uncomfortable,
yet it feels so good.
It is so sexually and energetically charged,
that it makes one restless.
But if one was to allow it to flow without offering any resistance,
it will flow as one, whole and complete.
It is not so easy to achieve and requires real work,
but once achieved, one wouldn't want anything else.
It is addictive.
It is desiring.
It runs head to toe, from one end to the other.
It makes one feel more alive than ever.
Sometimes, one feels the desire to squeeze it out of the body,
but when one closes their eyes and pays attention to it,
one realises, it is part of their prana, it always has been there.
Only awareness and sensitivity has increased now,
which has made it possible to connect with it.

The more I explore it, the more I fall in love with it.
The more I experience it, the more it needs to be experienced.
The more it makes me curious, the more I long for it.

I am deeply and immensely in love with it,
My Orgasm Love.

CONTENTS

PREFACE

When I tell people that I am an orgasm coach and bodyworker, I tend to get mixed reactions. Some joke about it, some are surprised, some are shocked, some get curious, and some run away.

- *Are you for real?*
- *Now, what is that supposed to mean?*
- *You must be one hell of a lucky guy!*
- *What exactly do you do?*
- *Excuse me, what did you just say?*
- *Thank God, there is someone who is doing this!*
- *Sorry, you are not allowed here.*
- *What do your parents think about that?*
- *How does your partner cope with this?*
- *Nah, we don't talk about this like that.*
- *You must be one hell of a busy man!*

While I really love where I am in my life now, the road has not been easy. It started with my teenage dream of pursuing a career in sexuality because I was unhappy with the way sex was treated in my native country of India, as taboo, and with the way rape, violence, molestation, and torture against women was the norm in our society. Growing up in India, hearing about the *Kamasutra*, the world's first sex treatise, and watching documentaries relating to ornate erotic temples and how sexual education was once a norm in our society, used to fascinate me. But I also used to feel extremely disappointed with what Indian society had turned into in regard to repressive attitudes about sexuality.

Something that was once so open, so deeply embraced, so part of our culture at one time, had become something that nobody wanted to talk about and that people felt shame to even mention. In our biology class, our teacher skipped the entire chapter on reproduction because of shame. As per our Indian culture, we were taught to treat women like Goddesses, but on the other hand, we had frequent inhuman incidents happening to women in the news. I felt that it was the lack of sexual education which was one of the biggest reasons behind these social ills. Hence, at the age of 17, I said to myself, "One day, I would like to work in the field of sexuality and bring a transformation in our society." Though at that time, I had no idea how I was ever going to fulfil my desire. I buried this desire of mine and continued my studies in accounting. Sexual teacher and an accountant? Hmm. Quite contrasting worlds, aren't they?

Between 2004 and 2013, I got a chance to live in the UK, the US, and Singapore. Hence, I also got a chance to explore various forms of sexuality ranging from BDSM, Shibari, group sex, various forms of sensuality, one-night stands, sex with multiple partners outside of a relationship, and engaging in various sexual fantasies. I really enjoyed all this exploration but, somehow, it felt that something was still missing. I would always want to have more sex, as if it was never enough.

In 2013 I started getting very serious about my journey to learn more about sex and orgasm. I began taking classes and joining communities of other people who were equally curious. I studied under teachers, read books, practised various techniques and modalities. Nine months into this journey, and things started to make sense. I realised that thing which had been so unknown all along in my sexual experiences but always there, the thing that I have been craving more of but couldn't name it, the thing I couldn't understand but was always ready to be uncovered and explored was orgasm itself. Huh? It was a strange realisation and I was shocked, bewildered, confused, and happy at the same time when it struck me. This orgasm was not the one I had known to exist since my adolescent days of watching porn and masturbating to ejaculation. It was something bigger and more profound.

I realised that orgasm was more than just climax. It was an experience that could celebrate the many dimensions of what it means to be human that went far beyond the physical into the emotional, energetic, mental, and indeed even the spiritual realms. I have come to call this expanded notion amplified orgasm.

For me, the transformation has been one of personal growth that has gone beyond the bedroom in many ways. I have experienced much deeper and more satisfying relationships with my lovers, become more self-aware, and expanded my consciousness of these many layers of my own embodied experience so that I can appreciate a much richer and more satisfying experience of life in each moment. And, once the transformation began to happen in me, I realised it was my life purpose to pass on what I had learned to others seeking to expand their sexual experiences to include deep and nourishing connections with others.

I became a certified bodyworker, certified coach, and have coached hundreds of clients over the last few years. I have given talks, online courses, and workshops on various aspects of sexuality to people from diverse backgrounds and experience levels. The work has been incredibly rewarding. I value each and every interaction and continue to learn and grow each and every day.

Writing this book has been a three-year journey, starting in 2017. It has been full of twists and turns, valleys and peaks, and itself a learning experience to help me clarify some of the ideas and knowledge I have gained during my journey so far. I hope you will find this book useful and transformative. If you do, then please drop me an email to let me know how this book has helped you. I hope that you will be able to find some nuggets in this book that will help you have better relationships, nourishing sex, and amplified orgasms.

If you notice anything that is incorrect or you believe will add value to the text in the next edition, then please do feel free to provide me with feedback. I have always learned so much from the people that I aimed to "teach" and I hope to continue on that path.

I look forward to hearing from and connecting with you, one way or the other.

I am sending you lots of love, hugs, and best wishes on your orgasmic journey. Have an exploratory, transformative, and safe journey.... Inwards and Outwards.

Michael Charming

Email: *coach@michaelcharming.com*
Website: *michaelcharming.com*

ACKNOWLEDGEMENTS

First and foremost, I would like to thank the Universe for showering me with blessings and gracing me with the courage and wisdom to carry on the work destined for me. This book is one important step towards my goal of bringing sexual transformation in our society as well as helping individuals love each other with more depth, passion, and compassion.

I am extremely grateful to my mom and dad as well as my brother and his wife for their prayers and continuous support throughout my life, and in particular, while writing this book. Without their sacrifices, love, and care, it would not have been possible for me to continue on this journey.

I would like to thank all my friends who have stood by and supported me while I have undergone this transformative journey. When I embarked on this journey in 2013, I didn't know where it was heading or what the future outcome would be. Having such amazing, accepting, and encouraging friends around me has definitely made the path easier to travel.

I would like to thank all my teachers who have shared their knowledge, love and guidance to help me progress in my path. Every single teacher that I have had a chance to study under has been an expert in their field and offered unique perspectives with humility. It is with the same level of humbleness, love, and care that I express my sincere thanks to them.

I would also like to thank all of my colleagues, course mates, community members, practice partners, and exploratory partners with whom I have had a chance to connect at various moments of my journey. Thank you for all your help in helping me understand different aspects of the teachings, for sending me the notes for the classes I missed, for guiding me and helping me get better at my practices, and for support during difficult times.

I would like to express my sincere and heartfelt thanks to all my lovers who I have had a chance to meet and become intimate with in one form or the other. I am extremely grateful for the love, support, and care that every single one of you have offered me during the time of our relationship. Thank you for coming into my life, for allowing us to spend some precious moments together, and for being yourself. I wouldn't be who I am today without the experiences we shared. I wish each of you best wishes, happiness, positivity, and lots of love.

I would like to express my sincere warmth and gratitude towards Cordelia Zafiropulo who has always been willing to help, support, and guide me throughout the process of this book journey. I am deeply grateful to be able to learn from her depth of insight, wisdom, life experiences, and profound knowledge. Her contribution towards this book has been tremendous, for which I shall always remain grateful.

I would also like to thank my editor, Sharon Elber, who provided thoughtful perspective on concepts and sound editorial advice with the intention of helping me carry my message through this vehicle, my first book.

Last, but not least, I would like to thank the readers who have had the courage to buy this book and invest their time, energy, and trust into the ideas and practices shared within it. I hope you will find the experience valuable and transformative.

Regards, Hugs, and Love,
MC

INTRODUCTION

ORGASM. We all want to have it, no matter who we are, how old we are, and no matter how many times we might have had one in the past. No matter how beautiful our past orgasmic experiences might have been, we always want to have a better one next time.

But what does it actually mean to say, "I just had an orgasm," or, "I want to have the best of the best orgasm in the world!"? What are we really talking about when we say the word *orgasm*?

In 2013, some of my friends and I did an informal survey in different parts of London. We asked people: "What does orgasm mean for you?" Some people were shy, some laughed hysterically, some were hesitant to talk about it, some got serious, some thought we were weird, and some thought we were doing some sort of prank. A few whispered in our ears: "We don't talk about this in public."

Here are a few of the responses:
- *Orgasm is oh, oh, aah, aah, followed by tingles*
- *27th June 2014, 23:50 hrs*
- *God*
- *Ecstasy*
- *Over the rainbow*
- *Peace*
- *Baby, I'm cumming!*
- *Splash*
- *A tall blonde in leather and a wet bed*
- *A dinner with the tall French man who has sharp pointed face and a beard*
- *Unexplored, never experienced*
- *A smiley face*
- *A dance to music*
- *I have never had sex*
- *A memory that I will never forget*
- *An unfulfilled desire*
- *Moksha*
- *A deep penetration that will blow her mind away*
- *I don't remember. I always have sex when I am drunk.*
- *A long, distant memory*

At one point during the survey, there was one very beautiful moment that stands out in my mind. One couple took a few steps back and discussed the question between themselves before sharing what orgasm meant for each of them individually and for them as a couple. I was deeply touched by this experience. It pleased me to see this couple realise that orgasm was a topic they could discuss and explore both as individuals and as a couple.

I am not interested in telling you what orgasm is. Rather, what really gets me excited as a speaker, coach, and certified bodyworker is helping my clients get a deeper, richer understanding of what orgasm is for them, how they would like to expand their experience of orgasm, and then help them find their own Path of Amplified Orgasm.

I invite you to take a moment now to reflect on what orgasm means to you here at the start of our journey together. Open your workbook to the very first exercise, *What is Orgasm for You?*

EXERCISE: What is Orgasm for You?

The Benefits of Orgasm

Beyond simple pleasure, orgasm offers many benefits to our overall physical health and well-being. Here are just a few:

- The activation of "feel-good" neurotransmitters that make us feel happier, more energised, and balanced
- The production of oxytocin, a hormone central to our feelings of love and bonding
- Reduces stress, provides relaxation, and fosters better and more peaceful sleep by boosting endorphin levels and flushing cortisol (an inflammatory hormone released by the adrenal glands) out of the body
- Improves blood circulation throughout different parts of the body which keeps our tissues healthy and our heart strong
- Increases the production of DHEA hormone (Dehydroepiandrosterone), which promotes healthy skin, improves brain function, and balances the immune system.

Physical health is certainly a great reason to enjoy more orgasms! Who doesn't want to get healthier while also experiencing joy and pleasure? However, this is just the beginning of the story. In fact, the benefits of orgasm, and amplified orgasm in particular, go well beyond our physical body.

In Western societies, the notion of "climax" and "orgasm" have been conflated. That is, many believe that orgasm and climax are the same thing. However, I invite you to see that climax is simply one kind of orgasm, one restricted to mostly physical experiences and sensations. Orgasm, on the other hand, is a much bigger event. Orgasm has the capacity to open up and celebrate many other aspects of our embodied being, that is, our human experience. This expanded notion of orgasm, once harnessed and developed, is what I mean to refer to as amplified orgasm. To help clarify and make use of this expanded notion of orgasm, this book will use the concept of The Layered Body.

The Layered Body

Figure 1: Getting ready for the hike.

Imagine that you wish to travel to a new place where you have never been before. You will be travelling on foot, and you have with you everything you need packed into a rucksack. In your hands is a map that has the trails between you and your destination marked in squiggly lines. Is this enough to get you to your destination?

Probably not. It really isn't enough information to help you decide what to pack in your bag for the journey or which paths to choose. They all look the same on the map, but you realise that the wilderness is full of challenges and you are not sure which is the best trail to choose in order to embark on the journey.

Imagine now that the map also shows elevation. Now that is helpful information! This will help you choose those trails with fewer steep inclines or choose those with steeper inclines if you are looking for a challenge. What if it also included the location of re-supply shops where you can pick up new supplies that you mailed in advance of your hike? Helpful indeed! What if it also included information on where the best water sources will be? Even better!

What does this example teach us? Information from a variety of sources, on different aspects of the adventure, can help us navigate on our journey. The same is true on the Path of Amplified Orgasm.

As we explore the exciting and rewarding Path of Amplified Orgasm, it is helpful to think of the body in new ways. Although we are accustomed to thinking about the body in terms of purely physical or anatomical terms, this map of the body is too limited to gain true insight into the experience of orgasm. Indeed, since orgasm is an explosion of pleasure that is happening on multiple dimensions, we must have a map that guides us in many ways.

This book encourages you to understand the body as layered, each layer adding important information to the overall picture. Each of the layers on this body map gives us new insight into how to achieve deeper, more fulfilling, and indeed, even mind-blowing orgasms. The layers of the body that we will explore in this book include: the emotional body, the mental body, the energetic body, the physical body, and the spiritual body.

These layers of our embodied experience of sexual pleasure, orgasm, and indeed even everyday life, are to be understood as interactive layers. That is, although looking at each in turn offers great insight into how we experience and can become intentional about sexual pleasure, orgasm, and intimacy, they must be also be understood as integrated systems. For example, our emotional bodies are not distinct from our mental bodies, as core beliefs tie these two layers together. Nor are emotions completely distinct from our physical bodies, since emotional states have complex biological markers located squarely in the physical realm.

My deep desire in writing this book is to give you, the reader, helpful maps to understand these different layers of the embodied human experience, as well as insight into how they interact, so that you may better navigate your own individual Path of Amplified Orgasm.

How to Use This Book

This book is designed to be read from beginning to end, rather than jumping into the parts that at first glance might seem the most interesting. The reason for this is that the concepts developed are cumulative, one building on the next. The terms and concepts used in Chapter Five will assume that you have read the previous chapters, for example.

As you read along, you will notice there are references to exercises which can be found in the workbook. Rather than reading on, I encourage you to stop and do these exercises, which offer a chance to reflect on, practise, or get in touch with some of the concepts in this book on an experiential level. This is actually central towards building a deeper sense of the layered body. While reading words on a page can help you develop a mental picture of the ideas, only by stopping and feeling and doing can we gain understanding through our other senses and ways of knowing.

I encourage the reader to use what I call "The Feeling Over Doing Formula." This means that instead of being goal-oriented with any of the exercises or practices that you do, you listen to your body (on all levels) and let it be your guide. If something starts to feel overwhelming, it is OK to back off and come back to it another time. Respect your own boundaries and limitations while continuing to approach learning more about amplified orgasm with the mindset of curiosity and exploration, rather than trying to force any particular goal into being.

Reading (and doing) this book will be a journey. The suggestions mentioned are only to be taken as guidelines and to be practised at your own risk. Please always consult the relevant specialist if you are not sure or seek their advice before trying any of the exercises mentioned in the book.

Transformation is a process when old patterns and behaviours begin to shift, when a new identity begins to get formed, when new experiences and new parts of your being begin to emerge which can feel exciting, adventurous, and also uncomfortable at the same time. If you feel something like this, then you know that you are definitely on the right track. Just like on any other path, we need to feel into the process of change rather than trying to jump over the parts we don't like. My invitation would be to see how you can quieten your mind and actually drop into your body; drop into your feelings, drop into your desires, and let them emerge and see what they would like to do. After all, the journey towards a happier, healthier, nourishing and amplified orgasmic life is worth taking as it impacts every aspect of our life and the quality of the way we live and our connections to others.

Please do not force this process of transformation. Keep it consistent, keep it persistent, and keep it to a pace you can digest and alchemise. Let the journey unfold itself, let the transformation show you what it needs to show you rather than aiming at something that you want to become. Most importantly, have trust in yourself, have trust in this process, and have trust in the universe.

While some of the exercises in the workbook are geared towards couples, certainly most of them can alternatively be explored on your own if you do not currently have a partner. Likewise, although many of the examples in the book reference heterosexual sex, as this is where majority of my experiences have been, I have made an effort to be inclusive of the LGBT community as well. I believe that amplified orgasm should be accessible to anyone interested in the journey of personal transformation and the growth that it offers.

Finally, although this book covers many basic principles on the Path of Amplified Orgasm in depth, Part II will go beyond the scope of this book to explore more advanced concepts, practices, as well as relationship dynamics relevant to amplified orgasm. In addition, although I have touched on the spiritual body in this book, Part II will include a more expanded exploration of this very important aspect of the human experience and orgasm.

Are You Ready to Begin Your Journey?

When we learn to see orgasm as a much deeper and richer experience than climax (a simple momentary physical release), we can realise that the Path of Amplified Orgasm is not just a means to an end. Rather, the journey itself is one that can lead to a richer experience of our life in general, a deeper connection to our life's purpose, and more satisfying relationships built on deep and fulfilling intimacy.

As we embark on this journey together, you will be encouraged to think about sex, orgasm, and indeed your own embodied experience in new ways. I hope you will bring an open mind, and a mindset of curiosity to this opportunity to learn more about yourself, your partner, and the world around you. Ready? Let's go!

THE EMOTIONAL BODY

Emotions are there to be felt, to be experienced, and not to be held or repressed.
Set them free to liberate yourself, your body,
your sex and your orgasm.
Michael Charming

Let's return to the metaphor of the layered body discussed in the introduction. This book will help you understand the body in terms of several different layers, similar to the different kinds of information you will find depicted on a map. On an actual map, these layers may include things like elevation, trails, terrain indicators, water sources, provision stops, or climate information. The first layer of the map to the Path of Amplified Orgasm is the emotional body, which we will explore in this chapter.

Most of us already have a language we use to talk about our feelings and emotions. However, sometimes we are not clear about these concepts, which can lead to confusion, miscommunication, and misunderstandings. In order to be very clear as we learn more about the emotional body and how it works, we have to agree on some basic terminology first.

As we proceed through this chapter, you will gain a better understanding of the difference between feelings and emotions, how culture and experience influence our feelings, and how feelings and expression play a vital role in creating intimacy in relationships. Finally, you will begin to see why learning to fully feel and express your emotional reality is critical on the Path of Amplified Orgasm.

Emotions and Feelings

We start our journey on the Path of Amplified Orgasm with two foundational concepts: emotions and feelings. Many people use these two terms as if they are the same. However, for our purposes, it is important to understand that these two related concepts are actually referring to something different. It's worth taking a moment to get really clear on what I mean when I refer to these terms as they will come up time and time again throughout this book.

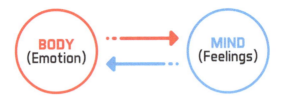

Figure 2: Emotions rooted in the body, feelings rooted in the mind

Emotions: Rooted in the Body

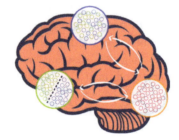

Figure 3: Brain processing and responding to triggers through neurotransmitters

NEURAL PATHWAY

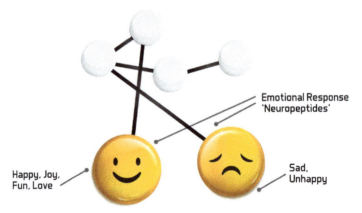

Figure 4: Transmitters and receptors working along a neural pathway to generate an emotion

One way to look at emotion is to understand it as the body's way of responding to stimuli (also called triggers) at a biological level. Emotion includes physical processes such as communication between transmitters and receptors along neural pathways, the release of endorphins throughout the body, and a variety of processes in the central and peripheral nervous systems. Areas of the brain involved in signalling emotion in the body include the subcortical regions of the brain, the amygdala, and the ventromedial prefrontal cortices, which alter our physical state through a variety of neurochemical reactions.

Figure 5-6: Emotion is also energy in motion (like electric energy, left or soft energy, right)

Another way to think of emotion is energy in motion in the body, or energy that moves or gets stuck depending on flow or blockages. This alternative way of talking about emotion has its foundation in the spiritual traditions of Hinduism, Taoism and many other similar philosophies. These ancient ways of knowing offer important tools for learning how to observe and make use of the energy flow in the body for the purpose of amplifying orgasm. We will discuss energy in more detail in Chapter Three.

Rather than thinking of these different ways of understanding emotion as opposing paradigms, I think of them as complementary. That is, the science of neurology and endocrinology complement those of Hinduism and Taoism, each offering a different but useful language to understand what is happening in the body during intimacy. Rather than choosing one or the other, I will use both, choosing the language that best clarifies how emotion is operating in the body.

Psychological research led by Paul Ekman led him to classify six basic, universally recognised emotions, which are: sadness, anger, fear, tenderness, excitement, and happiness.[1] You can probably identify with having experienced each of these emotions yourself. However, you may not be used to thinking about them as states that are recognisable as specific kinds of physical (and energetic) states in your body.

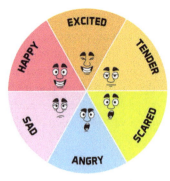

Figure 7: Paul Ekman's six basic universally recognised emotions

Learning to identify how emotion feels in the body may be very new to you. I encourage you to open your workbook and take some time to complete the exercise Emotions in the Body. This exercise is designed to help you learn to get in touch with how your body feels in specific emotional states. If you find yourself feeling "out of touch" with your body, this exercise is one you can return to time and time again to get used to using your body as a source of information about your emotional state.

EXERCISE: Emotions in the Body

Emotional Sensitive Spots

Emotional states in the body are more or less the same for all of us. That is, anger is characterised by the same physical states in the body, the same endorphins, the same basic energy state, regardless of who is experiencing this emotion.

However, one of the things that makes us unique as individuals when it comes to emotion is that we are each more sensitive to some energy states over others. In this book, I will refer to this phenomenon as emotional sensitive spots. If we have anger as our sensitive spot, then we will get angry very quickly, likely in response to a variety of triggers. On the other hand, we may be more inclined to tend towards sadness, fear, or other types of emotional states. Each of us has our own emotional sensitive spots, usually deeply influenced by our individual life experiences.

Imagine for a moment someone that has been a victim of physical abuse. They may have experienced a great deal of trauma from conflict with an intimate partner. Having been physically hurt and having been powerless to stop it, such a person may be much more inclined to experience the emotion of fear at the first sign of conflict. After all, conflict has preceded violence against them in their past.

On the other hand, someone with the experience of successfully intimidating others with outbursts of anger may be more inclined to default to an angry emotional state in response to the trigger of conflict. These two different kinds of patterned response to the same trigger, namely conflict, demonstrate different sensitive spots.

In a healthy relationship, it is important to be aware of each other's sensitive spots as much as possible. Empathy and understanding for our partner's emotions, as well as the past experiences that have created these sensitive spots, are among the foundations of intimate bonds. However, on the Path of Amplified Orgasm, it becomes all the more important to be aware of our own and each other's sensitive spots, as these can get triggered when an orgasm starts amplifying.

In terms of neurobiology, this concept can be understood as your "neural superhighway."[2] The theory is that the more often you exercise certain neural pathways, the more these emotional states become habitual. (We will discuss neurological theories and their applications more in Chapter Two.) For most of us, certain emotional states are our "go to" for a large range of triggers. Part of getting to know yourself is to identify which emotions are your sensitive spots and learning to use these insights as tools for healing, connecting with your partner, and personal growth.

EXERCISE: Identify Your Emotional Sensitive Spots

Feelings: Rooted in the Mind

Now that we have defined emotion as rooted in the body through biochemical processes and energy states, we turn to feelings. Feelings are instead rooted in our psychological states. In other words, feelings are in the mind and represent the meaning we make of the different physical states we call emotion. As we take our journey in life, certain emotional states take on certain meanings for us. As such, emotions become reflected in our feelings.

A feeling is the mental portrayal of what is going on inside our body when we have a certain emotion and feelings are considered to be the by-products of mental processes. Our brain perceives the emotional state and then projects meaning onto it using past experiences and associations as a guide. Feelings use cognitive input to make sense of the physical emotional states, which are rooted in the body, by incorporating the present context, past experiences, memory, and conscious and subconscious beliefs.

One way to think of it is this: The six emotional states covered above are more or less measurable biological states corresponding to certain brainwaves, endorphins, and indicators such as pulse, breath, and sweat. In other words, these emotional states are physical states found in the body.

Any one of these six emotional states can be interpreted in context into any number of feelings. This work is done in the mind in relation to the subjective meaning we are making of both our physical emotional state and the contextual triggers we are being exposed to. This means that feelings are subjective relative to the meaning we make of our emotional experience in each moment.

Take for example the emotion of sadness. On a certain level, sadness is an emotion that is a body state (specific hormone concentrations, for example) which also corresponds to certain energy states (more on that in the next chapters). However, clearly there is a range of feelings associated with this general emotion of sadness. And these feelings are generated as we attempt to make meaning of both our body and our situation.

Perhaps we have a history of severe depression. Association with this particular type of sadness might make us tend to feel depressed when our body experiences a sad emotional state. For others, sadness may be experienced as bittersweet in the moment, for example, as they ponder the loss of a pet who brought a great deal of joy into their lives.

The feelings of bittersweet sadness and depression are qualitatively different, created by the meaning we make of each moment. And yet, they share similar biological emotional states which underpin the feeling at its root. This is what it means to understand feelings as reflective of our emotional states, and yet more subjective in nature.

Equally important to understand is that since feelings represent a state of mind, they affect how we see the world around us. They encourage us to weigh certain kinds of information more heavily than others. For example, when we are experiencing the feeling of hopelessness, we tend to see the parts of our lives that are not working as much more significant than those parts of our lives that we can feel very grateful about. When it comes to our experience of sex, for example, a feeling of hopelessness from past negative sexual encounters can culminate in a loss of desire for any physical intimacy.

EXERCISE: Getting to Know My Approach to Feelings

Expression

Although emotion and feelings are internal states, we externalise them through expression, in other words, through behaviour that we enact to communicate a particular emotion/feeling. We do this both consciously with the intent of communicating a certain feeling, as well as subconsciously, in other words, without realising it.

Expression is sometimes very stable across cultures and time. For example, the smile is universally understood regardless of the society we find ourselves in. Other expressions are highly cultural and still others are highly personal.

Expression can be a way to cultivate a common understanding or form a bond. For example, a "high five" is a way of mutually expressing joy, victory, or accomplishment. On the other hand, expressions can be a source of misunderstanding. We will see how differences in expression styles can play out during our intimacy, sometimes bringing us together, other times creating some disconnect. A good example of this would be when one partner doesn't want to have any kind of physical intimacy with his/her partner but then continues to keep touching his/her partner, giving mixed signals resulting in confusion and misunderstandings. Having a higher level of awareness of what is happening on the inside and how it is showing up on the outside plays a huge role in creating great orgasmic flow between partners.

When we are our relating with our partner, our behaviour and responses will have an effect on them and their desire towards us. The more often we remain in touch with our emotions and feelings, and the more we convey the same, the more it will create a space of openness and trust. When there is openness and trust, it allows our body to relax more and makes way for us to be able to go into involuntary states.

Many women become open to physical intimacy only when they feel they have emotional intimacy. That is, when they feel heard and emotionally supported by their partner, they are more likely to want to experience sexual intimacy with them. While women need to learn to express their feelings, men also need to understand that listening and supporting their partner on the emotional and feeling levels is important to opening up receptiveness on the physical and sexual levels. That is, helping a woman become orgasmic is not just about touch, contrary to what many men have come to believe.

EXERCISE: Expressing Emotions and Feelings with Our Partner

Conditioned Emotional Response: Rooted in Experience

It is important to realise that both our emotions and our feelings are conditioned by our life experiences, our culture, and our belief systems. What this means is that we each have a set of emotional responses we tend to associate with certain triggers. We have learned these responses over our lifetime, most of the time without even being aware of them. Since we are all on unique life journeys, our conditioned emotional responses are also unique.[3]

Let's take a look at what this might look like in practice by way of an example:

Context: *It is a first date for a couple. They are having a romantic dinner.*

Trigger: *The man insists on paying for the meal.*

Female #1: *This woman came from a family that emphasised the gender story that good men are strong providers. Her own father exemplified this principle and routinely showed his love with gifts and surprises for both her and her mother as she grew up. She associates this gesture with a showing of love and caring. When her date takes the check and pays for the meal, she feels warmth and is comforted by the gesture. She smiles and thanks him, expressing gratitude and appreciation for his act of kindness.*

Female #2: *We can also imagine a second scenario where the details are all the same, with one exception: A different woman with a different life history is on this date. This second woman had an experience in college where she felt pressured into sex after a man paid for the meal on their first date. He said something like, "Well, I did pay for your dinner and I thought your acceptance of that meant you were interested in sex." Feeling guilty and pressured, she went through with the sexual encounter and it was a terrible experience that made her feel violated and manipulated. Because of this past traumatic sexual experience, which was coerced, she has a different feeling/emotion in reaction to the same trigger, that is, the man offering to pay for dinner on the first date. She feels nervous and tense and her emotional state turns to one somewhere between fear and anger. Although she had been enjoying the date until that moment, she coldly insists on paying for her own meal. Her reaction is confusing to the man, who honestly intended the offer to be an act of kindness.*

This example offers us a chance to realise that external triggers can mean very different things to each of us. If we think of the external stimulus or trigger (the man paying for the meal), we can see that although it remained the same, it evoked a very different emotional state and feeling response in two different women with different past experiences. Notice that this was a different reaction that happened both on the biological and psychological levels. And, the same trigger evoked a different behaviour/ expression from the person as well.

Figure 8: Female #1 — Good men are providers.

Figure 9: Female #2 — Sex is expected after being treated for a meal by a man.

Society, Belief, and Feelings

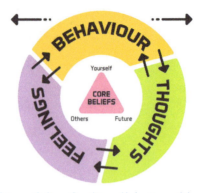

Figure 10: Interrelation between feelings, thoughts, and behaviour and the role these play in shaping and being shaped by core beliefs

One of the most overlooked aspects of understanding our emotional and feeling response is the role that core beliefs can play in terms of shaping our responses. (We will be exploring the concept of core beliefs more in Chapter Two.) This is particularly true when it comes to sexuality.

A prime example includes how societal beliefs about masculinity and femininity have shaped us as men and women, and how those beliefs have impacted how we tend to deal with feelings. One result of these core beliefs about gender results in the fact that women tend to be more connected to their feelings than men. For most men, feelings may be something to avoid, dismiss, or suppress. If you ask many men, "How are you feeling?" you might find that the majority may find it difficult to express and answer this question. On the other hand, women tend to be more comfortable with naming and discussing their emotions and feelings.

Of course, this is not to say that every woman and every man follow this pattern. It is simply a trend that is created by learning to embody core beliefs spread in our culture that men "should" be emotionally stoic, and women "should" be emotionally expressive. Once we recognise that sometimes our core beliefs were handed down to us through society, rather than rooted in biology, we can make the decision to change our core beliefs to those that are more supportive of our whole potential as complex human beings entitled to the full range of emotional experiences.

We will be discussing how belief shapes our emotional reality in more detail in the next chapter. However, now is a good time to just remind you that all feelings and emotions are an important part of the human experience. There are no "wrong" feelings or emotions. And, feelings must be felt in order to move through them and release them.

Sometimes cultural norms, particularly if we internalised them as core beliefs, pressure us to feel a certain way in a given situation. When we don't, we sometimes feel shame, guilt, or other unwanted feelings. These negative feelings can then block us from fully feeling and expressing our true feelings and thus they can become trapped, creating blockages in the body. In order to experience amplified orgasm, it is important to have this vessel of energy flow clear so that orgasmic waves can flow freely. In my bodywork sessions, when I clear these energy flow pathways, many of my clients either start connecting with their own orgasmic energy or experience whole body orgasms for the first time.

In my own life, I have seen the benefits of learning to feel and express the full range of feelings. There was a time when I was pretty much happy all the time. It was my strongest "sensitive spot," my default emotional state. However, as I learned more about myself and the world around me, I realised that I wasn't really willing to experience other feelings to the same depth, and was thus missing out on the richness of the human experience.

In addition, by expanding my bandwidth to be able to feel a different set of emotions at various intensities, I have become more able to connect with others at their emotional level, which often can create deeper levels of connection between us.

Would you agree that sometimes the greatest connection with others happens in sadness or when we are sharing our pain and hurt with each other? Previously, I had always been happy, so it was not possible for me to deeply relate to my lovers when they were feeling sad or when they were in pain. Instead, my default tendency was to try to cheer them up, to move them into my comfort zone (happiness). However, because the ultimate source which was making them feel sad or causing pain would never be explored and looked into, this tactic, while well meaning, was cutting off opportunities for intimacy and connection.

When I coach men, one of the first things that I ask men to do is to start having conversations in terms of their feelings. I find that men often want to rush into expanding their orgasm, they want to become multi-orgasmic overnight and are often looking for quick fixes. It takes a good amount of effort for me to rewire my male clients' thinking and have them understand that the Path of Amplified Orgasm is a path of transformation. It is a journey which will take its time, just like planting a seed will take time to grow into a tree and give fruit.

EXERCISE: Identifying Social Influence on Our Core Beliefs

Sensations

We have talked about emotions and feelings, but in order to gain a deeper understanding of orgasm, it is also important to understand and be able to talk about the different kinds of sensations that we feel in our body. In our day to day life, we are not used to talking with each other in the language of sensations. In this section, I encourage you to learn to recognise different kinds of sensations that exist in your body and then work on being able to express them.

Generally speaking, our body structure is essentially the same. We all have one heart, two eyes, two lungs, and so forth. All of these systems function more or less in a similar way in every person's body. No doubt, anatomically male and female bodies are structured in a different way, but what I am pointing out is the fact that the feeling of our hearts beating is similar in both men and women. Likewise, the tingling sensation in the genitals of men are similar to the tingling sensation in female genitals.

When someone tells us that they are feeling happy, we sort of get an idea of what they are feeling, but we don't really know how happiness feels in their body. As you have seen above, happiness is not a feeling. It is an emotion given to a feeling. Expressing feelings is enhanced by also expressing the sensations happening within our body such as pulsating inside the lips, hot liquid warmth in the belly, or a tingling sensation in the genitals.

When we express in terms of sensations, it allows us to be able to associate and relate to what the other person might be experiencing in their body. In a deeper state of orgasm, you will find the sensations of your partner will have an impact on how you feel inside your own body in a kind of feedback loop. This is part of the orgasm amplification process.

For example, when someone says to you, "I feel love," it has the possibility of creating a feeling of love within you. But imagine instead someone actually says, "I feel love. I feel warmth in my heart. I feel my body expanded and I feel light." From this you can gain a better sense of the quality of the feeling of love by way of sensations in different places in their body. It also gives you an opportunity to look and feel in your own body and to see what kinds of sensations are arising.

In Chapter Three you will see how our bodies are composed of different energy centres, and how awareness of those centres allows you to promote better energy flow between them, identify blocks, and open pathways to amplified orgasm. Expressing feelings in terms of sensations plays a very critical role in amplifying our orgasms as well.

For example, if a pot is filled with boiling water and we continue to apply heat, the water will be converted to steam and/or will begin to boil over and out of the pot. Similarly, if a woman is feeling too much energy in her pelvis, or if a man is too aroused and close to climax, and this couple continue to do the same motions with the same intensity, very likely, the energy will make her feel uncomfortable and the man will end up ejaculating. However, if both are aware of their feelings, sensations, and energy movement, and where in the body those sensations are, then both will have an option to adjust their energy, their penetrative strokes, and touch accordingly. This will enable them to not only prolong the overall orgasmic experience but also start helping them move towards experiencing full-body orgasms.

In addition, naming the feelings, emotions, and sensations is a great way for each partner to keep in check with the other. One of the biggest reasons women end up having a dislike for sexual connection with men is because somewhere during the love-making process, the resonance between the two partners gets broken with him getting overwhelmed by his own feelings and sensations and ejaculating or finishing long before she is ready.

Types of Sensations

When we speak of sensations, we generally talk in the following categories. Please note this is not an exhaustive list and I invite you to remain curious and explore sensation more on your own and together.

- Temperature
- Degree of intensity
- Texture
- Taste/Flavour
- Colours
- Where in your body (which part/organ)
- Motion
- Pressure
- Shape
- Atmosphere
- Direction.

Notice the difference between saying, "I feel orgasm" vs "I feel hot and tingling sensations rising in my genitals and moving towards the centre of my chest. I feel a watery and creamy feeling in my lips, explosive and expansive feelings in my pussy/cock, and circular moving heat around my head." Which of the two sentences gives you more insight into how the other person is actually feeling in their body?

When someone says they are feeling explosive and expansive feelings in their pussy/cock or a circular moving of heat around their head, a follow-up question might be, "Does this feel comfortable or uncomfortable?" If the person says "uncomfortable," then there has to be a change of stroke, a change of pressure or/and intensity, etc. The more we are able to check in with each other, the more we will be able to enjoy having sex and experiencing deeper realms of orgasm. The more we have the capacity to experience deeper realms of orgasm, the more we can amplify our own orgasms.

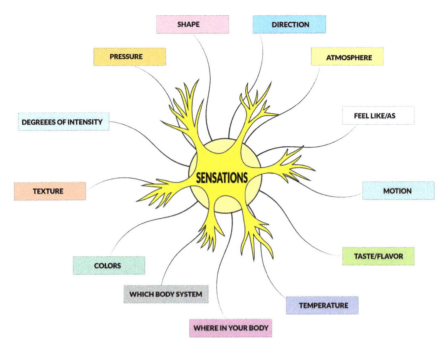

Figure 11: Qualities of sensations

Learning to speak in terms of sensation takes time and a commitment to practice. When I made a commitment to become more willing to speak of my emotions and feelings in terms of sensation, it took me six months of constant practice and continuous support from my partner before I was consistently expressing myself in this way. So, when she would ask me, "How are you feeling?" my response was not, "I am feeling good," but rather "I feel happy, especially in the centre of my chest." Or "I feel slightly sad. I feel heaviness in the right part of my stomach, a bit of contraction in my heart, and a hot liquid feeling in the centre of my chest."

EXERCISE: Naming Sensation

What Does All This Have to Do with Orgasm?

When it comes to orgasm, being able to cultivate intimacy is critical. One way we create space for intimacy is through sharing our feelings with our lover, both in terms of sex but also in the relationship as defined more broadly. Most of you already know this, although this book will give you some new and surprising tools to do that.

However, less known, and equally important, is learning to process emotion. As we have learned, emotion is in the body. Many people lack the knowledge and experience to learn to fully experience, embrace, process, and release emotional energy. Without this ability, most of us get "stuck" in terms of our energy flow, preventing us from experiencing the full potential of our orgasms. As you will learn in this book, these emotional and energy skills are both central on the Path of Amplified Orgasm.

Since all of these emotions, feelings, and sensations reside and emerge from within us, in order for us to be able to feel more orgasmic, it is important to be able to understand and relate to each of these feelings and emotions. And, because of conditioning, the meaning and significance that we assign to any particular stimulus will depend on this deeply rooted individual programming. Culture, life experiences, personality, values, beliefs, as well as parental and societal circumstances, all play their part in shaping our emotions and feelings.

To learn more about how this happens, we will turn next to the mental body, adding yet another layer to our map. You will discover how neural pathways in the brain, belief systems, social norms, and indeed our consciousness all play a role in helping or hindering our orgasmic potential on the Path of Amplified Orgasm.

Chapter One Summary:

- Emotions are rooted in the body and are characterised by physical states. They are universal and can be identified by physical sensations and measured by biological markers such as pulse or hormone levels.
- Feelings are rooted in the mind and are subjectively experienced.
- Life experience, culture, and beliefs shape the feelings we associate with certain triggers and emotions.
- All feelings have value and need to be felt in order to have access to the complete human experience.
- Learning to feel and express the full range of feelings allows us to know ourselves more deeply, as well as connect with others more fully.
- Learning to express the sensations we feel in our body can help facilitate better communication during love, allowing for better energy exchange, and ultimately lead to amplified orgasms.
- The Path of Amplified Orgasm requires that we learn to more fully feel and express our emotions, feelings, and sensations with our intimate partners.

THE MENTAL BODY

The human brain is an intricate organ which contains about 80-100 billion neurons and 100 trillion connections. It interprets sensations and experiences, it signals feelings and emotions, and it helps us make decisions and gives us choice over our actions. The brain is part of our body's central nervous system and it plays a huge role in our feelings of arousal, desire, pleasure, and ultimately feeling orgasmic. Taking the Path of Amplified Orgasm, therefore, requires that we dive into this most amazing layer of the human experience and formulate a useful map of the mental body.

Perhaps you are familiar with this saying:

Watch your thoughts, they become your words; watch your words, they become
your actions; watch your actions, they become your habits; watch your habits,
they become your character; watch your character, it becomes your destiny.
Anonymous (some credit Lao Tzu)

As you will discover in this chapter, this old saying has actually been shown to be largely true by modern research on the brain. Even if you have some understanding of the brain from biology classes, it may surprise you to learn that a revolution has taken place in the science of the brain over the last 20 years or so. While the brain was once perceived as a "blank slate," a kind of empty container to be filled with information as we learned, we now know the relationship between the brain and our lived experience is much more complex.

Modern theories of the brain focus on the interaction between the brain, the body, subjective experience, the mind, behaviour, belief, and more. Rather than understanding the brain as a fixed and passive container, scientists now understand the brain itself to evolve and change as a result of our experiences, environment, behaviours, and habits. In this chapter we will be looking at each of these step by step. After all, our brain deeply influences how we experience an orgasm. It is therefore important to gain a basic understanding of the brain and the role it plays in our sexual experiences.

This chapter will explore:

- How the brain and central nervous system work
- The concept of "neuroplasticity" and how it applies to orgasmic states
- How our thought processes, and indeed orgasms, create neural pathways
- The difference between the brain and the mind
- How different belief systems influence our perceptions, which in turn shape our realities around sex and orgasm
- The difference between attention, intention, presence, and awareness, and why they are important for amplified orgasms.

Anatomical Structure of the Brain

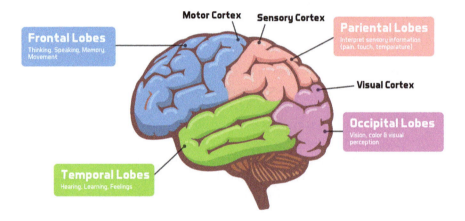

Figure 12: Anatomy of the brain: the four lobes

Let's start our exploration of the brain with a quick primer on its anatomical structure. There are four main lobes of the brain, each of which perform a specific function. These lobes and their functions include:

Frontal Lobes

The frontal lobes control motor skills and cognitive functions like thinking, planning, organising, movement of the body, short-term memory, and problem solving. So, thinking, planning, organising about sex or physical intimacy, movement of the body as a result of touch, short-term memory, and problem solving like putting a condom on the penis or working out a particular sex position, will be performed by this lobe.

Parietal Lobes

The parietal lobes interpret sensory information, such as the soft touch of lips. This includes both pleasurable experiences, such as a kiss, as well as the sensation of pain.

Occipital Lobes

The occipital lobes process images from the eyes and link that information with images stored in memory. They will be active in processing anything visual during your sexual experiences, such as looking at your partner's physical appearance, the shape of their genitals, or noticing the reactions of another person through visual cues such as seeing them blush.

Temporal Lobes

The temporal lobes process information from our senses of smell, taste, and sound. Examples during a sexual experience may include experiencing the taste of vaginal fluid, interpreting the different sounds of orgasm, or noticing the scent of your partner.

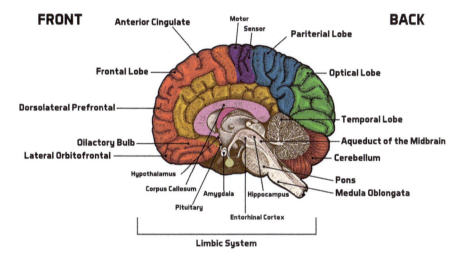

Figure 13: Anatomy of the brain: the limbic system and brain stem

Other important parts of the brain and their primary functions include:

Brainstem

The brainstem consists of three major parts and it links the brain to the spinal cord. These three parts are:

- The **medulla oblongata**, which controls involuntary processes like digestion, breathing, heart rate and also manages reflex behaviours like coughing, sneezing, vomiting, and swallowing

- The **pons**, which regulates sensations from the head and movement of the eyes and mouth
- The **midbrain**, which collects sensory information relating to eye movements, visual, and auditory processing.

Limbic System

Structures deep within the brain, known as the limbic system, control emotions and memories. In orgasmic states, when we are deeply in resonance with one another at a physical level, it is the resonance of this limbic system that we generally experience. The limbic system includes several structures including the corpus callosum, olfactory tract, the cingulate gyrus, mammillary body, the amygdala, and the hippocampus.

When people who are in healthy, caring, and loving relationships, whether as couples or in a family, interact with one another, the interaction results in the release of certain neurochemicals in the limbic region of the brain.[4,5] These neurochemicals are important for one's well-being. If we do not have enough limbic resonance with others, then our brain and well-being tends to suffer over time. People who lack loving, caring interactions, those who are lonely, or those who have had experiences of being taken away from maternal touch during birth or infancy, are often more easily prone to depression and anxiety.[6,7] Some may also find it difficult to experience orgasm. As a bodyworker, I have worked with a number of such clients and have had great success helping them access sexual pleasure, and indeed, amplified orgasm.

Amygdala

The amygdala acts as a hub in the limbic system and forms connections with a diverse array of structures. The amygdala influences autonomic processes, memory formation, and neuromodulation.[8] The positive correlation that we all experience between erotic stimuli and feeling sexual-arousal is due to the activation of the amygdala. Importantly, the feeling of safety is also controlled by the amygdala. If at any point during a sexual experience you are not feeling safe, it is because the amygdala has become hyper-vigilant. Men often associate safety with feeling physically safe, but in fact, safety also includes the mental, emotional, and energetic layers. We will be covering the topic of safety in more detail in Part II.

Thalamus

The thalamus acts as a gatekeeper for messages passed between the spinal cord and the cerebral hemispheres. The thalamus transmits incoming sensory pathways to appropriate areas of the cortex and is responsible for facilitating communication between several regions in the brain.

Hypothalamus and Pituitary
The hypothalamus, along with the pituitary gland, are responsible for controlling various visceral functions, including regulating body temperature, behavioural responses, sexual reproduction, eating, drinking, growth, and lactation. Your eating and drinking habits, your sexual responses, the feeling of different kinds of temperature during sex, the feelings of aggression and pleasure, are all controlled by these areas of the brain.

Hippocampus and Cerebellum
The hippocampus and cerebellum are two regions of the brain (along with the amygdala and prefrontal cortex) where memories are stored. Scientists believe that specific kinds of memory are stored in different areas of the brain. For example, the amygdala is thought to store memories associated with fear. The hippocampus stores what scientists call "declarative" and "episodic" memories, both of which are long-term memories that can be consciously recalled. On the other hand, "procedural" memory, such as how to play a musical instrument, is stored in the cerebellum.

Central Nervous System
The central nervous system is composed of the brain and the spinal cord and is responsible for integrating the information received through the senses and coordinating and influencing the activities of the different parts of the body. It sends messages to and from the body and brain through motor and sensory nerve fibres located on the spinal cord. If you have been touched on different parts of the body, especially the erogenous zones, and if you have felt aroused or pleasure, it is because signals of pleasure and arousal are being received by the brain's reward system and the central nervous system.

Peripheral Nervous System
The peripheral nervous system acts as a communication channel between the brain and the extremities. For example, if you touch a sensitive spot like a nipple, the sensation travels from the nipple to the brain in a split second. Within just an instant, the brain tells the body to react, often without having to involve the cognitive process of the brain at all.

Pineal Gland
In many ancient Hinduism and Taoist practices, the endocrine system which consists of the pituitary gland, hypothalamus, pineal gland, adrenals, pancreas, thyroid, parathyroid, ovaries, and testes, is considered to play an important role in combining physical bodily function with mental and spiritual development. In Chapter Four, you will get to know that these glands produce hormones which act as neurotransmitters and bring changes in our body, energy, emotions, and impulses. The relationship between the hypothalamus, pituitary gland, and pineal gland is considered to be of paramount importance if one is to grow beyond physical dimensions.

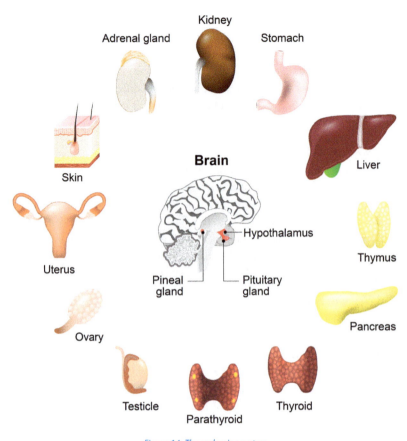

Figure 14: The endocrine system

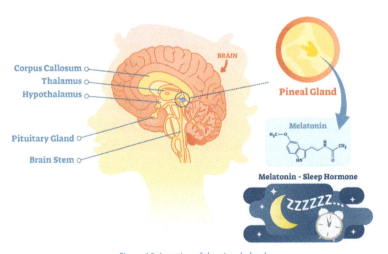

Figure 15: Location of the pineal gland

Greek anatomist Herophilus (4th century BC), referred to the pineal gland as "A sphincter which regulates the flow of thought" while a Latin anatomist referred to it as "the master gland."[9] Scientists have been baffled by the pineal gland for centuries. So what actually is the pineal gland and why does it really matter?

The pineal gland is a tiny, pea-sized gland shaped like a pinecone, which is located in the centre of the brain, beneath the cerebral cortex, above the third ventricle. It is considered to have a higher concentration of energy in the body due to it being filled with highly charged cerebrospinal fluid (CSF) and more blood flow per cubic volume than any other organ in the body. It is the dominant source of the body's melatonin, dimethyltryptamine (DMT), pinoline and serotonin. These hormones affect our mood, sleep, biological rhythms, blood pressure, body temperature, and many other bodily functions, including sex drive.

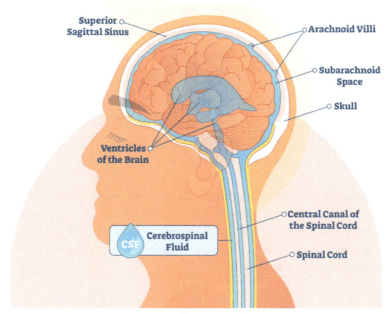

Figure 16: Cerebrospinal fluid, which is a clear and colourless liquid, acts as the shock absorber for the nervous system and also circulates nutrients and chemicals from the blood.

Have you wondered why the sunshine feels so good on your body? The pineal gland is made up of cells that have characteristics of the rod-shaped light sensitive cells found in the retinas of our eyes. It acts like a third eye by detecting light and releasing a hormonal response. Sensitivity and activation of the pineal gland is important for our physical, mental, emotional, and spiritual health while also enhancing our intuition, creativity, wisdom, consciousness, and deeper feelings of orgasms.

For deeper states of orgasm there needs to be a resonance called rhythmic entrainment (energetic waves oscillating together and the more aligned they are, the more resonance it will have). In Amplified Orgasmic Method (AOM) we are working on creating resonance with our energies and with our partners' energies. In bodywork, I am working on creating resonance with different energies present in different locations of the body so that we can become more aligned and real alchemy can take place. In order to be involved in deeper states of love-making, we need to have awareness of resonance between the two bodies at all layers.

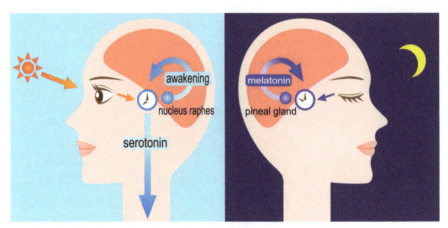

Figure 17: Role of serotonin and melatonin which makes us all have a good night's sleep. Serotonin is the hormone of lightness and melatonin is the hormone of darkness.

The pineal gland is activated by light, vibration and even magnetic and orgasmic fields.[10] Our different energy centres have different electromagnetic fields so activation, especially the sexual energy centre and the heart energy centre, will cause the pineal gland and the third eye to vibrate and activate, which will create stronger intuition, better creativity, and profound vision.

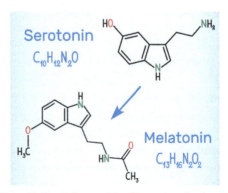

Figure 18: Chemical composition of serotonin and melatonin.

On an energetic level, the pineal gland gets blocked due to exposure to various toxins in the environment, poor diet, stress, pesticides found on food, electromagnetic fields by electrical gadgets, especially mobile phones, fluoride, and other chemical substances like chlorine.[11] All of these cause calcification of the pineal gland. Detoxification of the body is important in order to decalcify the pineal gland. Meditation, yogic practices, and sun-gazing at dawn are considered to be great ways to activate the pineal gland. Whole body orgasms are very good for activation of the pineal gland, although people who have not been on the Path of Amplified Orgasm might believe that orgasm is something only to be experienced in the genital area, so they might struggle to see the connection between the pineal gland and orgasm.

As you can see, our brain performs so many important functions! Don't you think we should really be taking care of our brain? Our modern lives have become robotic. We run around on autopilot, scarcely aware of the incredible feats of internal processing that our brain and nervous system are doing just so that we can move around and make sense of our world. Most of us do not allow enough time to engage ourselves consciously, including engaging our brain in ways that go beyond merely thinking and into the realm of gaining a deeper understanding of how it operates to create emotion, feelings, sensations, thoughts, and indeed, our perception of reality itself. And of course, on the Path of Amplified Orgasm, these are all important insights.

EXERCISE: Exercising Different Parts of the Brain

An Orgasm is a Whole Brain Experience

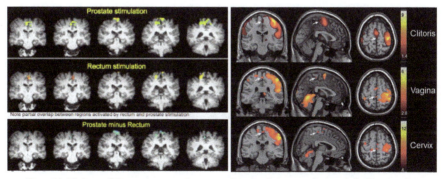

Figure 19-20: Areas of the sensory cortex that respond to stimulation to various genitals. (Komisaruk et al 2011). https://www.lelo.com/blog/wp-content/uploads/2015/09/male-mapping-poster.pdf.

According to neuroscientist Barry Komisaruk, fMRI scans performed on various people at different stages of orgasm (covered in more detail in Chapter Seven) showed that the brain is completely activated during this experience.[12]

We see activation in the nucleus accumbens, the pleasure centre of the brain, and the hypothalamus, which secretes oxytocin. We see activation in the cerebellum, which is involved in muscle tension; we see activation in the insular and cingulate cortex, which are interesting because those same areas react to pain, so it may be inhibiting pain in its processes; we see activation in the amygdala, which increases heart rate and blood pressure and sweating. They're all activated, and they're all activated maximally.[13]

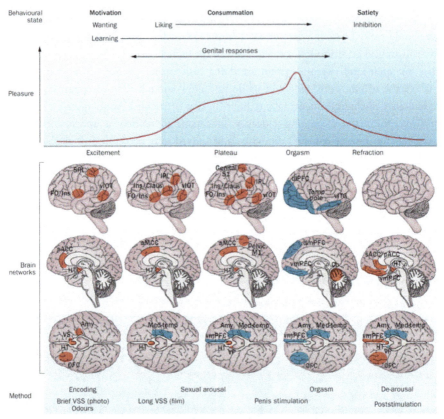

Figure 21: Activation of different parts of the brain during different phases of the sexual response cycle. (Credit: Sex for fun: a synthesis of human and animal neurobiology, Janniko R. Georgiadis, Morten L. Kringelbach & James G. Pfaus.)

His research also shows different parts of the brain lighting up when different parts of the body are touched, although the brain can't really tell the difference between whether you are stimulating yourself or getting stimulated by someone else.[14] In fact, recent research shows that even thinking about the genitals can light up these regions in an fMRI scan.[12] Other areas of the brain responsible for other functions also become activated one after the other as a person progresses towards climax. These include the limbic system (memory and emotions), the hypothalamus (signals hormonal releases), and the prefrontal cortex (problem solving).

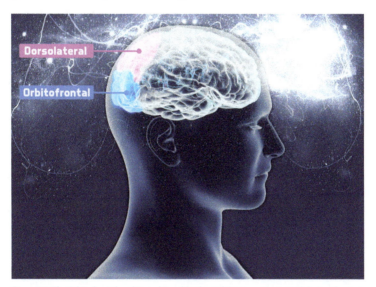

Figure 22: The Orbitofrontal and Dorsolateral Prefrontal Cortex get activated during the state of orgasm.

During orgasm, the orbitofrontal cortex (OFC), which is located right above and behind the eyes, gets activated when we are aroused and the dorsolateral prefrontal cortex (DPC), which is located above the orbitofrontal and roughly behind the hairline, keeps us in check to act consciously and gets activated to suppress our impulses. Neuroscientist Dr Heather Berlin argues that when people talk about getting in their heads and not being able to be present or enjoy sexual pleasure, it is because of the activation of the DPC, which can result in performance anxiety.[13]

According to her, when we are stimulating ourselves, these frontal cortices are free to turn their attention to fantasy. However, when another person is stimulating us, then our mind wanders. In anxious people, it wanders not to fantasy, but to self-consciousness or distractions such as other parts of their day. Hence, it is important to decrease activation of the DPC to be able to be in a flow state and allow the subcortical parts of the brain to take over. Although we can't consciously tell ourselves to decrease dorsolateral prefrontal cortex activation, we can figure out what makes us in the "flow state" by losing the sense of self, time, and space.

Neurons: Communicators of the Nervous System

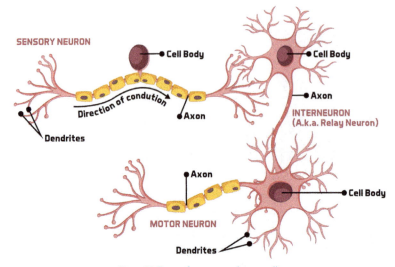

Figure 23: Types of neurons and nerve cells.

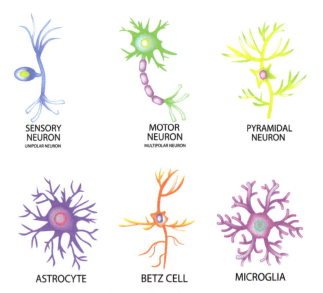

Figure 24: Types of neurons

Of course, each region of the brain works in concert with signalling from other areas as well as the rest of the peripheral nervous system. It is through the activity of special cells called neurons that this communication takes place. These neurons (nerve cells) are intensely interconnected with each other and are responsible for efficient and lightning-speed communication.

There are three basic parts of a neuron. The cell body or soma contains the nucleus and endoplasmic reticulum. Inside the cell body we also find ribosomes which are responsible for building proteins and mitochondria which generate energy. And, there are two main types of branches coming off the soma: dendrites (which receive incoming messages from other nerve cells) and axons (which carry signals from the cell body to other cells). A nerve cell communicates with other cells through electrical impulses when these nerve cells are stimulated. These impulses move to the tip of an axon, which stimulates the release of chemicals known as neurotransmitters that act as messengers. The gaps between the nerves are called synapses.

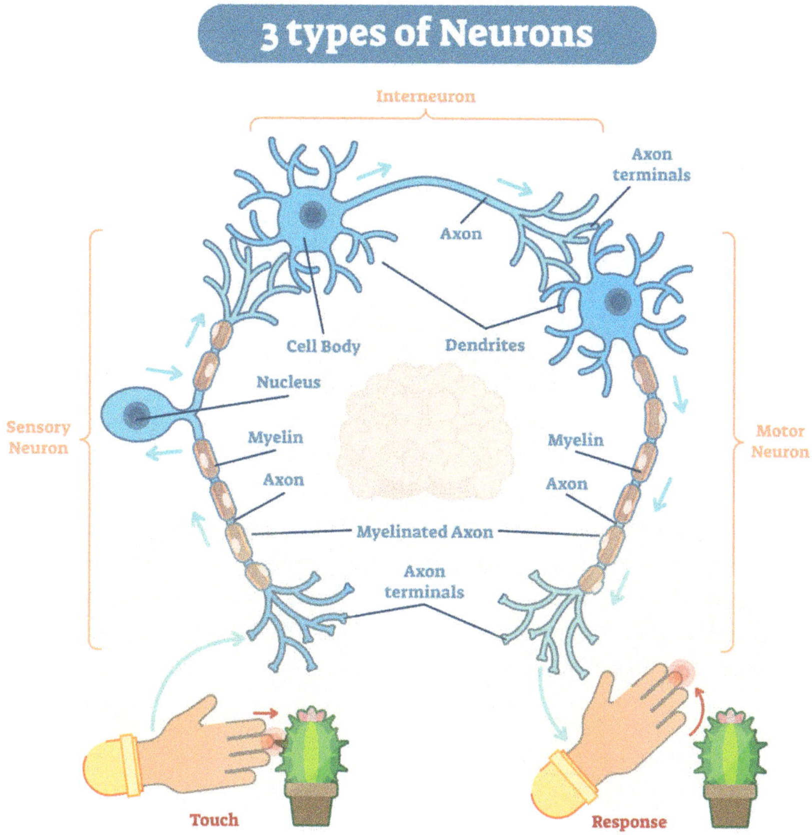

3 types of Neurons

Figure 25: Neurons and our responses

Neurotransmitters pass through the synapse and get attached to receptors on the receiving cell. This process keeps repeating from neuron to neuron allowing us to move, think, feel, and communicate.

There are three basic types of neurons: motor neurons which control muscle contractions, sensory neurons which carry signals from the peripheral nervous system to the central nervous system, and interneurons which connect neurons in the central nervous system.

Any muscular movement in the form of a jerk during hard and fast penetration or the movement reaction due to pinching the nipples is felt by sensory neurons, which then pass the message to motor neurons that control those muscles. This jerk-like reaction doesn't involve the processing of the brain.

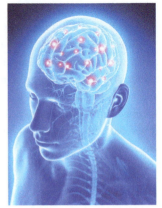

Figure 26: Neurons in the brain firing together through neural pathways

Neural Pathways and Conditioning

A neural pathway is the connection formed between neurons, which enables a signal to be sent from one region of the nervous system to another. Neurons are connected by a single axon, or by a bundle of axons known as a nerve tract, or fasciculus.[15]

One way to think of a neural pathway is like a road that connects one town to another. Imagine the road is a dirt path, and only one person travels on this road each day. It is not very wide, and the weeds on either side threaten to overtake it. On the other hand, imagine the road is a major highway in a modern city, carrying hundreds of thousands along its path each day. Which is stronger? Bigger? Faster? Offering more efficient travel? The highway, of course.

In a similar way, neural pathways are influenced by our behaviours, beliefs, and environment. The more we use a pathway, the easier travel along that route becomes. This process is known as conditioning in psychology circles. The associated strengthened neural pathways have been called "neural superhighways" by brain researchers. Interestingly, researchers in artificial intelligence also use this insight from human learning, known as Neural Network Theory.[16] Habits offer a good example of how this process works in practice.

Habits

Do you find yourself repeating the same patterns, even when you would rather not? Perhaps you have tried to give up alcohol, sugar, or porn but found it difficult to do.

Our habits are the result of the process of conditioning on the brain. As you have seen above, when we repeat certain thoughts, feelings, or actions, these repetitions strengthen neural pathways. Neuropsychologist Donald Hebb, often named as the father of Neural Network Theory, explained what he termed the Neuropsychological Postulate in his landmark 1949 book, *The Organization of Behavior*. This concept has since been paraphrased as: "Neurons that fire together, wire together."[17] At a deeper level, it is these neural pathways that create habits – some of which we like and some we don't.

EXERCISE: Identifying and Evaluating Habits

Neural Pathways: The Case of Porn

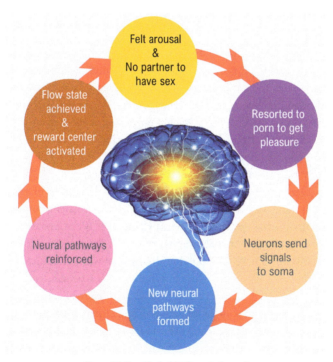

Figure 27: How the habit of porn is formed

Here is an example of how a habit is formed. As a man, you may have felt arousal, but you don't have a partner to have sex with or your partner doesn't want to have sex. So, you resort to porn to get pleasure. This billion-dollar industry has become all the more easy to access thanks to the internet. It is easy, free, and fast. However, what happens when it becomes a habit?

As you watch porn repeatedly, neurons housed in the area of your brain that's storing desire for pleasure send electrical messengers down the axons to the cell's centre (soma) where it is then routed to a particular group of connected dendrites which would then release a chemical messenger to the new, targeted group of neurons that are located next to it. New neural pathways begin to be formed to acquire and store these new ways of seeking pleasure as a substitute for actual sexual connection.

Neural pathways get reinforced through repetition. Because sexual energy is so powerful, without knowing how to harness it effectively for the purpose of our well-being, it overpowers us. The more these pathways are used, the stronger they become, resulting in the likelihood of new long-term connections and memories of watching porn and seeking pleasure through the hand and the specific visual stimulation of pornography, which is disconnected from other stimuli such as emotional connection with another person. With enough "practice" this association between porn and sexual satisfaction can crowd out other paths of arousal and stimulation, such as sexual experience with our partners.

The neural pathways of repeated exposure to porn can eventually crowd out other ways of enjoying sexual pleasure, creating what amounts to a porn/pleasure neural superhighway, meanwhile, making it harder for us to access the pleasure of sex on other levels, impeding our ability to enjoy sex with real people. As per Dr Norman Doidge, a researcher at Columbia University states, "porn creates the perfect conditions and triggers the release of the right chemicals to make lasting changes in the brain."[18]

The state of being in flow is the most ideal state for forming stronger neural pathways. Flow is "a deeply satisfying state of focused attention."[19] When we are in flow so deep that nothing else matters – we can even lose track of time. You have experienced this state numerous times in your life – whether having conversations with friends, focusing on a task, playing a game, or having sex. When one watches porn, the flow state is easy to achieve. After all, there is no person there to distract you, make you feel self-conscious, or to have to respond to. Many men who are addicted to porn find it difficult to find that flow state when interacting with a person, and soon the path to a healthy sex life with a partner can begin to close. Meanwhile, the neural pathways connecting pornography to stimulation, arousal, and climax continue to get stronger.

Like other addictive substances and behaviours, porn activates reward centres in the brain and releases specific chemicals, one of which contains a protein called DeltaFosB. This is the same protein which is used for learning a new skill, but it can also lead to addictive and compulsive behaviours. In the case of porn, DeltaFosB enables the brain, especially with the release of dopamine, to make strong connections between watching porn and the pleasure one gets from it. This protein stays in the brain for weeks or months, thus making it difficult to get rid of porn or any addictive habit.

Although I have chosen porn addiction in a man as an example, it is important to understand that porn addiction can also happen with women. In addition, other addictions and compulsive behaviours such as having frequent risky sex with strangers or compulsive cheating on your partner are habits that are formed in the same way for both women and men, that is, at the level of brain chemistry.

At this point, you may be feeling depressed, particularly if you or your partner suffer from porn addiction or other equally problematic addictive behaviours. However, hang in there. In fact, by understanding the mechanisms of how habits are formed, we can learn to become intentional about our brains, and rewire them using the same principles.

EXERCISE: Build a Healthy Habit

Neuroplasticity: Remapping Orgasm

We end up doing the same things over and over because we are wired to follow the path of least resistance. Repeated behaviours become habits which can be healthy or unhealthy.

Figure 28-29: Neuroplasticity in the brain due to repeated behaviours. Different neural networks throughout the body

Meanwhile, habits also build in specific associations. We are often not aware of these associations, but even though they are not necessarily intentional, they are still part of the neural pathway we have built.

For example, if someone with a porn addiction also chooses only to view certain body types, for example very slender young women with large breasts, then this body type can become central to the neural pathway for the rise of sexual energy, and can eventually become essential to feelings of arousal. This can then become a kind of block to achieving sexual arousal with partners that do not have that body type. And, if you plan to enjoy sex with a partner who ages alongside you, then consider the problems that being exclusively stimulated by images of young models will create in the long term.

Likewise, repeating sexual encounters under certain types of emotional states such as stress, pressure to perform, and even pain can eventually become required parts of the sexual experience, leading in some cases to destructive and unhealthy patterns. By seeking climax, by forcing it, under stress, or during pain, you are creating a neural superhighway that connects orgasm to desperation, stress, and pain.

The good news is that when we become aware of the habits around sex that we have formed, we can make a choice to change them. These habits can be transformed by choosing to condition new neural pathways so they become our paths of least resistance. On the Path of Amplified Orgasm, we look at the ways to create new neural pathways in a healthy manner by looking at the existing patterns and behaviours then creating new, healthier pathways. For example, in bodywork sessions, clients learn to create new pathways. Likewise through the practice of the Amplified Orgasmic Method (AOM), clients learn how to get in the flow state, further deepening new pathways.

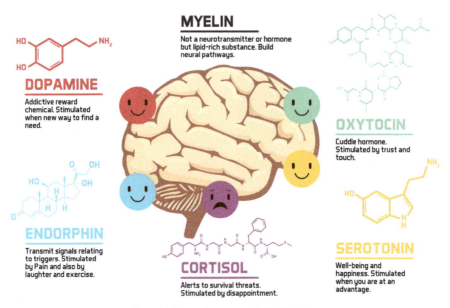

Figure 30: Various hormones and their functions

Regular orgasms, AOM sessions, or bodywork sessions are so powerful in creating new neural pathways because of the release of stagnant and unwanted cellular memories, the creation of new memories, and the release of hormones (dopamine, oxytocin, serotonin, endorphins). Repetition of newly formed circuits strengthens neural connections with one another and creates a new path to orgasm that can then be reinforced through repetition and practice.

Orgasm and Mental Health

The World Health Organization defines mental health as:

> Mental health is not just the absence of mental disorder. It is defined as a state of well-being in which every individual realizes his or her own potential, can cope with the normal stresses of life, can work productively and fruitfully, and is able to make a contribution to her or his community.[20]

Mental health problems may be caused by excessive stress from a situation or series of events, genetic factors, biochemical imbalances, substance abuse, poor coping skills, or a combination of these. There are many ways to address mental health, including learning how to handle stressors in healthier ways, having a supportive network, self-care, mindfulness, and counselling.

In some cases, psychotropic drugs are prescribed to address neurochemical imbalances. The drugs that are used to treat many mental health conditions can often interfere with a person's sex life as well as their ability to feel orgasms. Patients on certain medications, such as antidepressants, mood stabilisers, or antipsychotics, can experience all forms of sexual dysfunction, including difficulties with sexual arousal, decreased desire, erectile dysfunction, poor vaginal lubrication, difficulty achieving orgasm, and reduced sexual satisfaction.

Even in instances where the mental health state has improved, sexually adverse effects can continue for a long time and are often not recognised or are under-recognised by doctors and therapists.

While I do not think that orgasm alone is a cure for mental health conditions, research does suggest that a healthy sex life can contribute to a more positive outlook. Sex can be a positive stress reliever, and it can increase our intimacy and emotional vulnerability with our life partners, all of which can have a positive impact on mental wellness. Dr Michael Aaron, a licensed psychotherapist, sexologist, and certified sex therapist, has noted that "Orgasms are a potent form of stress relief, bringing calm and relaxation. Much of this is due to the release of oxytocin, a hormone that is sometimes referred to as 'the love hormone' for the feeling of well-being and bonding that it brings."[21]

In addition, I have seen with my own eyes that bodywork sessions can impact people in positive ways through my own coaching. I have often had clients who have experienced severe depression in their life due to relationships, family issues, career issues, and other stressors. After our bodywork sessions they have found themselves feeling better, stronger, and more positive towards life.

The sessions help them to connect with themselves at a deep core level, help them to let go of things that they may be obsessing about, or help them to release negative experiences they have been holding onto that have become trapped in their body at the cellular level. Orgasms, especially whole body orgasms, help in the flow of sexual energy moving from head to toe, and as such, they affect every body part in between. Orgasms not only provide physical benefits, they can also help with improving self-esteem, lowering anxiety, and creating new positive cellular memories and neural pathways. In addition, they can unblock areas where negative energy and emotions have been stored in the body, thus releasing them from our energetic selves.

The Mind

Western societies often confuse brain and mind, a symptom of the mind/body dualism that was deeply reinforced during the Enlightenment period. Rather than making room for scientific discussion of such concepts as spirituality, morality, souls, and emotional reality, such topics were deemed irrational and thus banished as serious topics for rational minds to ponder. This hyper-rationalism collapsed the aspects of the mind (memory, emotion, thought, sensory processing, belief) as simply effects of the mechanisms of the brain.

As a result of this tradition in the history of science, many people in Western cultures have come to understand the mind in this way. However, there are major disadvantages of this model, the main one being that it does not allow for a robust language capable of analysing and becoming reflective about the aspects of human existence that are perhaps the most unique to our species: self-awareness, the formation of belief, a sense of identity, spiritual connection, mindfulness, morality, emotional richness, and the list goes on.

Post-structural (also called post-modern) philosophers of the mind have, over the last several decades, challenged the mind/body dualism at the heart of modernist (or Enlightenment) philosophy. Interdisciplinary research combining insights from neuro-imaging, linguistic, and cognitive theories, psychology, and philosophy of knowledge has revealed new paradigms, such as the concept of *the embodied mind*, which better capture the complex interplay between the mechanisms of the brain, the deep influence of personal experience, and the construction of our sense of reality and identity.[22]

The best way to discover the secrets of the mind is to understand the mind as separate from the brain, yet deeply shaped by it. That is, the brain is the anatomical structure of the body that is visible and tangible which is made up of neurons, lobes, different systems, etc. The brain is responsible for providing the structure and mechanisms to keep our bodies operational and it is the canvas upon which the mind is painted through subjective and intersubjective experiences. Perhaps in this analogy, the brain may also provide brushes, paints, and hands to move the oil onto the canvas. However, the mind conceives and manifests the painting itself, which is our view of reality, our sense of self, and our efforts to make meaning out of our world.

The transcendent world of thoughts, feelings, attitudes, beliefs, desires, emotions, sensations, consciousness, and imagination are the products of the mind. In addition, the mind is not confined to the brain, and the intelligence of mind permeates every cell of the body. The mind is some sort of energy which can flow either positively or negatively through various senses and facilitate the functions and processes of brain which manifest through our relating, behaviour,

Figure 31: Our mind, which is separate from the brain, is shaped by it.

and perceptions. Negative or disharmonising energy impacts the brain negatively while positive and harmonising vibrations impact the brain positively.

The mind is awareness of consciousness, the ability to control what we do, why we do it, and how we do it. It is the reasoning, the know-how, and the ability to understand. The mind is also largely involuntary although various practices and techniques like tantric sex, amplified orgasm, meditation, and yoga attempt to gain voluntary control over the involuntary functions of mind. This concept is widely known as *intentionality*.

Figure 32: Different categories of mind and their functions

43

In order to have deeper and amplified orgasms, it is important to have alignment of the mind between lovers, not just the body or the brain. An example of how this can break down can often be seen in the ways many women and men (much of which has been reinforced by cultural norms) approach sex. If a man is mostly tuned in to the physical aspects of sex, and his female partner is tuned in to the emotional aspects of sex, then a disconnect is created. Energy flow is blocked.

Amplified orgasm becomes impossible unless the couple is able to recognise and open themselves to the other ways of experiencing sexual energy. When this happens, then emotional and physical interplay develops both *within* each man and woman as well as *between* them. Once both learn to also be open to these other ways of experiencing sexual energy, men often feel more loving, caring, compassionate, and connected with their feelings while women feel more physically turned-on by their partners. Once women and men have been on the Path of Amplified Orgasm, both of them learn how to develop the resonance with each other, even before even sex has started.

Beliefs

Until you make the unconscious conscious, it will direct your life and you will call it fate.
Carl Jung

During my coaching sessions, I often find my clients having a lot of limiting or negative beliefs about themselves, about their sex lives, or negative feelings relating to orgasm. Much of the work we do is to convert limiting or disempowering beliefs into empowering and supportive beliefs. In order to understand this at a deeper level, we will be looking at what beliefs are, how are they formed, how the different kinds of beliefs play a role on the Path of Amplified Orgasm.

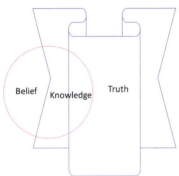

Figure 33: Beliefs are subjective and form a smaller part of the overall truth.

Belief is the attitude when we take something at face value and regard it to be a fact. For example, if one woman has a belief that she is beautiful, then she has the belief *I am beautiful* stored in her subconscious. If another woman believes that she is ugly, then she has the belief *I am ugly* stored in her subconscious. The way each of them operate in the world would be different in many ways because their beliefs would influence their behaviour.

44

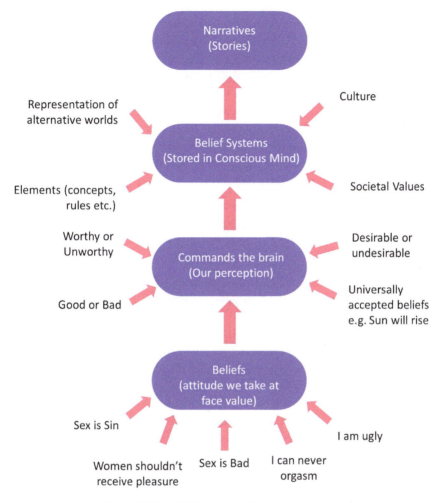

Figure 34: How the belief systems and narratives are formed.

Beliefs help us to understand and navigate this world. They are like the internal commands to the brain relating to how we represent ourselves and perceive what is happening around us when we believe something to be a fact. Some beliefs do not require much critical thinking. For example, we simply believe the sun will rise tomorrow, and of course, it does. Some beliefs keep us safe so we try to preserve them once they are formed and guard them carefully. Beliefs play an important role in serving our subconscious mind and often we take them for granted, assuming them to be factual, without ever really wondering if they are true or not. It is our beliefs that determine whether anything is good or bad, sexy or not sexy, desirable or undesirable, worthy or unworthy, acceptable or unacceptable, achievable or impossible.

When a set of beliefs gets stored in our subconscious mind, a belief system tends to emerge. These belief systems are often passed around on a social level. When they are, they are known as narratives or social scripts by researchers in the social sciences.[23] Narratives or scripts become like stories that we believe about the world, ourselves, and others. These narratives about the world are not only something individuals hold (beliefs), but we also pass these stories back and forth, creating social narratives which either reinforce or challenge current cultural norms and values.

Here are a few examples of these narratives or scripts that you are probably familiar with, even if you have personally rejected them:

- *Real men are strong and emotionally stoic.*
- *Women are supposed to be emotionally giving and supportive.*
- *Survival of the fittest means that competition is the natural state of all animals, including humans.*

Please notice a few things about these narratives. First, they are not just beliefs, because they are ideas that are regularly passed around socially through conversations, media, even children's stories.

Second, these types of stories or narratives tend to reinforce what *should be*. That is, we tend to notice when the exception to the rule is present (a man who is emotionally present, a woman who is cold). Often times, rather than realising the exception is proof that the narrative itself is flawed, we tend to see the individual that breaks the rule as flawed. And, we can also internalise failings, we perceive in ourselves along these same lines.

Third, these narratives provide a tremendous amount of background assumption about the way the world is, and as such, are constantly reinforcing our own beliefs and belief systems. And, because many of the beliefs are shared through social narratives, we are often reinforcing our individual belief in these ideas through social interactions every single day.

In a belief system, it is not uncommon for different beliefs to reinforce each other. This is true whether or not they are factually correct. The fact that different beliefs in a system support each other can give a false sense of "truth" to beliefs. In addition, belief systems usually contain conflicting beliefs. We have all probably experienced the realisation that we sometimes hold beliefs that are in conflict with each other. Totally normal!

Beliefs are formed throughout our life but the ones formed during our childhood are so deeply rooted that by the time we are adults some of our beliefs are engrained so deeply that it feels like they are part of our core, they are part of our body, living inside the marrow of our bones, living inside our soul, and are met with huge resistance when they are challenged. And, because they are intertwined, challenging one belief can begin to unravel our entire belief system. Since our sense of identity is deeply related to our belief systems, challenging our beliefs can feel very threatening indeed.

Formation of Beliefs

The subconscious mind, which is a storage device that contains all the data and information one is ever exposed to in life, including past memories, experiences, thoughts, and ideas, uses this information to form beliefs. Beliefs are generally formed in two ways: by our experiences, inferences, and deductions or by accepting what others tell us to be true.

Most of our core beliefs are formed when we are children, and because we are unable to question these beliefs or distinguish between truth and falsehood, we often accept them as they are told. However, life experiences at any age can cause the formation of core beliefs. Our parents, schooling, culture, religion, and social environment play a big part in creating and shaping our beliefs from an early age onward through social narratives. For example, in certain religions, sex is considered to be sinful. Good girls are taught to obey their partners and fulfil their demands. Men are taught to be courageous and strong and not show emotions to the point that being vulnerable is considered to be a sign of weakness.

As we grow older, our beliefs are influenced by a new set of environments that have their own native narratives. For example, porn persistently represents the narrative that great men are those who have large penises and who can fuck women for a long time, women are sexy if they make sounds and noises during sex, lubricants are good for sex, beautiful women are more orgasmic, and so forth.

Our sense of identity is shaped by these narratives if we internalise them as beliefs. The more we invest in these beliefs, the harder it becomes to untangle them in order to liberate ourselves from them.

Scripts: How We Turn Belief into Our Reality

Man is what he believes.
Anton Chekhov

Let's review quickly: Beliefs are ideas that individuals hold to be true. Belief systems are constellations of individual beliefs that reinforce each other in the mind of an individual. Narratives are socially held beliefs that are constantly passed around through culture, media, and personal interactions.

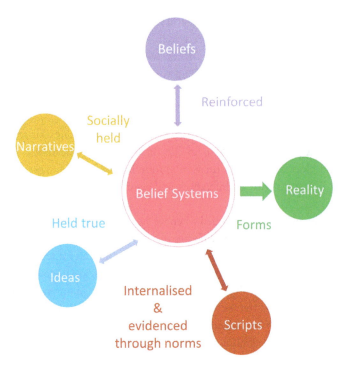

Figure 35: Formation of reality through belief systems

So, what about this notion of "scripts"? Influential sociologist Erving Goffman developed this term to bridge the gap between culturally held ideas, and individual actions and behaviours. In a nutshell, the idea is that normative social narratives (that is those social stories that imply the way the world *should* be) encourage us to internalise these ideas and become congruent with them. That is, social scripts offer insight into how cultural norms are first in the collective mind, and then manifest in the world as individuals internalise these stories and actually become them for fear of social punishment.

One can see how notions about hypermasculinity have shaped men in ways that have encouraged them to limit their existence by suppressing their emotional selves in favour of the more accepted rational expressions. Of course, since scripts about masculinity also encourage men to dominate both other men and women in order to show their true manliness, men are encouraged to express certain emotions, such as anger.

Meanwhile, as we make ourselves into the social scripts of our culture, we also then look around and see that compliance with these norms is evidence that this way of being is "natural," thus "true." For example, statistical rates of men and violence seem to confirm that men must be, by nature, prone to violence. This kind of circular reasoning then feeds into a self-fulfilling prophecy: *The world is this way, the world should be this way, the world can only be this way.* Rather than understanding toxic masculinity as something that can be changed at the level of societal norms, many people then participate in keeping it as a kind of status quo. For example, a mother sees her boy bullying another child in the neighbourhood and says: "Well, boys will be boys."

When we understand the role that these scripts play in creating our reality, we can become aware of the tremendous capacity for human beings and society to change, and become both willing and able to participate in that change. However, liberation from such damaging social scripts begins in our individual mind.

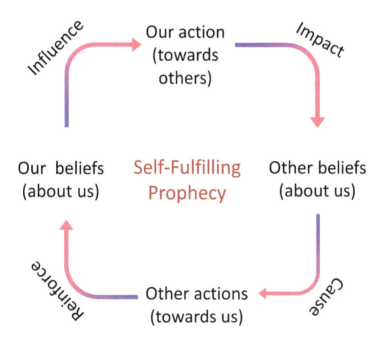

Figure 36: The cycle of self-fulfilling prophecy

EXERCISE: Identifying Social Scripts About Gender, Love, and Relationships

Liberation of the Mind

There is nothing inherently wrong with the process of the formation of belief and even the formation of socially held ideas. However, when we buy into narratives that are fundamentally limiting, then we are choosing to enslave ourselves to these ideas. And, we are often profoundly psychically damaged when we choose to do so.

Take for example a woman who believes in the narrative that "good girls" don't enjoy sex. Only "sluts" enjoy sex. And, "sluts" are bad girls. This constellation of linked social narratives exists in many cultures. The woman who allows these stories to become her core beliefs is very unlikely to be able to have access to her own beautiful and amazing sexual being. Until she is able to shed belief in these narratives, she is trapped in a very limited reality where sexual pleasure is denied to her.

Here is the good news:

Beliefs are not static and we have the power to choose our own beliefs.

However, we need a framework to help evaluate our beliefs that is not tied to outdated traditions, brutal or repressive regimes, and gatekeeping methods designed for social control rather than the liberation of the human spirit.

EXERCISE: How Belief Becomes Reality

Limiting Verses Empowering Beliefs

In my work with clients over the years, I have found many whose journey on the Path of Amplified Orgasm was blocked by damaging beliefs about themselves, about sex or gender, or about the body. In working to help them find a healthier approach to the sexual experience, I have found it exceedingly helpful to evaluate beliefs as falling into two main categories: limiting or empowering.

Empowering beliefs (non-limiting or positive) are beliefs that don't hold us back. They help us fulfil our true potential and give rise to positive thoughts, feelings, and emotions. They allow us to explore ourselves, the world, and each other. They create a sense of the infinite journey of life, love, and spiritual connection. They contribute to our overall well-being. Empowering beliefs open doors to allow us to use our incredible power of self-awareness and intentionality to become a human being who is aligned with our deepest desires. Empowering beliefs also encourage us to empower others.

Limiting beliefs are those that are disempowering, hold us back, prevent us from fulfilling our true potential, and give rise to negative thoughts and emotions. They tend to create a narrow passage point through which we must pass to love ourselves or others, rather than to accept the inherent beauty and value of all ways of being. Limiting beliefs also take the form of confusing what *is* with what *could be*. In other words, limiting beliefs close the door on personal growth because they imply that we cannot change to experience new ways of being.

Most of the time we are not even aware of what kind of beliefs we have stored in our subconscious mind. Since they have a profound effect on our ability to actualise our best self, beliefs are at the root of your capacity to grow in your journey, in terms of both the Path of Amplified Orgasm as well as other aspects of life such as your relationships with other people.

My recommendation is to self-reflect on your beliefs from time to time. Identify your limiting beliefs and consciously change them to empowering beliefs so that you can open your mind to becoming the person who makes the most of your potential and who can experience the most of this life you have been given.

Limiting Beliefs	Empowering Beliefs
I will never be able to be orgasmic.	*I can learn to become orgasmic and I choose to invest some time, energy, and practice into growing my ability to enjoy sexual pleasure.*
I am too fat (too thin, too tall, too small chested, etc.) to be attractive.	*Sexual attraction is about connection on many levels. I choose to seek partners with a broader view of sexual attraction rather than those with limited perceptions, focused on the physical only, and/or narrow conceptions of sexy body types.*
I am afraid to be vulnerable again.	*I choose to be brave knowing that intimacy requires vulnerability, but the benefits of feeling connected on a deep level are worth sometimes getting my feelings hurt.*
I am a victim of sexual trauma and I am broken from those experiences.	*I am a survivor of sexual trauma. I know that others have recovered from abuse, and so can I. I am willing to get help and try to overcome the effects of abuse. I refuse to allow my abuser to rob me of access to sexual pleasure.*
I can never let go of my porn addiction.	*I can recover from porn addiction with proper training, education, and discipline.*

Supporting Your Partner's Empowering Beliefs

Before we move on from the concept of empowering beliefs, it is important to reflect on what we know about the formation of beliefs in order to best pave a map towards transforming our belief systems. Although one can certainly make a lot of progress in shifting from limiting to empowering beliefs on their own, it is beneficial to enlist those we love, especially if we are finding resistance to change within ourselves.

For example, let's say you have identified the limiting belief *I must be thin to be sexy* and decided to replace it with *My curvy body is very sexy*. You can ask your partner to participate in this shift by reinforcing it through words, touches, kisses, caresses and other ways to put some intention on helping you to invest in this new empowering belief.

The Mind and Orgasm

As we delve further into the relationship between the mind and orgasm we see that the mental body provides a meaningful map. There are five keys to understanding how to best bring the mind into alignment on the Path of Amplified Orgasm: Consciousness, Awareness, Attention, Intention, and Presence.

We might understand their relationship through this framework:

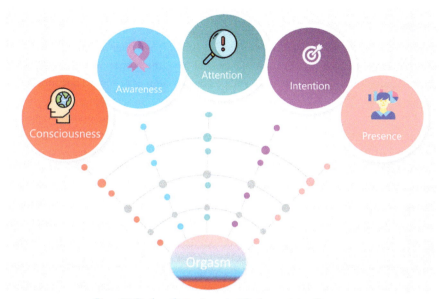

Figure 37: Five keys that are important for deeper states of orgasm

Consciousness

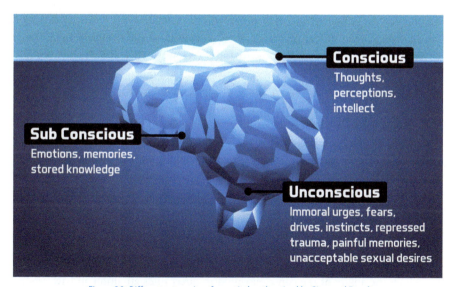

Figure 38: Different categories of our mind as theorised by Sigmund Freud

Sigmund Freud, the famous Austrian psychologist, first theorised the concept of the three categories of our mind.[24] Our three minds – conscious, subconscious (preconscious), and unconscious – work together to create our reality. They offer insight into how we can change our habits, increase confidence, and have the deeper and better orgasms that we desire. It is important to note, only a small fraction or our mind operates at the conscious level.[25,26]

The conscious mind uses words, images, writing, movement, and thoughts to communicate with the outside world as well as our inner-self. The subconscious mind takes care of recent memories and is in continuous contact with the resources of the unconscious mind. It is also referred to as the "sixth sense." The unconscious mind stores all those memories and past experiences which have been repressed through trauma or have been consciously forgotten and are not required on day-to-day basis. It is from these memories that our beliefs, habits, and behaviours that can't generally be explained are formed. Communication among the three minds happen through feelings, emotions, imagination, sensations, dreams, thoughts, etc. The term unconscious is not the same as used in medical terminology, which means knocked out or anesthetised.

If we focus on negative things, our subconscious mind will deliver feelings, emotions, and memories associated with negativity. On the other hand, if we focus on positive things, it will deliver positivity. A never-ending loop of negativity, fear, and anxiety gets created when one continues to keep thinking about negative things. However, it is important to note that feelings, emotions, and memories associated with negativity are important and are not to be dismissed, as these exist in our conscious, subconscious, and unconscious minds. We need to acknowledge their existence and then use tools to alchemise and either release these negativities or move towards positivity in a way that allows it to grow to such an extent that it surrounds negativity, slowly diminishing its very existence. When you do this, the subconscious mind will make connections with feelings, emotions, and memories of past events associated with positivity. If you consciously use tools, then you can direct this energy to more rational and constructive aspects and also calm yourself while still honouring negative feelings.

In AOM we allow our conscious mind to make way for the subconscious mind to connect, emerge, and become our navigator. In bodywork, while we work on the conscious and subconscious mind, we are also working on the unconscious mind, bringing the unwanted and disharmonised emotions to the surface so they can be released. Day in and day out, our automatic routine makes it difficult to bring the shift from the conscious to the subconscious mind. But for old programmes to re-emerge and their blueprints be transformed, it requires a great shift at the physical, mental, emotional, energetic, and spiritual layers.

The type of programming at the level of the subconscious and unconscious minds determines the ability of the conscious mind to direct one's attention and awareness. The more control we have on our conscious mind, the more we will be able to direct our attention and awareness to where we would like it to be. Certain techniques such as free will of mind, mental power, and visualisation can be used to direct our energy towards our goals.

The conscious mind can imagine what is totally new and unique but the subconscious mind can only offer versions of memories that have been stored as a result of past experiences. The subconscious mind cannot distinguish between what the conscious mind imagines and what is real, so whatever is focused at the conscious level also brings up emotions and feelings associated with it in our mind for us to experience. For example, if we have felt justified jealousy in the past as a result of actual betrayal, then we have probably also felt being surrounded by thoughts about jealousy even though intellectually we knew that there was nothing to worry about.

The subconscious mind also plays an important role in day-to-day functions like behaviours, habits, mood, etc. Our subconscious mind obeys orders from the conscious mind unless we bring awareness and make a shift. Negative conscious thoughts will direct the subconscious mind to deliver negative feelings, memories, emotions, and positive conscious thoughts will direct the subconscious mind to deliver positive feelings, memories, and emotions.

The conscious mind gives the direction; the subconscious will deliver the emotions and feelings of what we continuously think about. Therefore, it is very important to pay attention to all kinds of thoughts that emerge from our mind, day in day out, as we do not know which of these thoughts could act as a command for our subconscious mind to work on.

Figure 39: Our consciousness is bigger than our physical body. When we interact, our consciousness is also interacting.

55

Consciousness is not something we see, it's something through which we see, which makes it challenging to study.
George Mashour,
Director of the Center for Consciousness Science
at the University of Michigan

Let's explore an example of this in practice. Consider a woman who has been in several abusive relationships. She may have come to believe that she deserves such abusive treatment. She may even have conscious negative thoughts along the lines of "I guess that is just the way love has to be, and I will always have to tolerate abuse if I want to be loved." If she does not come to recognise that these conscious thoughts can fuel her subconscious, then she is unlikely to stop the cycle of abuse in her life. For example, she may be attracted to abusive men and draw them into her life, without even realising it, through small signals she sends out, and her subconscious mind ignoring the red flags of abuse when meeting her next partner. Only by making a conscious shift to replace these negative thoughts with more empowering ones, such as, "I deserve a love that doesn't come with abuse, and I will not settle until I find it," can she begin to reprogramme her subconscious to work towards seeking and finding a loving and compassionate man.

The same applies during orgasm. If a man is able to direct his consciousness to the sexual experience rather than becoming singularly focused on climax, he will be better able to hold off his ejaculation and more fully experience sexual pleasure as well as extend the experience for his partner. With practice, this kind of conscious awareness will allow men to expand their consciousness in a way that will play an important part in their overall growth and journey to becoming multi-orgasmic.

Rhythmic stimulation and awakened energies during sexual and orgasmic connections alters brain activity and it is very important to be completely conscious to experience every single moment of this exchange. Are you conscious of the speed of interaction and thrusts, the kind of sounds and noises made, the kinds of feelings that arise, the kind of smells, the temperature of your body, your partner's and the room? Or are you focusing on sensations alone? Or you are not even conscious of what is happening because you have been occupied with the act of doing?

Adam Safron, a neuroscientist, explains, "Sex is a source of pleasurable sensations and emotional connection, but beyond that, it's actually an altered state of consciousness."[19]

In order to achieve orgasm, one must actively engage in being present, surrender to the experience, while recognising our feelings and everything that is happening within us, around us, and in connection with our partner.

Sometimes I hear from men who are single but do not understand why they are still single even though they want to be in relationship with someone and have lots of sex and physical intimacy. I ask them, "Do you watch porn, masturbate, and ejaculate regularly?" Generally, the answer is yes, and I believe this is where one of the biggest issues lies. If you are watching porn, masturbating, and ejaculating, you are automatically feeding your subconscious mind with stimuli that doesn't help you manifest the relationship you desire. Our subconscious mind can't distinguish between what our conscious mind imagines and what is real. So, even if you do not have a partner, but you are masturbating, your subconscious mind thinks it is getting what it needs, hence it feels no need to work on something extra. It is only when you don't masturbate, that the subconscious mind will start feeling panic and start thinking of solutions to do something about the unmet need. This is when the irresistibility kicks in; neural pathways overpower and you end up watching porn. Hence, a never-ending loop gets created. You can apply this in any scenario and mostly like this will hold true.

While men and women are individuals with their own life experiences, I have seen certain patterns that hold true in most cases. Men often feel a loss of consciousness during sex, while women often disconnect from their bodies. Men get overwhelmed by sensation, while women continue to remain disconnected from sensations they are feeling in their bodies. By altering our state of consciousness, we can address these barriers to amplified orgasm.

Consciousness is a subjective phenomenon. Orgasms, if experienced in the right way, should expand our consciousness. When we are conscious about the reason we are engaging in sex, the way we are having it, the impact it is causing moment by moment, then the more our consciousness will be driven to an altered state. When old and unwanted stuff starts coming up during sex, then it means through the help of sexual and orgasmic energy our conscious mind has penetrated through to the unconscious mind. This is one of the reasons why sex is often considered sacred and intimate. It will bring old memories and you want to be with someone you trust and who knows how to work through them with you. If the impact of sex only stays at the conscious level, it means you are not going deep enough.

Our subconscious mind obeys orders from the conscious mind unless we bring awareness and make a shift. Negative conscious thoughts will direct the subconscious mind to deliver negative feelings, memories, emotions, and positive conscious thoughts will direct the subconscious mind to deliver positive feelings, memories, and emotions.

EXERCISE: Reflecting on the Relationship Between the Conscious and the Subconscious

Attention

Figure 40: When there is chaos, we can still pay attention.

As we all know, our brain receives millions of stimuli every minute, but it has a filtering mechanism through which some stimuli are selected, whether consciously or subconsciously, while other stimuli are partially or completely ignored. Attention is the act of directing the mind to focus on an object or phenomenon.

This process is actually happening across all the bodies and not just the physical. So, the question is, are you aware of this process? Do you know that you are selectively ignoring the pieces of information coming at you? When she says, "I desire to cuddle only tonight and not have sex," what is it that's actually coming to your mind? When he says, "I will be coming home late tonight as I am meeting a woman to discuss a business proposal," what is it that's actually coming to your mind? Where does your attention go?

Characteristics of Attention

Mentioned below are some of the characteristics of attention:

- **Attention requires a clear object**. The clearer the object of attention, the easier it is to put and hold our attention on it and the easier it will be to receive the stimuli in the way it should be received without getting fogged by one's own judgements or errors in perception.
- **The process of selection also implies de-selecting everything else**. When someone is inattentive to something, they are attentive to something else, and vice versa. Inattentiveness and attentiveness go hand in hand. Inattentiveness on important things is attentiveness on unimportant things.
- **Attention happens at all levels**. That is, attention is happening at the physical, emotional, mental, energetic, and spiritual layers of the body. Those layers where

attention is more developed have more energy flow which in turn results in better understanding and more awareness at those layers. Layers where we lack developed attention result in misunderstandings, inhibitions, and lack of awareness.

- **Attention flexibility or mobility refers to the ease and speed with which we can move our attention from one thing to another.** Higher flexibility can mean a higher degree of spontaneity, a higher range of frequencies and energies that one can perceive, better capacity for multi-tasking, etc.
- **Attention span refers to the stability and/or durability of our attention.** It is possible to improve attention span with practice. Take a moment to notice if you can hold attention, or if your attention fluctuates often in space and time.
- **In an overwhelming state we lack the ability to distribute our attention.** When this happens we often get consumed by the energetic or physical state. The more expanded our consciousness, the more our attention can be distributed and the less overwhelmed and more grounded we will be.

For orgasmic amplification, we can think of the following as goals of sharpening our attention to more fully experience the many layers of the body during our sexual experiences:

- Improve clarity of mind and body
- Become aware of the process of selection and stay curious to observe things coming at you and the impact they are creating
- Learn to put attention at all levels: physical, emotional, mental, energetic, and spiritual layers
- Become more flexible and spontaneous with regard to different peaks, frequencies, emotions, and energies
- Build and strengthen attention span as much energy will be required to penetrate through to higher levels of consciousness
- Practise distributing attention while staying grounded during periods of high stimulation to really experience every single part of the layered body during sexual experiences.

Attention Expands Where Consciousness Expands
You might have heard the phrase, "Energy flows where attention goes."

When we are putting attention on something, we are actually putting energy into it and the quality of energy will depend on the quality of energy we have for it. For instance, you might have found that someone who has an awakened heart energy centre or has had deeply nourishing sex will often have love and compassion which will be of an amazing quality in comparison with the person who is more focused on the physical aspects of love-making or hasn't had sex for a while.

In my coaching over the years, one of the biggest concerns that I often hear from women relating to men is that they wish men could pay more attention to them and listen to what they have to say. If a woman feels this way in relating to a man, just imagine the seeds of conflict, disconnection, and dissonance already sown in the relationship. How would you as a man feel if the person you were talking to was not really paying attention or allowed his/her mind to wander somewhere else while you were sharing intimate thoughts and feelings?

Back in my college days, I used to get advice from my friends that if I wanted to last longer in bed I should either drink loads of beer or think about something else during love-making, especially right before I was about to climax. In that way, I was told, I would not ejaculate quickly. Perhaps you have heard the same advice? Pause for a moment to consider this. Don't you think it is disrespectful to be with someone, in such an intimate space, performing such a loving act, while deliberately directing your attention elsewhere?

During sex and love-making, where is your attention when you start? Where is your attention when you are in the middle? And, what happens to your attention after you have finished the act of love making?

Once my girlfriend and I were having sex and were deeply immersed in it. Suddenly, I felt a sort of disconnection at the mental level which I ignored. A few minutes later, it happened again. I started paying attention to that disconnection and noticed that my mind started going in random thoughts, which was so unlike me. I asked my partner to pause the act of sex for a second and asked her, "Where are you?" which then brought her attention back into the room, back with us. She said that for the past few minutes she had been thinking about a few things that had been bothering her but she wasn't conscious enough to know that she had not been present. We then spent some time talking about things that were bothering her and then continued our love-making once she was able to bring her attention back to both of us.

Another example: Once I was with another lover of mine and just a few minutes into our sexual engagement I felt some sort of disconnection/resistance between us. I started paying attention to it and then asked her, "Are you OK? Is there anything that you feel needs to be communicated?" She opened up and said, "After our last sexual connection, you sort of left the house without giving enough time for us to cuddle and come down together. That didn't feel good to me and I am now concerned that the same thing could happen again today." We paused our sexual act, had a conversation where I assured her that we would make enough time for connection and cuddles afterwards. Once we were reconnected, we continued happily with our love-making.

These two examples show how becoming more attentive to the emotional and mental levels was required to establish a good connection and to open up the sexual layer of our connection.

It is true that the more orgasmic energy we have in our body, the more attention we will be able to put on this experience. However, the more attention we have at all layers of the human experience, the more we will be able to experience amplified orgasms with our partner.

Intention

INTENTION
Opens up

Figure 41-42: It is better that we start everything with the right intention. When we are open and positive towards our intention, our intention is also open and positive towards us.

What is intention and why does it matter? What role does intention play in orgasmic amplification? Before we begin to answer these questions, I would like you to ask yourself: What is your intention when you are having sex with your partner and what is your intention when you are engaged in love-making? What happens to your intention throughout the course of a sexual encounter?

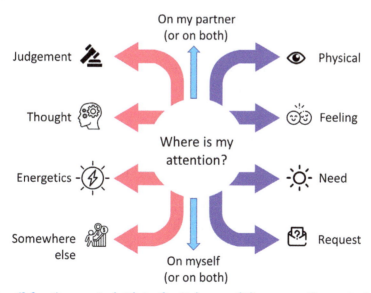

Figure 43: Sometimes we get so lost that we forget to be aware of where we are putting our attention.

Sexual energy and orgasmic energy are very powerful energies, but if used with the wrong intention in the form of rape, abuse, or molestation, they can be detrimental to the overall well-being of everyone involved. In our culture, where casual sex, friends with benefits, flings, sexual exploration partners, and hook-ups are so prevalent, it generally becomes very difficult to know what the real intention of each person is. People often end up engaging in sex while having an emotional, mental, and/or spiritual disconnect from each other and are fulfilling their needs at the physical level only, which in turns leads to creating intimacy issues, pain, and fear. Over time, these kinds of experiences can rob of us the real and deeply satisfying pleasure of this deeply intimate experience.

Dr Wayne W Dyer, in his book, *Power of Intention*, mentions the definition of intention as "a strong purpose or aim, accompanied by a determination to produce a desired result. People driven by intention are described as having a strong will that won't permit anything to interfere with achieving their inner desire."[27] He further states that some prominent researchers believe that our intelligence, creativity, and imagination interact with the energy field of intention rather than being thoughts or elements in our brain.

Intention is the starting point of every goal, every dream, every desire. Upanishads, the Indian Vedic scriptures, state: "You are what your deepest desire is. As your desire is, so is your intention. As your intention is, so is your will. As your will is, so is your deed. As your deed is, so is your destiny."

When we are putting our intention onto something, we are investing energy and creating an imprint. Imagine if a man is fucking his lover from place of ego. He is leaving the imprint of that kind of energy in her body. If a woman is feeling love and turned-on, she is inviting the man with the intention of experiencing that amazing love and engaged in love-making in a way that they both end up bathing in the orgasmic ball together.

We have sex for numerous reasons (enjoyment, pleasure, to get rid of headaches or pains, attraction, to stir jealousy, to celebrate, to de-stress, insecurity, obligation, etc.). The question is how many times are you aware of the reasons you have sex? Do you discuss what the intention of that love-making session should be/would be? Throughout our day we are generally working with some or the other intention, whether we are conscious about it or not, but don't you think it would give our life and love-making deeper meaning if we actually consciously laid down what the intention should be?

Just like we have different bodies, in the same way, these different layers of our bodies have different intentions too. What is our physical intention, mental intention, emotional intention, energetic intention, spiritual intention? If we are only focused on the physical, then our experiences will be limited to the physical realm. If we focus on the mental body, only then we will be able to amplify our experiences at this mental layer. Similarly, if we want to experience the interplay of energetic orgasms, we have to shift our intention to experience them and then put our attention towards energetic movements happening in and around our bodies.

Our intentions should be to connect with each other at the deepest levels possible. When we do that, amplified orgasm will begin to flow automatically. If our intention is to experience more love energy, then we need to pay attention to our heart energy centre, and if our intention is to connect telepathically, then our attention should be on third eye or crown energy centre. If our intention is to experience amplified orgasms, then our attention should be in understanding what would cause orgasms to be amplified.

Orgasmic energy and sexual energy are very powerful energies and if we have the right intentions set, we can harness them in a very positive way. In each of my sessions with my clients, whether it is the practice of Amplified Orgasmic Method (AOM) or whether it is a session relating to bodywork, both my clients and I always discuss our intention for the session. During love-making with my partner, I often aim to talk about our intention for the love-making session (although I still need to get better at it as sometimes I miss talking about this). One of the biggest reasons why the practice of AOM or bodywork is so healing is because the intention (energy being directed towards a purpose) is being laid down so our conscious and subconscious mind are both working on it in the background.

Imagine in real life you are working with someone or a group of people but you are not aware of what their intentions are or what they want to do. What kind of messy situation or trouble could that lead to? When we do this in other aspects of our life, don't you think it is important to incorporate the practice of intention-setting in the most intimate act with our partner? If the intention is simply to have pleasure through sex, then most likely all the acts of that experience will be directed towards that end. However, if the shared intention is to make spiritual advancement, experience deeper and amplified orgasms, then the actions would be directed towards that. As you can see, in order to be effective, intention must also be communicated clearly. We will talk more about guidelines for effective communication in Part II of this book.

I desire to spend the rest of my life with him. I desire to finish writing this book. I desire to create change in this world. In each of these we are laying down our desires but also setting our intentions. We will discuss more about desires in Chapter Six of this book. For our desires to be fulfilled, intention needs to be laid down. So, once the intentions are set, any action taken in that regard will only make us get closer to the fulfilment of our desire. Our intentions direct our subconscious mind to work at something, hence it is important to be conscious of the kinds of intentions being set.

The clearer the intention we have, the more we will be allowing energy to move towards that cause. The more awareness we have of each other's intention, the more we will be able to synchronise with our partner during love making and experience the joy of amplified orgasms.

EXERCISE: Learning to Share Intention

Presence

What does it mean when we talk about being present with someone?

When we are present, we are not only experiencing the moment in the way it should be experienced, but we are also allowing our conscious and subconscious mind to be willing to receive new information in its truest sense possible without adding our own filters and judgement.

Figure 44: Presence involves more than just being physically present.

Like attention, presence happens at all of the layers i.e. the physical, mental, emotional, energetic, and spiritual. True presence implies integrating all of this external information coming at you along with sensations, emotions, and feelings arising within your own body. Presence is observing everything that is happening in the moment, as much as possible.

Notice next time when you are present with someone. Which of these levels of presence do you notice in yourself? Chances are you may tend towards being more present at certain layers over others as a kind of automatic way of being. For example, an engineer may be very used to being intellectual and analytical, and he or she may bring this kind of mental presence to areas of life outside of work, including relationships. While there is nothing wrong with being mentally present, it is only one aspect of presence. To become more present, we must learn to expand our ability to "be in the moment" with the other aspects of human existence including energetic, emotional, spiritual, and physical.

A common dynamic in relationships that reveals a lack of emotional presence is when a woman shares with her male partner the frustrations of her day. Many men will follow an impulse to start "fixing" the problem by rationalising, analysing, and troubleshooting. Meanwhile, the woman in this scenario has already "done the math." What she is looking for from her partner is emotional resonance which can only happen if the man is able to be emotionally present. Of course, this can also happen the other way around. However, social scripts of masculinity often train men from an early age to choose mental presence over emotional presence, thus this common pattern plays out over and over in relationships. (We will be sharing deeper aspects of these relationship dynamics and how they contribute towards affecting each other's amplified orgasms in Part II.)

Imagine the impact that genuine presence can make in a relationship. Now imagine the impact presence can have in the sexual context. Presence is not only about hearing or making sounds, or experiencing intense body convulsions and shaking during orgasms, but it is also about paying attention to small nuances, the minute details, the slight twitching, the low voice that wants to come out, the highly aroused clit or vagina that doesn't want his cock to move an inch, the heartbeat that wants to just stop for a mini-second so that it can capture this whole magical moment, the orgasmic sensation that doesn't want you to do anything more but be in the moment for it to be felt and experienced, noticing the faith and trust in the eyes of your partner, the energetic push and pull happening in between, that aroused nipple that wants you to lick it with your tongue gently and softly, those lips that want to feel you but still maintain a distance, the curling of those toes in appreciation of how the body is feeling in the moment, noticing that deeper part of your partner which doesn't generally come out and remains hidden but now feels safe and wants to come out and play with you. This is what an experience of real sexual and orgasmic presence feels like.

Being able to tap into deeper thoughts, feelings, and sensations of each other while also paying complete attention to all the nuances happening at all levels is possible when we learn to expand our presence. When we create a space of such presence, repressed old emotions begin to come out which then gives us an opportunity to work through them so that release can happen and newer and positive memories can be created. This is where real transformation takes place.

Orgasm and Presence

After reading Chapter Seven, you will get a deeper understanding of what masculine and feminine energies are and how masculine orgasm differs from feminine orgasm. Both male and female, once they have been on the Path of Amplified Orgasm, can experience either of these orgasms at any given time. Through the principle of polarity, you will get to understand why it is important for both the partners to be operating on different ends of the polarity spectrum. The awareness of when to make a shift to move from one side of this spectrum to the other will be determined by the level of presence you have in the given moment.

Presence in the truest sense will help in amplifying each other's orgasms while the lack of presence will end up crushing either or both orgasms. It is like windsurfing. The more attentive and present you are to the movement of air and water as well as your own position and inner state, the balance of the board, the distance from the other surfers, and so forth, the more you will be able to navigate and enjoy the waves. The less present you are in any of these aspects, the more likely you are to wipe out.

Amplified orgasm requires expanding one's presence, that is, the ability to be "in the moment" with all layers of the experience including the mental, emotional, energetic, physical, and spiritual bodies.

People may not remember exactly what you did, or what you said, but they will always remember how you made them feel.
Maya Angelou

Awareness

What does it mean to be aware of something?

How is awareness different from consciousness, presence, and attention?

Why does having profound awareness matter for orgasmic amplification?

Being aware means having knowledge or perception of a situation, fact, or state as well as ourselves and/or our partner in relation to it. When applied to different layers of the body, it refers to having knowledge or perception across these different domains, often more than one at a time. Examples include:

- **Physical**: *I'm aware that I have not been taking good care of myself.*
- **Mental**: *I'm aware that I've not allowed my mind to rest for a minute.*
- **Energetic**: *I'm aware that I've been feeling low in energy ever since I've stopped my yoga class.*
- **Emotional**: *I'm aware that you have been desiring intimacy, love, and connection which has been missing in our relationship for a while.*
- **Spiritual**: *I'm aware that for spiritual growth I should be doing meditation and my daily practices.*
- **Combination of all layers**: *I'm aware that when I am near her, I feel overwhelmed, excited, and often lose myself.*
- **Combination of physical and energetic**: *I'm aware that when I am close to climax, I need to slow down and let you know that I'm close.*

Each of these levels of awareness impacts the other. And, when we interact with others, our awareness also interacts with theirs. The more open-minded we are, the more others will be able to influence our consciousness.

Awareness is created by both the conscious and subconscious mind, and the latter is the stronger force. The more we work with the subconscious mind, the stronger sense of awareness will emerge, often referred to as the "sixth sense."

At any given point, our body knows what it knows but it is not until we put our attention onto that thing or aspect that the awareness of that thing can come to our conscious mind. So, we can say that awareness requires putting attention onto a certain thing or aspect. For example, when we put our attention consciously on an apple lying on the table, then everything we know about apples starts coming into our awareness. But what actually comes into our awareness is mostly from the subconscious. For example, it may be a recent memory of eating an apple pie or a time you almost forgot from your childhood picking apples in an orchard with your family. Until we put attention on the apple, those aspects of the subconscious remain hidden from our awareness. This same process is happening in terms of our awareness of sex and orgasm.

Most likely, it is either the most recent experiences we have had or the most impactful experiences we have that tend to emerge first. If we keep on putting awareness to all that is emerging (without switching to analytical mode), we will notice that we are starting to have a heightened experience relating to that which we place our attention on. This experience will be determined by our past experiences, our present condition, our level of attention, and our ability to stay present during this emerging process. It also relies on our ability to allow the conscious and subconscious mind to continue to keep interacting with each other, without allowing the conscious mind to take over with judgement about these thoughts. Note that in both the above examples, both apple and orgasm have always been there on the table or in the body respectively. This is one of the reasons why the practice of AOM increases the feeling of orgasms as our awareness is drawn in and we move away from the act of doing to the act of being.

Orgasm increases the ability for us to become aware of different aspects happening at multiple dimensions. How often are you aware of your own emotional needs or the emotional needs of your partner during sex? How often are you aware of your own physical needs or the physical needs of your partner throughout the course of sexual activity, especially when both of you start experiencing deeper states of orgasm? Orgasm is an energy which flows like waves and it will require you to be on top of the wave sometimes, under the wave sometimes, and at other times deeply immersed. The more awareness you have about where the wave is within you, within your partner, and between you, the more you will be able to navigate yourself, enjoy this experience, and amplify your orgasms.

EXERCISE: Growing Awareness Through Practice

The Importance of an Open Mind

What do the concepts of "open-minded" and "close-minded" mean to you?

How often do you find yourself closed off to your partner emotionally?

How openly do you share yourself to your partner at all levels?

Have you ever experienced that sometimes both of you are so deeply aligned that even if you don't say anything to your partner, they will be able to start picking up your thoughts and feelings?

Figure 45: An open mind is key to learning and self-improvement.

Take a moment to be honest with yourself and consider these questions. The Path of Amplified Orgasm will require you to become willing to acknowledge your strengths and weaknesses when it comes to fully relating to your partner, and become willing to address those ways of connecting that may not always feel comfortable, especially at first.

In one of my previous relationships, we became so aligned, especially after sexual connections, that we started picking up on each other's thoughts even before the other person had expressed anything to the other. This started to happen in spite of us being in two different locations, sometimes miles apart. Perhaps you have also experienced this kind of connection. When this kind of alignment happens, it takes the experience of orgasms to a different level because during love-making one is able to pick on the other person's thoughts and energies, even when they have not been expressed. This allows the person during the act of love-making to adjust his/her strokes, intensity, pressure, and closeness accordingly without disturbing the flow of love-making.

This ability to be able to navigate the mind and all that comes with it is extremely beneficial in relationships. When we are open-minded, we are opening ourselves to not only receive more energy from our partner, but also to develop a greater perception of our own feelings, thoughts, and sensations. We are opening ourselves to newer levels of attention, presence, awareness, and consciousness that come along with an open mind. In this way, we can become more able to experience, as well as intentionally create, amplified orgasm.

EXERCISE: Opening the Mind to New Ways of Experiencing Sexual Energy

The Brain, the Mind, and Orgasm

As we have explored in this chapter, orgasm is a whole brain, and maybe we should also say, a whole mind, experience. As we become more aware of the ways in which the brain and the mind provide the tools through which we mentally process orgasm, we find many opportunities to amplify orgasm by accessing and becoming more skilled at navigating this aspect of the sexual experience, that is, the mental body.

In this chapter we learned more about how the specific functions of the brain operate to create the perception of the experience of orgasm and may enhance or block our access to orgasm depending on the kinds of experiences we have had, along with the new experiences we can intentionally create. We learned how the tools of neuroplasticity can be used to amplify orgasm, create healthy habits, and reprogramme old neural pathways that had become dead ends, blocking our full experience of orgasm.

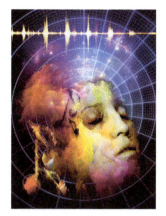

Figure 46-47: When we have an open mind and a well-stimulated brain, then our experiences of orgasm is expanded.

Extending the concept of the mind to include several ways to enhance our consciousness offers yet more tools to open our sexual experiences to a wider range of alignment and resonance with our partner as well as greatly increasing the depth to which we can experience intimacy, connection, and sexual pleasure.

Perhaps most importantly, we learned the role that belief plays in providing a framework or lens through which we understand ourselves, others, and make sense of our gendered, sexual, and romantic experiences. The concepts of limiting and empowering beliefs offer us a chance to become liberated from those ideas that hold us back from personal growth and identify and eliminate the feelings of shame and guilt passed on to us through family, cultural tradition, and societal norms.

We also explored state of mind through the interrelated concepts of consciousness, attention, intention, presence, and awareness. Further, we have explored these tools in relation to the Path of Amplified Orgasm and discovered that they are each multi-dimensional and give us access to the many layers of the embodied experience. By learning to expand our mind in these specific ways, across the various layers of our existence, we can truly connect in a more profound way during our sexual experiences.

Finally, we learned the importance of an open mind. Being receptive to new ways of understanding your body, the sexual experience, and even being willing to hold your beliefs up to the light for questioning, offers you the opportunity to grow and expand. And now I will ask you, dear reader, to bring that curious and open mind to the forefront as we embark on the next layer of our map of the Path of Amplified Orgasm, one that you may not be familiar with and may even have some preconceived notions about: The energetic body.

Chapter Two Summary:

- Orgasm is a "whole brain experience." By understanding how the different parts of the brain work to create this experience, we can learn to amplify our orgasm by exercising and strengthening these aspects of brain function.

- The brain and the rest of the body communicate along neural pathways. The more these pathways are used, the easier they are to travel, thus creating "Neural Superhighways."

- Habits, both healthy and unhealthy, are formed by repeatedly using neural pathways. This is true whether we are intentional or unintentional about our habits.

- Insights from research on neuroplasticity suggest we can intentionally change our neural networks by becoming aware and deliberately having new kinds of experiences.

- Sex and orgasm are experiences that utilise neural networks, and thus, can be "remapped" as a tool on the Path of Amplified Orgasm.

- The brain and the mind are different. The brain is the structure that lays the foundation for perceiving, interpreting, and storing information. However, the mind is what makes sense of our world, and it does so in concert with individual life experiences as well as social/societal influences.

- Although many of our beliefs may have been passed down to us through society, family, and friends, we can become aware of and intentional about the ideas we choose to believe in.

- Limiting beliefs encourage us to see limitations in who we ourselves can be, or who we "should" be, and are often the root of feelings such as shame, guilt, and other harmful thoughts.

- Empowering beliefs encourage us to see ourselves as beings of infinite capacity and generally support our path to personal growth.

- We can transform our limiting beliefs into empowering beliefs and reinforce these beliefs in ourselves and our partners through regular practice.

- The Path of Amplified Orgasm requires enhancing our consciousness by harnessing the power of attention and intention and expanding presence and awareness along all of the bodies: emotional, mental, physical, energetic, and spiritual.

THE ENERGETIC BODY

The physical body has limitations. Physically, one can only go to a certain extent. Physically, one can only penetrate the other to a certain depth. If you want to penetrate one's soul, one's mind, then you have to be willing to go beyond the physical; you have to be open to possibilities of other dimensions.
Michael Charming

In the previous chapters we learned about feelings, emotions, and sensations as well as the role the brain and mind play in terms of the nervous system and the construction of our subjective experience. In this chapter we will be spending time getting to know our body in a way we may not have seen, felt, or sensed before: the energetic body.

Up until many years ago, I spent the majority of my life looking outwards, travelling around the world, staying distracted by the events, people, and happenings around me. I hardly inquired within. I hardly asked myself: *Why is it that when I am in love, I feel soft, caring, and happy but when I am angry, I feel charged, energised, and tense at the same time? Why is it that after kissing and sex, I feel closer to her and the world and life feels amazing, but if I haven't had sex for a while, I begin to feel agitated, start to feel distant from my partner, and life feels less amazing?*

During some of my sexual encounters, my female lovers would express experiences of sex that were not only in their body, but also on other levels that I did not fully understand. At the time, I found this puzzling. It is only after learning more about the various subtle bodies, the different energy centres, along with gaining a deeper understanding of the physical body, that it all began to make sense to me.

No wonder I am so excited to share this insight with you! For me, it was transformative, both in terms of the pleasure I experienced from orgasm, but also the pleasure I was able to give to my partners.

The aim of this chapter is to explore how the physical body, in cooperation with energy centres that exist within each of us, creates the orgasmic experience. Most importantly, we will begin to dive into how we can make use of these centres to create alignment and resonance with our partners to become more orgasmic.

As you read this chapter and do the corresponding exercises in the workbook, you will come to understand your body in a whole new way. While biology certainly informs this approach, we will also draw on ancient ways of knowing such as Hinduism, Taoism, and Buddhism to come to understand your body via the energy that moves within it.

In addition to learning how to sense and influence the energy in your own body, you will also begin to see that energy moves between people as well. In fact, it is happening all the time and is especially active during intimate moments. As you will soon find out, getting to know your body in this way is a critical step on the Path of Amplified Orgasm.

We will use two main ways of mapping the non-physical body: energy centres (also known as chakras) and subtle bodies (also known as auras). One thing to notice about these two systems is that energy centres are within the body, while auras exist outside of our physical bodies.

Remember, if you are new to talking about the body in these ways, try to just have an open mind. In fact, you may discover that you already have experience with these forces, but you may not have had the language to better understand them and learn to become aware and intentional when it comes to the energy that flows inside and outside your body every day.

And, you probably didn't know that by learning to control (and, ironically, sometimes let go of control) these systems, you can greatly increase your orgasmic potential. And, it doesn't stop there. By understanding how energy moves within and in connection to your partner, you can become a more responsive and intuitive lover, deepening your intimacy, and unlocking new levels of love, passion, and orgasmic states in your relationship.

EXERCISE: Becoming Curious About Energy

Would you agree that everything that moves in this world is due to energy or vibration? This includes all that is lively on this planet, and indeed, the universe itself. Whether natural or man-made, when the energy stops, the object or being that contained it stops moving or responding.

Figure 48-49: Earth energy interacting with other solar energies. Even vibrations has its own energy.

Would you agree that when you are in love with someone, you feel this magical feeling within you and around you, even though the world around you hasn't really changed on a physical level?

And would you also agree that if you were to lay next to your lover without actually touching them, you might start feeling inclined to reach out to cuddle, caress, or touch them? This feeling is not so much a thought, rather a physical urge to move closer. What do you think is actually happening in this case?

One way to understand that urge is through the actions of human energy fields which are both around us and external to us. We will explore how we can make use of these centres to realise our full potential, which will then enable us to attain higher states of orgasm.

Human Energy Field

Over the past few decades, there has been a great deal of research done in this field and numerous books have been written about human auras, chakras, and different energy centres within our body.[28-30] These days there are many retreats, workshops and various kinds of seminars and modalities that take place throughout the world relating to energy healing such as Reiki, acupuncture, EFT (emotional freedom techniques), polarity therapy, quantum touch, shamanic healing, Theta healing, and more. The main purpose of these modalities is to help us understand and align our bodies beyond the simply physical dimension.

Energy goes by many names, depending on the discipline one is drawing from:

- Aura
- Qi (Chinese)
- Prana (India)
- Mana (Polynesian)

- Ki (Japanese)
- Barraka (Islam)
- Vital energy
- Biofield.

This vital life energy comprises the non-physical aspect of our energy system. The meridians through which this vital life energy flows are the energy vessels similar to the blood vessels in the body which allow the blood to flow. In order for one to feel orgasmic, one must:

1. Generate better blood flow throughout various parts of the body, especially around the genital areas.

2. Increase the flow of specific types of energy through various energy centres and meridians.

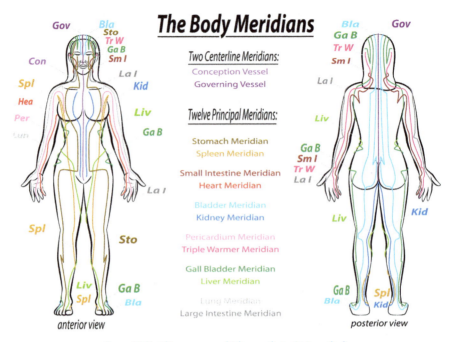

The Body Meridians

Two Centerline Meridians:
Conception Vessel
Governing Vessel

Twelve Principal Meridians:

Stomach Meridian
Spleen Meridian

Small Intestine Meridian
Heart Meridian

Bladder Meridian
Kidney Meridian

Pericardium Meridian
Triple Warmer Meridian

Gall Bladder Meridian
Liver Meridian

Lung Meridian
Large Intestine Meridian

anterior view

posterior view

Figure 50: Meridians, or energy highways, that exist in our bodies

When discussing energy, one concept that is very helpful is the term meridian. Just like we have various nerves that branch off in different parts of the body as part of the nervous system, we also have large and small meridians that branch off to carry energy throughout the body. The meridians flow throughout the body and the seven energy centres correlate with various meridian points. Generally, we cannot feel the flow of blood through the veins, however the flow of these vital forces can be felt when a person's inner senses are properly aligned and when one has developed a high level of sensitivity and awareness.

> **EXERCISE: Learning to Tune in to Energy**

Energy Centres or Chakras

Certain places in our body are associated with certain emotions and sensations. For example, we feel love in our hearts, not in our toes. We may feel fear on the back or our neck or in our stomach, but not in our nose. Energy centres help us make sense of why and how these different areas of the body seem to contain the capacity for certain types of emotions and feelings.

In addition, understanding energy in this way allows us to make sense of the fact that sometimes we may be blocked from fully experiencing certain kinds of feelings. It may be helpful to use a metaphor here to make this idea clearer.

Take, for example, a smart home system which you control from your mobile phone. It can remotely control various systems in your home such as the heating and cooling system, the window shades, the lights, etc. It is clear that in order for the entire system to work, both the central processor (your phone) and the various components (the heat pump, the lights, the thermostat) must all be operating well. In addition, the lines of communication must also be allowing information to flow; usually this is done over your home's Wi-Fi. If any system fails, the flow of information is blocked, preventing the system from working properly.

Likewise, energy meridians in the body are designed to allow energy to flow to different areas of your body, each with their own function relative to different types of energy, and different kinds of feelings. By looking closer at chakras and energy centres, we can see how this works in greater detail.

Within the non-physical aspect of our body, we have seven main energy centres. Although it is estimated that there are actually as many as 88,000 energy centres, the rest are extremely small and play only a minor role in our energy system. Please note that although there are many other important chakras which are located inside and outside of the physical body, for the purpose of this book, we have focused on seven main centres which exist within the space of the physical body.

Chakra is a Sanskrit word which means **wheels or centres of radiating life force**. They are named as such because of the circular shape to these spinning energy centres. These wheels are actually a series of vortexes within our body, five of which are located along the spine. Keeping these centres balanced is a very important part of our living, especially if one wants to take the journey of self-discovery and to achieve higher states of orgasm.

I have experienced different kinds of circular motions, waves, vibrations coming out of each of these energy centres with different intensities of speed and pressure. I spend between five and seven minutes a day connecting with each of these energy centres. Similarly to the way we like to know how much of a charge our phone has, it is important for me to know how my energy centres are doing and what intensity and vibration they are operating at.

The Law of Conservation of Energy, a foundational idea in physics, states that energy cannot be created nor destroyed, however, it can be transformed. Hence, it is important to keep this law in mind when talking about these energy centres as well. For example, we always have the choice to use energy in fighting with each other and creating disharmony, or we can align ourselves to remain in harmony with ourselves and those around us. Hence, the energy in our bodies can be used for constructive, positive, and supporting purposes rather than destructive, draining, and counterproductive purposes.

Each of these energy centres has certain specific qualities and vibrations associated with them. The lower energy centres have lower, thicker, and denser vibrations and these fulfil the base-level materialistic self-identity, fundamental emotions, and basic needs, while the higher energy centres have higher, lighter, and thinner vibrations. These fulfil our higher selves, sense of purpose, and our spiritual-related identities. They bring more awareness to our consciousness. Being important and essential parts of us, it therefore becomes all the more important to pay good attention to each of these, understand them, and align them all into a unified field of brilliance.

We all know that an atom is composed of electrons, which orbit around a nucleus of neutrons and protons. Electrons are negatively charged, protons are positively charged, and neutrons are neutrally charged. It is this balance in an atom that makes it stable. In the same way, every energy centre has positive and negative energies and our efforts should be directed towards bringing these energy centres into balance or in harmony.

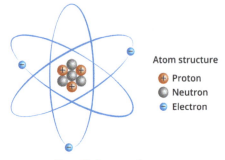

Atom structure

⊕ Proton
◯ Neutron
⊖ Electron

Figure 51: Structure of an atom

The interaction between the physical body and the energy field takes place through a flow of energy via consciousness and through various parts of the physical body such as the endocrine and nervous systems. The tension or contraction in consciousness and each of these systems will impact each of the energy centres and auras associated with them.

The energy at these energy centres rotates in a clockwise direction to move the energy from the body into the field around us and in anticlockwise direction to pull the energy from outside to inside our body. The direction and flow of these energies are determined by the frequencies and how blocked or clear they are. Clear, vibrant and strong energetic flow within these energy centres makes us feel energetic, positive, and brings the best of the qualities of each centre while the blocked and weak energetic flow will make us feel negative, lethargic, and brings the worst qualities of each centre.

These energy centres are formed at the junction of three connected energy shafts, called Nadis, that move along the spine. The central channel is called the Sushumna, while the two other channels, which are slightly lesser in frequency, are called Pingala, which is on the right, and Ida, which is on the left. Ida is white, feminine, cold and represents the moon. Pingala is red, masculine, hot, and represents the sun. Both of these originate in the Root energy centre and end up in the nostril – Ida being in the left nostril and Pingala in the right nostril. Each of these energy shafts run parallel to the spinal cord. That is why it is always advised to keep the spine straight as much as possible so that the energy flow through each of these channels can flow smoothly. Sushumna originates just below the Root energy centre and it runs up the body all the way to the Crown energy centre. When we talk about these Nadis, you will often hear about Kundalini energy.

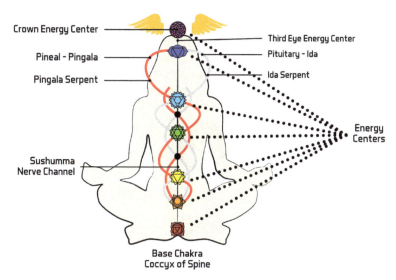

Figure 52: Energy centres (chakras) and the three most important nadis that run along the spine

Kundalini energy rests like a snake which has been coiled into three-and-a-half circles at the base of the spine. This serpent lies blocking the entrance to Sushumna, which remains closed at its lower end as long as Kundalini is not awakened. Kundalini Yoga is an ancient practice that helps to channel this powerful energy and transform life. The technique of Kundalini Yoga consists of using the life-force energy guiding its circulatory movement through Ida and Pingala down to the base of the spine into the space where this Kundalini lies coiled. When Kundalini energy arises, it rises up the Sushumna and energises the seven energy centres. If one is on the path of spiritual development and if one continues to do the relevant practices, then in my view, the rising of the Kundalini is a completely natural process and it will happen to you, just like it happened for me.

When I had my Kundalini energy awakening experience, I wasn't even sure what it was until a few days later when I was doing some research and I came across a few articles which mentioned the Kundalini awakening. The experiences and the effects mentioned in those articles were very similar to my own experiences and effects I was feeling and when I joined the dots together, it all made sense. The most important point I would like to make here is for one to remain curious rather than aiming for anything in particular, carry on the daily/weekly practices, pay attention to your feelings and little voices inside your body as an observer, and follow your intuition/gut feeling.

Every energy centre is associated with a certain part of the body and their function is to take up and collect the life-force energy, transform it, and then pass it on. Depending on how well developed an individual is in terms of spiritual awareness and wisdom, and how balanced he and his subtle bodies are, these energy centres vibrate at different levels.

How would you feel if both of you can live in total harmony with each other, where discussions can take place without resorting to violence, where each of you can feel each other's energy, and where each of you can have deep awareness of yourselves? Then that relationship will definitely be primed for a great transformation.

Figure 53: Seven main energy centres in the body

Where there is peace and harmony in the relationship between lovers, orgasm tends to flourish more because there is more trust, love, connection, and resonance not only at the physical layer but also at the mental, emotional, energetic, and spiritual layers. That is when one can say that both the individuals are so immersed in each other that they end up forming a big orgasmic ball around them which makes them feel complete, whole, full, and as one.

So, let's find out about each of these centres one by one so that you can start exploring each of them and begin creating energetic balance within yourself. Please note that working with these energy centres, especially the Kundalini energy centre, should not be taken lightly. Any misuse or improper way of awakening these energy centres can have negative effects on all your subtle bodies, including hindering your orgasmic growth. Do the research before you start working on them and make sure that you are working with someone who is an expert in this field. I have come across a number of cases where people have ended up feeling somewhat short-circuited, have energy stuck in the head or at any place in the body for months, and have even ended up in hospitals because of physical discomfort, pain, loss of identity, etc.

Just imagine the electric wires that carry current. There is a reason why they are coated with plastic. The same electricity which is used for multiple purposes like giving us light, warmth, and heat can also kill someone. In the same way, it is the same love energy that conveys warmth and compassion, if the heart energy centre is not properly awakened, can remain very focused on the self and selfish needs.

Let me share a few examples from my life. When I started on the Path of Amplified Orgasm, I really had no idea about how too much energy could go wrong. In the initial stages of trying a clit-stroking practice, I felt so much energy in my head that it would keep me awake for hours. Imagine coming home from the practice session and then sitting on the bed for hours, where you are unable to think, feel, or do anything! Although, I was awake, fully conscious, and aware of everything around me, I wasn't able to go to bed. The energy was too much and it was stuck in my head. A few days later, during discussions, it was mentioned that my experience was like this because of a lack of proper grounding after the practice session.

Figure 54-55: Heart energy experienced in the form of amazing electric sensations, warm and love energy

Take another example. Once I was going to work in the morning and as soon as I got out of the station, I experienced a very severe pain in the centre of my chest. The pain was severe yet unharmful, noticeable, yet I could still carry on my work. After a few hours the pain had subsided and a few days later I felt so much love coming out from the centre of my chest. I didn't have any teacher at that time to guide me as to what was happening, so I did some research on my own to find out exactly what happened. The symptoms were very similar to having the heart centre opened. It really felt like petals opening, but since energy is making its way through this area, it tended to impact the physical body, and as such, the pain was felt on the physical plane. I remember those moments very well. Since then, my feeling of love towards myself and towards others has changed and I have come to understand what real love, compassion, and care means, which goes beyond one's own selfish love and care.

In my view, everyone is unique and on their own journey, so everyone's experiences will be different. Remember in an earlier part of this book where we talked about going on a hike? If you had been on a hike you would have experienced that there are so many trails that lead to the same destination, and even though people might be following the same trail, everyone has their own experience of it. Likewise, you can use other people's experiences as a guideline to know what could be possible, but please do not think that this or that detail is going to happen for you in just this or that way.

I find many people who have been on so many spiritual courses, healing modalities and so forth, getting stuck because they are looking for a particular kind of experience which they might have heard somewhere from someone. My invitation to you would be to know the qualities of each energy centre, stay committed to your practices, remain curious and observant, and listen to your intuition. Have someone you can discuss and share your experiences with so that person can offer guidance if need be, and then let your path unfold itself.

First Energy Centre

(Also known as Root energy centre or Muladhara) It is in this energy centre that the powerful Kundalini energy resides. This centre relates to feeling grounded, supported, and secure, which in modern times, for some people can refer to financial security, having personal space, a strong career, and other forms of security. I have found that the stronger this energy centre is, the more grounded the person will be, which means they will not be impacted quickly by life's day-to-day ups and downs.

Figure 56: Symbol of Root energy centre, red colour, and mantra sound LAM

This centre is also linked to feelings of confidence and trust. If you are feeling low in your libido, performing certain exercises that will activate and strengthen this centre will also strengthen your sacral and make you feel more aroused. This centre is linked to sex muscles as well, so a stronger root centre means better self-control of those muscles, more vitality, better stamina, and increased endurance, all of which are essential for deeper orgasms and extended periods of sex.

If the energy at this centre is too strong, dominant, and out of balance, then a person may show habits of hoarding, self-centredness, dominating others, and defensiveness. During a bodywork consultation, if my client's life experiences tell me that they don't feel grounded in life, have an inability to trust (especially men), feel insecure with worldly needs, or feel unsafe, then it gives me an indication that I need to devote a part of the session to work on the root energy centre.

EXERCISE: Exploring the Root Energy Centre

Second Energy Centre

(Also known as Sacral energy centre or Swadisthana)

It is in this centre that we feel pleasure, desire, sensuality, intimacy, connection, creativity, and emotions. If this centre has a strong energy and is balanced, then a person will be good at socialising, be adaptable to different situations, will feel emotionally balanced, and would be very nurturing and sensitive towards others. When sexual arousal is full of affection, it makes this chakra stronger and harmonious. However, if sexual energy is full of selfishness, aggression,

Figure 57: Symbol of Sacral energy centre, orange colour, and mantra sound VAM

and tightness, then this chakra is closed and disharmonised. Rape, infertility, deep sexual trauma, and misogyny are all the result of excesses or imbalances in this centre.

Sexual fantasies, obsessions and restlessness, excessive indulgence, addictive behaviour such as porn addiction, unhealthy co-dependency in the relationship, as well as negative and unwanted or destructive emotions like shame, guilt, and sexual repression, are all symptoms that result from imbalances in this energy centre.

If the energy in this centre is too strong and imbalanced, then the person might be attention-seeking, indulge in social gossip or over-eating, neglect self-care, put others' needs in front of his/her own needs, become emotionally dependent, react to other people's expectations, and might end up engaging so much socially that they neglect taking time for themselves.

If during a bodywork consultation my clients exhibit the tendencies of having difficulty expressing feelings or are disconnected from themselves, have relationship, reproductive, or sexuality problems, are not easily adaptable to change, or have low self-esteem, then it gives me an indication that I need to spend a part of the session working on the sacral energy centre.

EXERCISE: Exploring the Sacral Energy Centre

Third Energy Centre

(Also known as Solar Plexus or Manipura)
This centre is situated between the heart and genitals and is associated with willpower, self-control, strength, dynamic personalities, ego, and feelings of intimacy. Thus, this centre helps two people really meet each other, become intimate, and allows orgasm to happen. In the second centre, people having sex aim to make orgasm happen, whereas it is when the third energy centre is aligned that orgasm actually happens.

Figure 58: Symbol of Solar Plexus energy centre, yellow colour, and mantra sound RAM

Since this centre is associated with ego, so it is through this centre that love-making actually starts. For real love-making to happen, ego needs to be worked on so that both can surrender to the energy and sensation that is arising and let those be the guide. A healthy ego contributes positively towards life. And if this centre is awakened and activated, one develops a sense of being able to differentiate between a healthy ego vs a destructive, self-centred ego.

The feeling of orgasm in this centre becomes the experience of a state of expansion, freedom, tenderness, and we develop a state of giving. Real love-making begins from this centre and prior to this centre, any physical connection is mostly related to sex.

If this centre has strong and balanced energy, the person will be action-oriented, will know one's self-worth, will have tolerance and acceptance, will have a good sense of humour, self-worth, strong willpower, and have a friendlier attitude towards life. If the energy in this centre is too strong and imbalanced, the person would have a high metabolism and might find it difficult to relax, would have an inflated ego, might show qualities of aggression, carelessness, lack of consideration towards others, or may get involved in multiple projects as part of indulgence but which are not necessarily successful. If this centre is out of harmony, a person will have a need to dominate and control, will keep up with fake personas, and ultimately will have a lack of self-respect.

If during a bodywork consultation, my client exhibits the tendencies of lack of motivation or poor willpower, fatigue, indecisiveness, or ego dominance, then it gives me an indication that I need to spend a part of the session working on the sacral energy centre.

EXERCISE: Exploring the Solar Plexus Energy Centre

Fourth Energy Centre

(Also known as Heart Centre or Anahata)
This centre represents unconditional love and compassion. It affects our sense of harmony, joy, and peace. This centre holds the connection to both the physical and spiritual aspects of ourselves. It is at the awakening of this centre that we can make the heart-genital connection. Having let go of ego in the previous centre, at this energy centre, we are now able to see beyond ourselves.

The orgasm experience leads to the amplification of love that is not attached, more profound, and brings a sense of inner peace and

Figure 59: Symbol of Heart energy centre, green colour, and mantra sound YAM

balance. The activating and feeling of energies at this centre lead to the disappearance of erotic satisfaction, which is replaced by feelings of fulfilment of intimacy, affection, and divine connection.

If the energy at this centre is strong and balanced, a person will generally have a healthy immune system, exhibit a sense of self-love and love towards others, will be reliable, practical and organised, and sensitive to other people's feelings and emotional states. If the energy at this centre is strong and imbalanced, the person might be overly sensitive, get easily lost in feelings, love others without any boundaries, and may at times become needy and dependent in a relationship.

If during a bodywork consultation, my client exhibits the tendencies of being disconnected from themselves, or consider themselves unworthy of love or lack self-love, or lack empathy for others, hold others responsible for their problems, are out of touch with their physical and emotional feelings, have a low immune system, or have a negative outlook towards life, then it gives me an indication that I need to spend a portion of the session working on this centre.

Fifth Energy Centre

(Also known as Throat energy centre or Vishuddha)
This centre represents listening, expressing, and manifesting abundance. Once the energies of these centres are aligned between the two lovers, then the experience of orgasms at this centre will be more refined, profound, and cosmic, giving glances of divine inspiration, inner beauty and perceptions of higher levels. If you have ever experienced a lover who has become quiet while having sex, provided the person is still present (i.e. not thinking about anything else) then most likely the sexual energy is getting blocked here.

Figure 60: Symbol of Throat energy centre, blue colour, and mantra sound HAM

In my view orgasm and expression are deeply connected. So if we are not allowing the other person in our relationship to express their feelings and speak about their experiences, especially sexual experiences, then in a way we are preventing their orgasm from coming out and expanding. Men often have the tendency to curb female expression and hold them responsible for not wanting to have sex or shaming her if she doesn't like sex a certain way, not realising they are equally responsible in creating that dynamic.

Communication relating to sex and orgasm between lovers needs to happen not only in the bedroom but also outside of the bedroom. We will be discussing this in more detail in Part II of the book. But for now, let's note that communication and one's ability to speak the truth is represented by this energy centre.

If this energy centre is strong and balanced, a person will be able to articulate and speak the truth, will be courageous, will love travelling and might even be a public speaker or teacher.

If the energy at the centre is strong and imbalanced, the person will be an excessive talker, will lack listening skills, will be impulsive, and might not be truthful.

If during a bodywork consultation, my clients exhibit the tendencies of inability to express, low voice, or feel judged for what they say then it gives me an indication that I need to spend some time during the session working on this centre.

EXERCISE: Exploring the Throat Energy Centre

Sixth Energy Centre

(Also known as the Third Eye or Ajna)

This energy centre is very symbolic in the sense that it is at this centre that the left and right eye dissolve to become one. This also means the feminine and masculine energies within oneself also dissolve and become one. If the energies of both the partners are aligned at this centre, then the capacity of self-control is amplified at the mental level, and both partners dissolve their individual identities and become one.

This centre is associated with a sixth sense, wisdom, spiritual insight, telepathy, psychic abilities, and self-realisation. Both partners become intuitive, experience enhanced imagination and creativity, and can also develop psychic abilities. They are thus able to make love that touches the pineal gland, giving both of them so-called "mindgasms."

Figure 61: Symbol of Third eye energy centre, indigo colour, and mantra sound AUM

If this centre is strong and balanced, a person will be intellectual, insightful, have a good understanding towards life, might have psychic abilities, and will have the capability of manifesting thoughts into reality. If the energy is strong and imbalanced, a person will be very analytical, judgemental, reject spiritual aspects, stubborn, will sometimes be delusional, can have mental imbalances, and may carry fear of inner wisdom.

If during a bodywork consultation, my clients exhibit the tendencies of lack of imagination or creativity, lack of sharp intellect, or are holding judgements, then it gives me an indication that I need to spend a section of the session working on this centre.

EXERCISE: Exploring the Third Eye Energy Centre

Seventh Energy Centre

(Also known as the Crown energy centre or Sahasrara)

Once this centre is awakened, a person will show curiosity, expanded awareness, spiritual aspirations, and will have energy that will be overflowing, almost giving the feeling of inexhaustible energy, provided other energy centres are not blocked or imbalanced. This centre is connected to spirituality, inner-knowing, enlightenment, and the expanding of consciousness.

During love-making, the two lovers will merge into unison and expand into the infinite feeling of vastness and dynamism of the universe, experiencing so called cosmic or transcendental orgasms. This is where individuals and lovers disappear in total orgasms with the merging of all the energies. The orgasmic states at this level bring deep satisfaction, universal bliss, radiance, infinite energy, and transcendental experiences.

Figure 62: Symbol of Crown energy centre, violet colour, and mantra sound AH

If the energy at this centre is strong and balanced, a person will have an open mind, will be reflective, calm, optimistic, and have a great level of curiosity. If the energy at this centre is strong and imbalanced, the person will be overly sensitive, have wavering mind and thought patterns, and can become ungrounded, that is, they may get lost in spirituality and disconnected from the physical or materialistic world. They also might have difficulty finding calm and peace.

If during a bodywork consultation, my clients exhibit the tendencies of a lack of general awareness, inability to find life-purpose, suffer from loneliness and/or depression, do not have an open mind or have a limited view and restricted belief system, disregard the spiritual aspect of life, then it gives me an indication that I need to spend a portion of the session working on this centre.

Figure 63: Affirmations of the seven energy centres

Symbols	Energy centre	Types of Desires	Types of Fears
	Crown energy centre	At this level, desire doesn't exists	At this level, fear doesn't exists
	Third eye energy centre	Desire for self-accomplishment and enlightenment	Fear of not being able to stay connected to reality and getting overwhelmed, fear of disconnected from intuition and wisdom
	Throat energy centre	Desire for knowledge, purity, knowledge, universal and divine beauty	Fear of being too outspoken or struggle to express one,
	Heart energy centre	Desire for love, compassion, kind heartedness, devotion	Fear of intimacy, unworthy of love, losing personal boundaries, betrayal, jealousy
	Solar Plexus energy centre	Desire for power, authority, fame, fortune, longevity	Fear of losing control, anger, indecisiveness, insecurity, chronic tiredness
	Sacral energy centre	Desire for sexual impulses, fantasies, family, reproduction	Fear of sexuality, impotency, lack of passion, addiction to pleasure
	Root energy centre	Desire for biological necessities, security, shelter, comfort	Fear of survival, being airheaded, not feeling grounded, anxiety, emotional neediness

Table: Attributes of Seven Energy Centres.

Where Do You Live?

Now that you have spent some time getting to know the different energy centres in your body, I would like to ask you: "Where do you live?" Just like different rooms of the house have different functions, in the same way, as you have seen above, different energy centres in our body have different functions.

Due to the demands of our lives, we are often required to use our mental and analytical decision-making processes so much that we end up living too much in the mental layer of our body and staying completely disconnected from our heart, crown, and other energy centres. If one hasn't worked on activating these centres, then one is not making the most of their capacity to operate from these vital sources of energy and wisdom, which offer important advantages in the right context.

If you would have asked me a few years ago how it feels like to live in the heart or root energy centre all the time, for example, I wouldn't have been able to understand the question. However, over the years, as I have embodied more of myself into my whole energetic body and worked on my energy centres, I now have the option to choose whether I want to live in my third eye energy centre or my heart energy centre or my sacral energy centre or alternate between in any combination of different energy centres throughout different parts of the day.

Figure 64: Next time when you are at the beach and sun rays are falling onto your body, pay attention to these energy centres and see if you experience anything different or if you experience them at all. Better if you use the mantra sounds of each energy centre and then pay attention to vibrations inside your body.

Instead of using different parts of the brain as mentioned in Chapter Two, if you end up living in the third eye centre, then wisdom, intuition, and imagination will automatically flow and you will develop a much more refined understanding. In order to optimise the use of the sixth energy centre, the mind-chatter needs to stop so that energy, vision, and deeper knowing can flow from deep within. Would you rather circle around the edges of the river or be fully immersed, swimming and drinking from the source?

Now I can make a conscious decision about which energy centre or centres give me the best perspective in the moment depending on the context. Do you believe me that this is possible? Do you think that this is fascinating? Yes, my friend, it indeed is fascinating! It has changed my whole view of how I see and experience life.

Imagine how it would feel if you could operate from your heart energy centre throughout the day, no matter how much stress there might be in life, no matter if the train is delayed, no matter if your boss is being demanding of you. When you operate from the heart energy centre, your mind is less stressed due to being less occupied, which in turn allows it to function better. You are less offended because you are giving out love, you have compassion towards others in spite of the busy and over-crowded trains, and you are not really doing anything to generate that compassion. All you are doing is staying (consciously putting attention) at the heart energy centre and allowing it to do what it is supposed to do.

Likewise, you can operate from the sexual energy centre when you are close with your partner or even when you are feeling tired during the day, as activation of this centre will bring energy in the body. Please note that for amplified orgasms, activation and strengthening of all energy centres are vital. You must have heard the phrase, "A chain is only as strong as its weakest link." In the same way, for energy to flow easily between these energy centres, each of them needs to be strengthened in equal proportion.

In addition to becoming conscious and intentional about entering and operating from specific energy centres, the process of mastering the art of moving between them allows us to better notice imbalances within ourselves, and this helps us both find our inner balance, as well as connect more deeply with our partner. First, we begin this process by simply moving our attention to these energy centres in the body. However, as with all things, practising moving between the energy centres means that it gets easier over time. I hope you will give this transformative practice a try!

EXERCISE: Navigating the Energy Centres

Just like the different parts of the physical body play an important role in amplifying one's orgasm, the different energy centres play a significant role in amplifying one's orgasms too, taking them far beyond the physical realm. If you are focusing on mastering the ancient disciplines, my invitation would be to also focus on those practices that will enable you to integrate embodiment within yourself, learning to be present with all your senses, and be willing to remain curious with an open mind and heart. Energy flows in waves much like water and the more we are able to develop sensitivity around and within ourselves, the more we will be able to relate with different energies, feeling them within, and then channelling through the different energy centres.

In the stages of deep love-making, the energy of lovers interacts, moves, and channels through different energy centres and creates higher orgasmic states. As you learn to tune in to these energy movements, you will gain access to new orgasmic experiences that you may not be able to imagine from where you are now in your journey. For example, an orgasm at the solar plexus energy centre might manifest as a sudden burst of uncontrollable laughter or crying, while an orgasm at the sexual energy centre might involve a lot of pleasure or pain, depending on the context. An orgasm at throat energy centre might invoke a lot of vocalisations such as screaming or shouting. Practise first becoming more aware of and then working to amplify these energy centres in concert with our lover is a skill set developed with practice and time.

Aura or Subtle Bodies

Have you ever felt specific feelings (such as happiness or anger) just because of someone's presence, even though no exchange of dialogue has taken place? Have you ever felt the entire mood of a room shift just because a certain person has walked into the space? What do you think is actually happening in these cases?

One way to understand these kinds of experiences is through the concept of auras, also known as subtle bodies. In addition to projecting their own energy field, our mind develops associations with auras, creating a kind of memory that is tied to a person's outward energy.

We all know that planets in our solar system, indeed the entire universe, are thriving on vibrations of various frequencies. Solid objects are made up of vibrational energy fields at the quantum level. There are also positive and negative charges that vibrate and cause electromagnetic waves with different wavelengths and speeds of vibration. These are simply the lessons of modern physics.

The body acts like a prism for these vibrations, just like a rainbow through drops of water. An aura is defined by the distinctive atmosphere or quality that seems to surround and be generated by a person, thing, or place. Sometimes they are seen as light or actual colour shades according to the specific sentiments that are present at that exact time. Humans are not alone in having auras. Even plants and animals have these energy fields. When you go to the park or enjoy your garden you may notice that you feel differently. And when you see an animal or get close to them, you feel differently as well. Take a moment to notice this common effect.

Each body generates its own vibrational energy through different energy points (or chakras) and projects them outwards, which is called the auric field or subtle bodies. The aura is an electromagnetic energy field that surrounds one's body. Every individual has their own energy system generated by thoughts, forms, genes, eating and living habits, substance intake, exercise regime, and so forth. How we feel defines our aura. Have you ever wondered why it is that the healthier you are, the more light and uplifted you feel? Likewise, the bigger and clearer your aura or energy field will be.

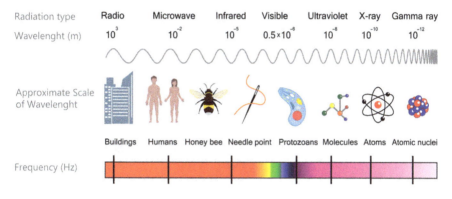

Figure 65: Electromagnetic spectrum

Would you agree that for an Apple phone to work on a mac, it needs to have a certain kind of compatibility and software that allows it to match the operating systems? In a similar way, a certain compatibility is required for us to be able to relate with others in the most effective way. When we relate with one another, our awareness is often based on the physical and mental aspects of each other, such as how we look, the clothes we wear, the words we say, the beliefs we hold. Often we are not aware that our interactions are also based on how we feel emotionally and energetically and how we receive others on these same levels.

Similarly, we have energy fields which get impacted and influenced by the environment we are in, although our physical form continues to remain the same in all those environments. That is the reason why going on holidays generally tends to have a positive effect on us while day-to-day life doesn't, even though at the physical level your composition has not changed whether you go on holiday or not.

Every personal energy field consists of seven layers which correspond to each of the chakras or the energy centres within the body, known as the subtle bodies or auras. Any disruption in the functioning of the energy centres will have an impact on the auras surrounding the physical body. The energy centres project and transmit energy vibrations in the form of colour. They also absorb energy vibrations from the surroundings. The energy fields act as a form of protection and, thus, they reflect the strength of one's immune system.

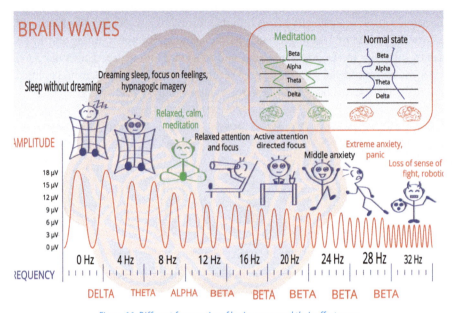

Figure 66: Different frequencies of brain waves and their effect on us

Human energy extends up to one metre on all sides, above the head, and below the feet into the ground. The concept of auras may sound like the result of a lofty imagination or colourful illusion, but in fact, they are a real phenomenon. Again, if you are sceptical, I invite you to simply keep an open mind so that you may continue to learn about these energy systems which will become clearer as you gain more understanding.

Chances are, you have already had experiences with auras, despite the fact that you may not be able to see them. Pause for a moment, and consider these experiences that you may find familiar:

- You and your lover have sex in the same way two different times. One time, the experience is amazing, and another time it is less exciting, almost as if the volume was turned down.
- You notice your body and energy after you exercise. You feel lighter, more lively, and energetic. Even the thin air around your body may feel different, as if it is vibrating at a higher level than normal.
- You stand next to someone you are highly attracted to. As your bodies get closer, you notice a kind of electricity or buzzing, tingling sensation, or some sort of love and affection energy that seems to have entered the air between you.

Figure 67: Our human bodies radiates with different energies at different frequencies

If you have not noticed these experiences, you may need to pay more attention, and intentionally begin to notice the way the people and experiences you are having affect not only the sensations within your body, but also the feeling of the atmosphere immediately around you.

Have you ever had an experience where you have felt drained in someone's company? The stronger your auras, the more you will be able to protect yourself from harmful or disharmonising energies which can become a drain on your different energetic fields.

Anyone with happy and positive thoughts will generally have wider, purer, brighter, and more vibrant subtle bodies. Those with sad and negative thoughts have smaller, more muted, muddled and faded or black auras. Colours range from deep orange to violet and white. As these are subtle bodies, they cannot generally be seen with naked eyes, although some advanced in specific types of training are able to actually see the visible spectrum of these energy fields. However, they can be felt by anyone through regular practice and mindfulness.

EXERCISE: Becoming Aware of Human Energy Fields

How Subtle Bodies Are Influenced

Just like if I were to ask you whether your thoughts, feelings, emotions exist even though we can't really see them with our eyes or touch them physically, similarly the subtle bodies are in a constant state of fluctuation. Just like a fire that is burning, they will always move rather than stay still because of the air around the fire constantly moving. Our auras are impacted by both forces inside and outside the body, for example:

- **Internal** – energy centres, hormonal levels, feelings, emotions, disease, etc.
- **External** – surroundings, other people's energy and projections, their subtle bodies, etc.

You might have noticed that sometimes you come across someone and you just don't feel safe around them. This may be true even though rationally you might not have anything to worry about. This is because of the energies of their aura which they themselves might not be aware of. However, we can learn to be perceptive at other levels as well, and learn to trust those feelings. As a bodyworker and coach, the reason my clients are able to disclose confidential information is because of the trust they feel which is often due to my own energy fields.

Have you wondered why we feel refreshed after taking rest but sometimes we don't feel refreshed even though we have taken rest? This depends on how well our energetic bodies are able to come together in alignment with our physical body while we are taking some rest. Our auras, which are like an outer wall or a shield, protect us from other people's energy. Taking a shower and going to bed often feels good because it provides relaxation to our physical body but also helps to cleanse all of the energetic mish-mash we have been carrying throughout the day and gives an opportunity for the layers of our aura to synchronise with each other as much as possible.

Some people's auras are more sensitive and affected by the auras of others. As such, these people may need more time and space alone to feel balanced. Just like at a physical level, we have different level of sensitivities in different parts of the body and it varies from person to person. Sometimes muscles are more sensitive than nerves. Likewise different subtle bodies reflect different sensitivities for different people, or even for the same person at different times.

We should develop a habit of feeling and paying respect to each other's sensitivity, as well as becoming aware of our own. When men are out with women for drinks, they often have the habit of wanting to have women stay longer, get them drunk, to spend more time with them, even though women have clearly expressed their desire to leave. I would like to ask such men: Why do you do that? And then the same men often complain that women don't join them for drinks the next time! This also applies in the sexual context when men barge into women's energy, making her feel collapsed, though this often happens unconsciously.

When I started on this path, my partner's energy and mine was completely 180 degrees opposite. Both of us would often feel collapsed once we had spent a little time together and I used to always wonder why, even though when both of us were alone we would be very energised, awake, and active. This went on for six months until one day it struck to us to explore our energetic bodies. From then on, our relationship started taking a new turn. We started noticing that the intensities of our energies were very different, and the reason we used to feel collapsed or even discomfort in our bodies was because our energies were striking with each other.

I used to do a lot of exercise at the gym and in sports so my energy would generally be heavy in comparison to hers. Hers would be more like a soft petal, or water. As we developed more and more awareness around this, I also developed practices of ensuring that before I met with her, I dilated my energy lower with the intention of meeting her at her level. And guess what? It worked! We started to become more and more energised in each other's company, our energies really started gelling with each other, which ended up creating unique experiences for both of us. Please note that in this case neither heavy nor light energy is "better." It was simply a matter of fact that when our energies were on the opposite side of the spectrum or polarity, it was exhausting and draining to be together. Perhaps that is why our sex was also so great because of this polarity of energy. We will be sharing more about polarity in Chapter Seven, but for the time being please keep an open mind towards these energies.

Have you ever felt that when you are in a relationship with a partner for a long time, you pick up their habits, their way of behaving, acting, responding, or even thinking? This happens more when we are in an intimate relationship because not only are our subtle bodies re-aligning with the other person, but also our energetic centres are developing a connection with the other's energy centres. That is why after a longer time, separation becomes very difficult and painful. It is not only due to recent memories stored in the conscious and subconscious mind, but also the separation of energetic alignment which had been happening at all levels.

The Seven Layers of the Auric Field (Subtle Bodies)

In an effort to gain a deeper understanding of our subtle bodies, which we will call auras, let's take a closer look at each of the seven layers of the aura using the Brennan model.[31] Understanding a bit more about the seven layers of the human energetic field is an important tool to have on the Path of Amplified Orgasm. For example, it will open the door for a conversation about masculine and feminine orgasm. In addition, this model gives us a better picture of how our energies interact and influence our state of mind, mood, and indeed even our physical health.

Different auras vibrate at different frequencies and show as colour vibrations in the form of shapes, fields, patterns, and colours. If you pay attention to these different layers of the human energy field, you will realise that they can even reveal when disease is about to set in on the physical body.

In the states of orgasm, especially in love-making, partners might experience orgasm in the form of energy, colour, vibrations, shapes, or patterns in the energetic field. The aura of a person plays a great role in creating such experiences.

Before we dive in, please note that no matter the layer you are currently operating at, there is no right or wrong. The important aspect to focus on is which layer you would like to operate on in your life, and how you can make that aspect your "home channel."

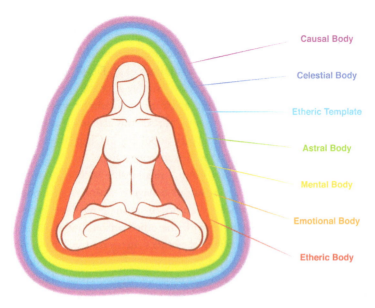

Causal Body

Celestial Body

Etheric Template

Astral Body

Mental Body

Emotional Body

Etheric Body

Figure 68: The seven layers of the Auric Fields

First Layer: The Etheric Auric Field

Sexual orgasm between two people results in the exchange of energies not only at the physical level but also at the etheric auric layer, one of the reasons why sex feels so great. For both women and men, the orgasm causes the two etheric auras to come closer to each other in a vertical direction, however for women, it also results in two etheric auras hugging each other. When men are compassionate, loving, and kind, the etheric layer of their auras can also interact in this way.

There was a time before I began to pay attention to the human energy field that I did not experience or perceive this level of connection during sex. However, when I started bringing my awareness around to myself and my partner on the energetic level, I began to notice how the sexual experience changed the energies around

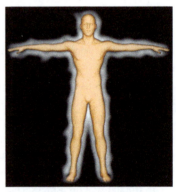

Figure 69: The Etheric Auric Field is associated with the Root energy centre and has a similar structure of that of the physical body.

us. Now I notice that there are times, during or after sex, when it actually feels that the auras are hugging and wrapping around each other.

If the etheric layer of the aura is not aligned between two individuals, then at the physical level, sex can feel like a rape, even if neither partner had the intention to violate the other. In other cases, misalignment at the etheric level can cause the sexual experience to feel disconnected even though, physically, both the bodies are connected. Sometimes, it can also feel that one's etheric energy is dominating the other, giving the feeling of rape or sex that is enjoyable to only one of the participants. In time, it is no surprise that a misalignment of this first layer of the energetic field can cause a general disinterest in sex.

EXERCISE: Noticing and Aligning the Etheric Auric Field

Second Layer: The Emotional Auric Field

Sexual experiences often include heightened emotional states. On one level, we can understand this as a series of chemical reactions in the body, including the release of various hormones that shape our emotional experience. However, in order to understand how emotional experiences are shared between two partners, it helps to understand the second layer of the aura or subtle bodies: the emotional auric field.

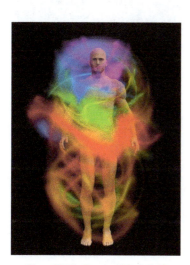

From an aura perspective, any unexpressed or suppressed emotions and feelings could be stored in this layer. The energies present here will communicate with the etheric layer and then the effect will be passed onto the physical body, which will then manifest symptoms such as pain, cramps, and tension.

Our emotional auric field becomes energised by internal emotional states and feelings, but also those of the people we interact with. If you have had the experience where you and your partner were experiencing different emotions during the same sexual act, it means that your emotional bodies were not aligned. For example, one may start bursting into tears while the other groans in extreme pleasure. There is no inherent harm in experiencing different emotions (although it can become a barrier to harmonising and resonating) during love-making. What is more important is

Figure 70: The Emotional Auric Field is associated with the Sacral energy centre, and is generally fluid and changes depending on our emotions and feelings.

97

to be aware of dissonance and then decide what to do. For example, on this occasion it would be better for the person who is experiencing pleasure to create and hold space for the person who is in tears i.e. dilating themselves to accommodate the vibration of the other person.

My sex went to another level when I started paying attention to how the emotional layer of my aura was responding during sex. Instead of focusing on what was happening to my partner on the physical level (for example, crying), if I paid attention to the feeling of her emotional auric field, I realised that it has a certain feeling, a certain energy, or a specific flavour associated with it. And, when I started connecting with that feeling, I felt so much more connected to my partner even though she hadn't even shared the reason she was bursting into tears.

EXERCISE: Noticing and Aligning the Emotional Auric Field

Third Layer: The Mental Auric Field

If by being physically intimate with someone you have noticed that your way of thinking or reasoning is changing to that of the other person and vice versa, it means both of your mental auric fields are becoming aligned. This layer of the human energy field gets energised through mental and thought processes. Clearer thoughts will illuminate the body more than ill-defined thoughts and ideas.

The first three layers of the aura (etheric, emotional, and mental) consume and digest the energies relating to the physical world while the fifth, sixth, and seventh layers of the aura consume and digest the energies of the spiritual world. The next layer, the subtle body known as the astral auric field, acts as the gateway through which energy must pass when moving from one world to the other i.e. from the physical to the spiritual and vice versa.

Figure 71: The Mental Auric Field is associated with the Solar Plexus energy centre and takes the structure of one's ideas and thought forms.

People who are strong in the mental layer of the aura may spend too much energy in their mind, which means they are using their energy vibration at a faster rate. Quite often, if the energy is only used in this layer without being put into other layers, it will result in mental fatigue and tiredness due to the over-consumption of energy. You may be

98

familiar with this feeling when you have felt stressed, zonked out, exhausted, are unable to pay attention or have no presence for anything else.

Since this aural aspect generally deals with mental reasoning, any issues relating to mental health could be present here. When one channels and ascends the energy through different energy centres and increases one's awareness and consciousness, it allows the mental body to open up, which then opens the whole reservoir of knowledge and logical reasoning.

Once I was with a partner, where after being deeply intimate with one another over a period of time, we could reach other's thoughts. Sometimes our physical body would react and behave slightly later with a time lag to the interactions that had already happened between each other at the mental body level. Over time, as I became more and more familiar with this process, I would let our mental bodies interact with each other while continuing to stay present in the physical body and observe and enjoy this interaction without acting on the mental dialogues happening. It was such a surreal experience.

> **EXERCISE: Noticing and Aligning the Mental Auric Field**

Fourth Layer: The Astral Auric Field

This layer is where the journey of a spiritual nature starts and separates from the first three aural layers, which are mostly related to the physical plane. When a person is operating in this layer of their aura, you will experience an abundance of love, compassion, and care as you get near them. You may even feel an impulse to hug them in order to get closer to this energy field. In relationships, this aspect of the auric field plays a special role in bonding.

In orgasmic states, if you have felt the irresistible strong desire of wanting to hug and cuddle up with your partner but have not acted upon it, it is because your astral body is engulfing or wanting to engulf the other person

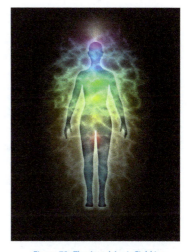

Figure 72: The Astral Auric Field is associated with the Heart energy centre and has a fluid like structure.

in that hug, but your physical body, which has not yet acted upon it, is feeling the itch.

Love-making in the astral layer of the auric field is governed by feelings of love and kindness, and it is often difficult to access logic or reasoning from this place. Sometimes, if you have felt the desire to have sex with your partner in the middle of the night all of a sudden, it is because your astral auric fields are interacting with each other during your sleep.

EXERCISE: Noticing and Aligning the Astral Auric Field

Fifth Layer: The Etheric Template

The Etheric Template serves as the blueprint or carbon copy of the physical body on the spiritual plane. The etheric template provides the structure for the etheric layer of the aura. It is associated with communication, and as such, it is at this layer when sound becomes more effective in healing. This is the place where spiritual enlightenment begins to take place. It holds the highest ideals for existence. The etheric template contains all the shapes and forms that exist on the physical plane.

Figure 73: The Etheric Template is associated with the Throat energy centre and is a structured body that provides the template for the Etheric Body.

EXERCISE: Noticing and Aligning the Etheric Template

Sixth Layer: The Celestial Auric Field

This layer is referred to as the emotional level of the spiritual world. It is associated with spiritual ecstasy, oneness with the divine, and unconditional love. It is connected with memories, intuition, dreams, and spiritual awareness. If during or after love-making and orgasms, you have felt the experience of being held together by something greater than each other, or if you have had emotional experiences which are not related to this physical world or which go beyond normal life occurrences and events, then most likely you are experiencing the harmonising of your celestial auric fields.

Figure 74: The Celestial Auric Field is associated with the Third Eye energy centre and has a fluid like structure.

Seventh Layer: The Causal Auric Field

The causal auric field is considered to be the mental layer of the spiritual plane. It is associated with the seat of divine wisdom, and an experiential connection with spirituality. The outer form of it defines the limits of the aura, contains all the other layers together, and it also contains the blueprint of our spiritual journey. At this layer, consciousness is often connected with Universal Supreme Source, God, Creator, Omnipresent, among other names for the divine. The outer part of this layer is very strong, resilient, and is protected by a thick field. Past life memories and imprints are considered to be stored in this layer. This layer is considered to be the last layer in the spiritual plane. Beyond this layer, we end up reaching the cosmic plane, which is beyond the scope of this book.

Figure 75: The Casual Auric Field is associated with the Crown energy centre and has a definite structure.

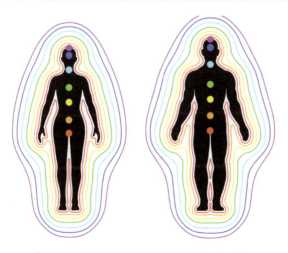

Figure 76: Seven energy centres and Auric Fields together

Energy Management and Accounting

I often come across clients who say they get tired easily or do not have enough energy on a day-to-day basis to live a healthy lifestyle and do what they would really like to do. I often ask them questions like what kind of exercises are they involved with, what are their relationship dynamics at the moment, how is their sex life, what kind of tasks do they do on a day-to-day basis, how connected are they to their energy centres, what kind of food do they eat, etc. Using their answers, I help them develop a plan to manage their energy more effectively.

As we have seen throughout this chapter, energy is always moving. No matter what we do, we are either cultivating more energy or spending it. The question to ask is: are you conscious and aware whether a certain action you are performing is cultivating or spending energy? For example, when you are spending time processing information or doing too much thinking, you are using your mental energy. Likewise, if you are not expressing and communicating what you really want to communicate, you are not only blocking the flow of energy but also using the energy to hold that expression.

Taking another example, kissing your lover is deemed to be energising for both the lovers, while having sex with ejaculation (for men) is depleting. If everything is energy, and we are energy beings carrying different kinds of energies within us, then ideally we should be able to have as much energy as we like and the kind of energy we like throughout the day depending on our needs. Whether we actually cultivate that level of energy or not depends on our presence, awareness, attention, and consciousness of the actions we are involved with throughout the day. Hence, I always recommend that my clients do energy management and accounting analysis periodically.

EXERCISE: Energy Management and Accounting

The Energetic Body and Orgasm

I hope this chapter has given you some new insight into the ways in which our energetic bodies are participating in our sexual intimacy, love-making, and orgasm. If you are new to thinking about your body in this way, perhaps this chapter has inspired you to learn more about this layer of the human experience. If you were already aware of energetic systems, I hope this chapter allowed you to make new connections in terms of how energy centres, auric energy fields, and orgasm are related.

On the Path of Amplified Orgasm, learning how to better tune in, control, and align your energy with your partner is critical to experiencing orgasms that reach beyond the purely physical realm. Perhaps you are looking to tap into the divine power of connecting at the level of your souls, or perhaps you wish to experience what people have termed "mindgasms." (Yes, that is a thing, I promise you.) It is through expanding our energetic flow and connection with our lover that these experiences will become accessible to us.

As we turn next to the physical body, you may wonder why I chose to share about the emotional (Chapter One), mental (Chapter Two), and energetic bodies first. After all, for many readers, the physical dimension is perhaps the most familiar way to understand, or map, the body. However, this decision was quite deliberate. As you will see in the next chapter, now that you have a clear sense and language for how emotions, the mind, and energy work, you are now ready to explore the physical body with a more enriched understanding of what else lives in the body beyond the organic material that makes up our muscles, bones, and blood.

Chapter Three Summary:

- The energetic body at the most basic level includes seven major internal energy centres known as chakras, meridians that circulate energy throughout the body, and the seven layers of subtle bodies or auras that are the external part of the human energy field.

- The energy centres are associated with specific types of energy and also correlate with specific areas of the body. This is why, for example, we feel the emotion of love so strongly near the heart, since the Heart Energy Centre is located in that region of the body.

- Auras or Subtle Bodies include seven layers of energy fields that are external to the body, experienced as a kind of vibrational energy. Our auras can be impacted by changes such as life experience, thoughts and emotions, habits, health, diet, the environment, and energetic practices.

- Many of us are stronger in some layers of the auras over others, and we can think of this as our "home channel." However, it is important to note that we can expand and grow the strength of our other subtle bodies through mindfulness and practice of different ways of feeling, sensing, doing, being, and processing our world.

- Aligning the auras during sexual intimacy becomes a powerful way to explore different types of orgasm including whole body orgasms and mindgasms.

- Learning to tune into your own energetic body, as well as that of your partner, allows you to gain access to new levels of the orgasmic experience. Ultimately, learning to create energetic alignment and resonance with your partner is a key skill on the Path of Amplified Orgasm.

THE PHYSICAL BODY

Learn to live in this body well and enjoy the greatest pleasure that this body has to offer. With so many erogenous zones available in our body, I see no excuse to not experience pleasure and orgasm to their fullest potential.
Michael Charming

Have you heard that sex and orgasm can help in fighting some diseases and make us feel healthier? Have you ever wondered why that is the case? Do you know why breasts are considered to be one of the erogenous zones of the human body? Did you know that the hands can also be explored as erogenous zones?

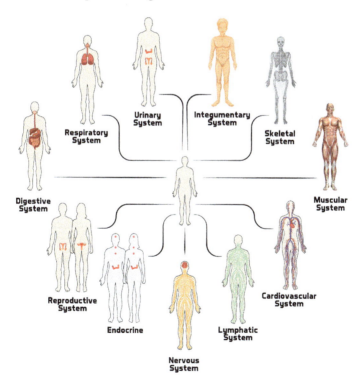

Figure 77: Our eleven human body systems

Perhaps the last time you thought about the human body was in high school or college biology class. Maybe you learned about the different systems in the body: the skeletal system, the nervous system, the circulatory system, the respiratory system, the digestive system, and the muscular system. You may remember diagrams like this one from those days:

Even if you did gain some valuable information about human anatomy and basic biological function, chances are good that your teacher did not spend much (probably none) on the relationship between these systems and sexual pleasure and orgasm. With that in mind, this chapter will explore the physical body with particular attention paid to the role these different systems play in orgasm.

In addition, we will explore the many different special areas of the body commonly referred to as erogenous zones (e-zones). While many texts on this subject treat these areas as "automatic" turn-on spots, this book will approach them with what we already know about emotion and energy to inform our view. That is, while many e-zones can indeed enhance and awaken our sexual energy, we also have to be aware that the degree to which this is true is highly individual and dependent on life experiences, blockages in the energetic body, and even our belief systems.

My hope when teaching about the physical body, whether in this book or during workshops and speaking events, is that my students will learn to develop a better relationship with their bodies and that of their partners. I have found that if you can bring the mind frame of "curiosity" to the table when exploring both your own body and that of your partner, it greatly enhances this relationship. To that end, the exercises in this chapter are designed to do just that.

Here are some fun facts about the physical aspect of the human body:

- The cornea of the eye gets oxygen directly from the air and is the only part of the entire body that has no direct blood supply
- A human brain has more or less the same capacity for memory as a hard drive with four terabytes of space
- Women's hearts beat faster than men's
- We lose 80 percent of our body heat from the head
- Nerve impulses in the human body move at about 90 metres/second
- An adult breathes in and out an average of 23,000 times a day
- The largest cell in the body is the egg and the smallest is the sperm
- Ounce for ounce, human bones are about five times stronger than steel
- Humans are the only species that produce emotional tears. Animals have strong emotions and tears, but it is yet to be proved that those tears are caused by emotions.

EXERCISE: How Well do You Know Your Body?

The Systems of the Physical Body

Because the physical body obviously plays a vital role in sex and orgasm, it only makes sense that we would dive into understanding the body in this way for this book. However, let's not get bogged down in the details, and instead focus on how each of these systems relates to orgasm.

Skeletal System

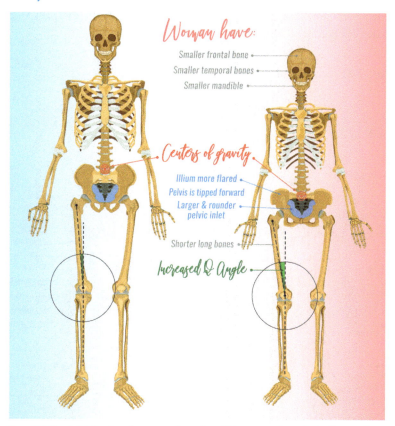

Figure 78: The skeletal system of women and men have differences as shown in the diagram above.

This system includes the body's hard framework of 206 bones which support and protect the muscles and organs of the human body.

It is divided into two parts: axial skeleton (supporting the head, neck, and trunk) and appendicular skeleton (supporting appendages or limbs and attaching them to the rest of the body). Different types of bones (long, short, flat, irregular, sesamoid) play different roles.

Women, relative to size, have a longer torso, shorter and more rounded pelvic bones, and the surrounding bones (tailbone, remaining hip bones, etc.) are designed to be more flexible to accommodate gestation and child delivery. Peak male bone mass is around 50% more than that of females, and women lose bone faster as they age.

Having a basic understanding of the different kinds of bones will help you with body mapping your lover, which will in turn assist in making the experience of love-making better. For example, knowing which part of the body one can put more pressure on to help with grounding or which areas of the body one can safely spank to create excitement can enhance love-making.

EXERCISE: Body Mapping Bones

Muscular System

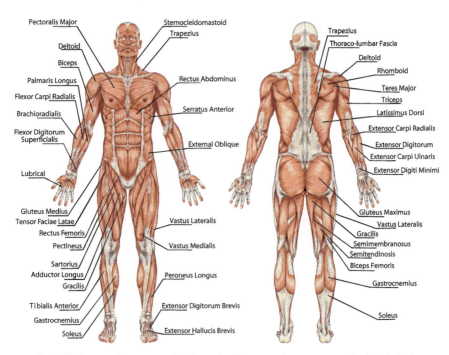

Figure 79: The muscular system – relaxed muscles allow orgasmic energy to move freely in the body and beyond while tensed muscles restrict the flow of energy movement.

This system is comprised of muscle tissue and its attachment tissues: tendons and fascia. When muscle fibres contract, the muscles change shape and move whichever part of the body they are attached to. This can be voluntary and conscious such as bending the knee, or involuntary, such as shivering.

A muscle's ability to contract is affected by the amount of energy available, strength of stimulus from the nerves, duration of the contraction, blood supply bringing oxygen and nutrients, strength of inhibitory nerve supply, the temperature of the muscle, and the presence of waste products like lactic acid.

Generally speaking, pound for pound, women can't match the bulk or strength of men's skeletal muscles – unless they artificially raise their androgens by a significant amount, which is considered to be dangerous. In an orgasmic state, muscles all over the body contract, the back arches, and muscles in the genitals contract and relax in different rhythmic patterns. Orgasms vary with individuals depending on stimulation, muscle tone, muscle contraction-release sequence, contraction intervals, etc.

Pelvic floor muscles (pubococcygeus) are the most important type of muscles which should be exercised for experiencing amplified orgasm (explored in more detail in Chapter Five). More toned pelvic floor muscles bring more intensity to muscle contractions during orgasms and help maintain continence.

In Chapter One, we learned that emotion is associated with three things: energy, movement, and feelings. Tensed and contracted muscles can hold back the emotional energy which affects the tissues surrounding those muscles, circulation, and nerves, ultimately stopping the flow of emotional and orgasmic energy. The pelvic area, neck, shoulders, and back are common places where muscles are tensed and emotions get held up. Have you wondered why massages feel so good? It is because, among other things, massages help to release tensions, contractions held in the muscles, which then brings relaxation to our body. In bodywork sessions, we go even deeper to clear the emotional energy held at the cellular level.

EXERCISE: Body Mapping Muscles

Cardiovascular System

This system is comprised of blood, heart, arteries, and veins. It includes two main systems: the pulmonary circulatory system and the systemic circulatory system. In order for one to feel multi-orgasmic, it is important that one has proper circulation of blood throughout the whole body. For example, addictions such as smoking, drinking, or binge-eating can lead to reducing the sensitivity of the body by restricting circulation, effectively making it become numb over time.

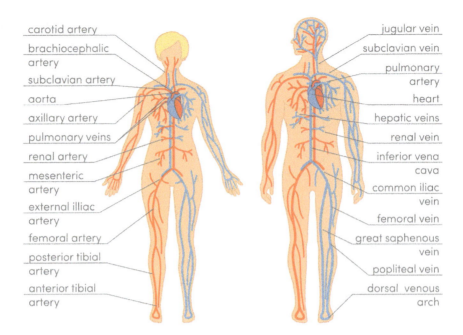

carotid artery
brachiocephalic artery
subclavian artery
aorta
axillary artery
pulmonary veins
renal artery
mesenteric artery
external illiac artery
femoral artery
posterior tibial artery
anterior tibial artery

jugular vein
subclavian vein
pulmonary artery
heart
hepatic veins
renal vein
inferior vena cava
common iliac vein
femoral vein
great saphenous vein
popliteal vein
dorsal venous arch

Figure 80: The cardiovascular system makes us feel aroused by circulating blood to our genitals.

Have you ever wondered what causes arousal in the body? In Chapter Five you will learn how blood circulation in the genitals brings arousal and makes us feel horny. During workshops, I often ask participants to list what they consider necessary to feel arousal. The answer is varied: trust, better communication, a loving partner, healthy diet, porn, physical beauty, hormones, etc. However, hardly anyone ever says blood circulation. While all the other factors are important and can play a role in making one feel orgasmic, it is good circulation that brings the turn-on to our genitals.

Symptoms relating to cardiovascular diseases can reduce sexual pleasure and enjoyment. As we know, blood is important for feeling arousal, so improper circulation affects the amount of blood flow that reaches the sexual organs. In men it can cause erectile dysfunction, while in women they might not feel arousal. Diseases like diabetes, high blood pressure, and depression can reduce sexual desire, arousal, and the feeling of orgasm. In my bodywork sessions with clients, I work to remove the knots, tangles, and sedimentation which result in blockages of the free flow of blood. Once these blockages are removed, clients begin to start feeling orgasmic again. No wonder, with their blood flow now restored!

Our blood transports oxygen, nutrients, hormones, and enzymes around the body, regulates body temperature, prevents the loss of body fluids, helps fight infection, and transports carbon dioxide and waste materials from the body to organs of excretion.

Our blood is made up of plasma, which consists of water and plasma proteins, red blood cells, white blood cells, and platelets. Many people often experience orgasm as a kind of chemical reaction, and this is because of the movement and chemical changes, such as hormonal shifts, in plasma during orgasm. Many people describe orgasm as an electric current that moves through the body. Plasma contains electrolytes which are energy carrying ions, so better circulation of blood will increase the feeling of healthy energetic vibrations. And, the feeling of love is often associated with a faster heartbeat, which is nothing but expansion and contraction of the atria and ventricles working together to pump blood through the heart. Its increased speed is triggered by electrical impulses that travel down a special neural pathway.

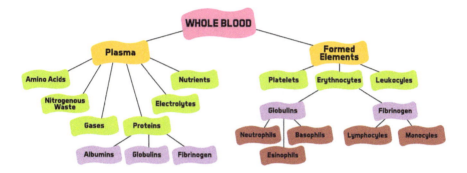

Figure 81: Components of whole blood

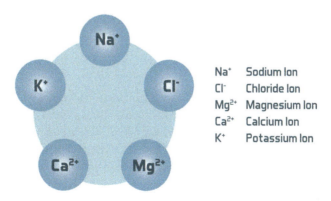

Na^+ Sodium Ion
Cl^- Chloride Ion
Mg^{2+} Magnesium Ion
Ca^{2+} Calcium Ion
K^+ Potassium Ion

Figure 82: Main electrolytes in body fluid

EXERCISE: Get to Know Your Blood Flow

Lymphatic System

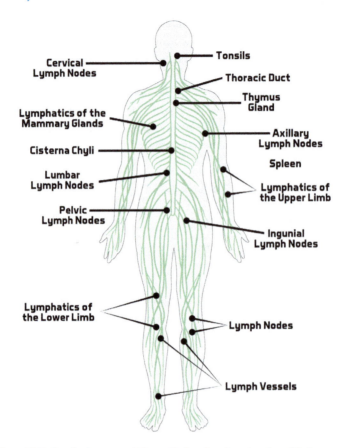

Cervical Lymph Nodes

Tonsils

Thoracic Duct

Thymus Gland

Lymphatics of the Mammary Glands

Axillary Lymph Nodes

Cisterna Chyli

Spleen

Lumbar Lymph Nodes

Lymphatics of the Upper Limb

Pelvic Lymph Nodes

Inguinal Lymph Nodes

Lymphatics of the Lower Limb

Lymph Nodes

Lymph Vessels

Figure 83: The lymphatic system, which contains lymph nodes, gets activated during orgasm.

This system includes the body's complex network of tissues and organs which eliminate waste and toxins while delivering white blood cells to various parts of the body to fight infection.[32] Unlike blood, the lymphatic system doesn't have a pump and it relies on your body's muscle and joint contractions. Physical exercise is one way to cleanse this system. In addition, the activities of sex and orgasmic states help to move stagnant lymphatic enzymes into circulation.

Orgasms provide an overall lymphatic massage to your body, which improves your digestion, mood, and flushes out toxins.[33] Sexual arousal and orgasm may stimulate the immune system and increase leukocytes (white blood cell) production, thus helping one increase immune-fighting hormones preventing common colds and the flu, for example.[33,34] No wonder sex and orgasms are considered to be important for our overall health and well-being!

EXERCISE: How is Your Lymphatic System?

Nervous System

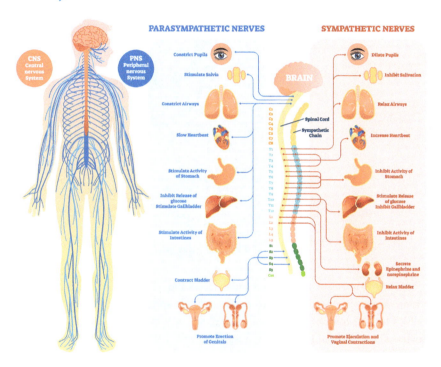

PARASYMPATHETIC NERVES

SYMPATHETIC NERVES

CNS
Central
nervous
System

PNS
Peripheral
nervous
System

Constrict Pupils
Stimulate Saliva
Constrict Airways
Slow Heartbeat
Stimulate Activity of Stomach
Inhibit Release of glucose Stimulate Gallbladder
Stimulate Activity of Intestines
Contract Bladder

BRAIN

Spinal Cord
Sympathetic Chain

Dilate Pupils
Inhibit Salivation
Relax Airways
Increase Heartbeat
Inhibit Activity of Stomach
Stimulate Release of glucose Inhibit Gallbladder
Inhibit Activity of Intestines
Secrete Epinephrine and norepinephrine
Relax Bladder

Promote Erection of Genitals

Promote Ejaculation and Vaginal Contractions

Figure 84: The nervous system, which sends signals back and forth from the brain to different parts of the body, is responsible for signalling sensations of pain or pleasure.

This communication and instruction network is categorised into two parts: the central nervous system (CNS, which consists of brain and spinal cord) and the peripheral nervous system (PNS, which consists of nerves throughout the rest of the body). The brain is the main unit and is connected to the rest of the body by nerve cells which function as messengers, carrying information to and from the brain. They report back on sensation such as pain or pleasure, as well as danger and safety cues, so the brain can make informed decisions that respond to the environment.[35]

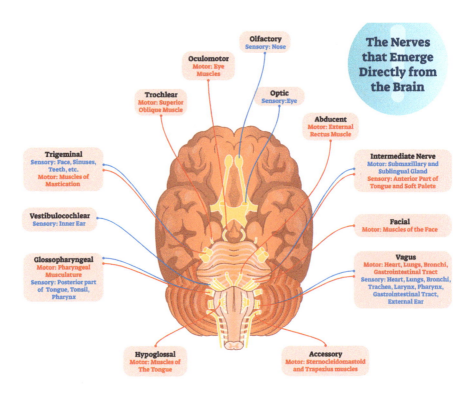

The Nerves that Emerge Directly from the Brain

Olfactory
Sensory: Nose

Oculomotor
Motor: Eye Muscles

Optic
Sensory:Eye

Trochlear
Motor: Superior Oblique Muscle

Abducent
Motor: External Rectus Muscle

Trigeminal
Sensory: Face, Sinuses, Teeth, etc.
Motor: Muscles of Mastication

Intermediate Nerve
Motor: Submaxillary and Sublingual Gland
Sensory: Anterior Part of Tongue and Soft Palete

Vestibulocochlear
Sensory: Inner Ear

Facial
Motor: Muscles of the Face

Glossopharyngeal
Motor: Pharyngeal Musculature
Sensory: Posterior part of Tongue, Tonsil, Pharynx

Vagus
Motor: Heart, Lungs, Bronchi, Gastrointestinal Tract
Sensory: Heart, Lungs, Bronchi, Trachea, Larynx, Pharynx, Gastrointestinal Tract, External Ear

Hypoglossal
Motor: Muscles of The Tongue

Accessory
Motor: Sternocleidomastoid and Trapezius muscles

Figure 85: The cranial nerves serves

The PNS consists of 12 pairs of cranial nerves and 31 pairs of spinal nerves. Motor division of the PNS is divided into Somatic (SNS) and Autonomic Nervous System (ANS). The SNS is largely concerned with voluntary movements, such as the use of our muscles. The ANS is an involuntary system controlled by the hypothalamus (the small region in the brain that plays an important role in releasing hormones, managing sexual behaviour, and regulating emotional responses). The ANS is further divided into two divisions: the Sympathetic, which is most active during stress, and the Parasympathetic, which dominates when the body is in a more restful state.

It is due to these nerves sending and receiving impulses back to and from the spinal cord and the brain that a person feels an orgasm in the body. In addition, a deep sense of relaxation is very important for higher states of orgasm. When you are asking your partner to relax, it is this Parasympathetic system that you are working with to keep them relaxed.

In my bodywork sessions, I have often come across clients who are hypersensitive to touch, noise, energies, and other environmental triggers. In my view, it is because of the nervous system which is highly sensitive and reactive to different things like touch, sounds, sensations, smells, movement. If you are with a lover who is very sensitive, it means you will need a lot more awareness of your own energy system, your touch, your tonality, your distance from them and so forth, with a strong understanding of how these are impacting them, especially during sex and physical intimacy.

EXERCISE: Identify a Few Key Pressure Points

Vagus Nerve

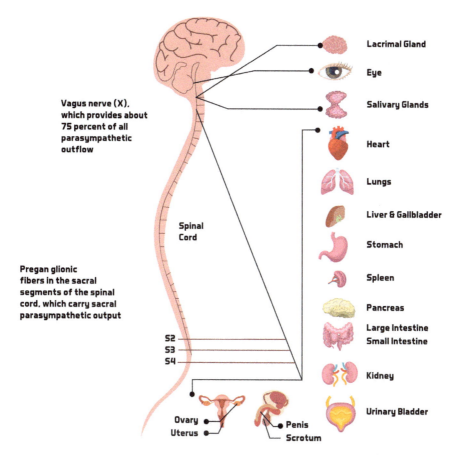

Figure 86: Triggering of the vagus nerve enables sensations to be transported to internal organs due to its connection with different organs of the body.

When we are talking about the nervous system, especially in terms of orgasm, it would be incomplete if we did not talk about the vagus nerve. The vagus nerve is the longest cranial nerve in the body and it controls the PNS and manages the motor and sensory impulses to different organs in the body. It is this vagus nerve that prevents inflammation from injury or illness, helps make memories, regulates heart rate, breathing, and the digestive system, stimulates muscle contractions, and helps in communication between the brain, gut, heart, and lungs. The better the tonality of the vagus nerve, the better our rest and relaxation is and the better management we have over our impulses.

The sensory function of the vagus nerve consists of somatic components (sensations experienced and felt on skin or muscles) and visceral components (sensations felt in different organs). The motor functions of the vagus nerve include stimulating muscles in different parts of the body. Stimulating the vagus nerve and increasing vagal tone helps to treat a variety of physical and mental health conditions like depression, migraines, and anxiety.[36 – 39]

If you have experienced strong gut instincts or intense emotional and mental states during sex and orgasm, or if you have started making deep sex and orgasmic sounds, it means the vagus nerve has been highly active and busy in communicating with the gut, brain, heart, and other parts of the body. Anything that increases the presence of the neurotransmitter acetylcholine will also improve the tonality of the vagus nerve. Considering the inter-exchange between the physical and energy centres, this nerve plays a vital role. So, increasing the tonality of this nerve becomes even more important if we are to strengthen the energy centres through the physical body. Besides the vagus nerve, the three important nerves that connect to the genitals which are worth learning more about are: the hypogastric nerve, the pelvic nerve, and the pudendal nerve.

EXERCISE: Toning the Vagus Nerve

Endocrine System

This system is another one of the body's communication systems and is composed of ductless glands which produce hormones (the body's chemical messengers) which tell the body what to do.

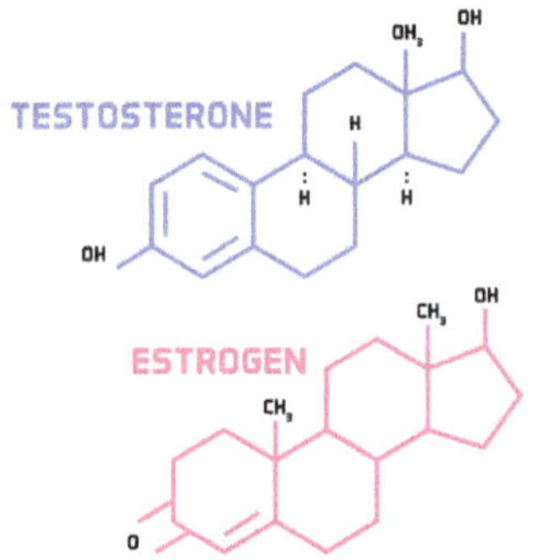

Besides ovaries and testes which are part of this system, the hormones which are most important relating to sex and orgasms are sex hormones – female: oestrogen, progesterone, male: testosterone. While women have higher

Figure 87: Chemical composition of two most known sex hormones

116

concentrations of female hormones, and men more male hormones, it is important to understand that all people have both of these types of hormones that play important roles when it comes to sexuality. For example, if a person has low sex drive, low sexual desire, arousal, or decreased orgasmic ability, it could mean that testosterones are not produced by the body in adequate quantity. In women, although we know that oestrogens control various female sexual and reproductive functions like arousal, menstruation and vaginal lubrication, testosterone deficiency in a woman can substantially impact her sexual and reproductive functioning as well. Age, chronic health conditions, use of some drugs (especially drugs used in chemotherapy), human immunodeficiency virus, obesity, primary or secondary ovarian failure, surgical menopause (in females), and dysfunction of adrenal axis are some of the reasons for the reduced production of testosterones. There are activities and dietary changes that can help bring sex hormones into balance in many cases.

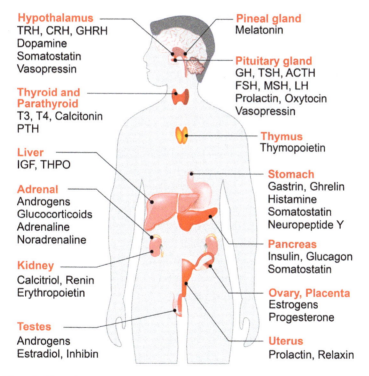

Hypothalamus
TRH, CRH, GHRH
Dopamine
Somatostatin
Vasopressin

Pineal gland
Melatonin

Pituitary gland
GH, TSH, ACTH
FSH, MSH, LH
Prolactin, Oxytocin
Vasopressin

Thyroid and Parathyroid
T3, T4, Calcitonin
PTH

Thymus
Thymopoietin

Liver
IGF, THPO

Stomach
Gastrin, Ghrelin
Histamine
Somatostatin
Neuropeptide Y

Adrenal
Androgens
Glucocorticoids
Adrenaline
Noradrenaline

Pancreas
Insulin, Glucagon
Somatostatin

Kidney
Calcitriol, Renin
Erythropoietin

Ovary, Placenta
Estrogens
Progesterone

Testes
Androgens
Estradiol, Inhibin

Uterus
Prolactin, Relaxin

Figure 88: The endocrine system and various hormones that play an important part in feelings of arousal

EXERCISE: Exploring the Endocrine System

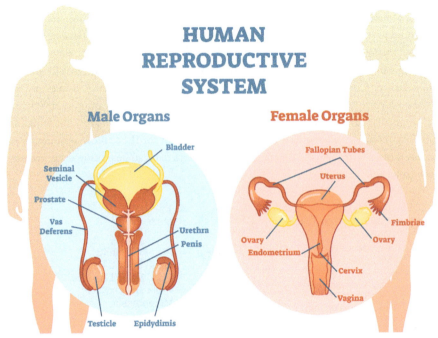

Figure 89: The reproductive system consists of both internal and external organs which play a role in reproduction and one's experiences of pleasure and enjoyment.

This system enables humans to reproduce and also to have sex and pleasure. Genitals, which make up much of the reproductive system and play a pivotal role in orgasm, will be discussed in more detail in Chapter Five. The hormones associated with the reproductive system are discussed briefly above as they are part of the endocrine system. However, let's take a brief look at the main aspects of the female and male reproductive system and how it relates to sex and orgasm.

Female Reproductive System

When it comes to the female reproductive system and how it relates to sex and orgasm, we should take a look at the womb or uterus. Orgasm in this area is generally caused by the stimulation of the cervix or the area just outside of the cervix. When a woman feels aroused, the uterus expands. The cervix is pulled forward, towards the front of the body, which creates a feeling of tightness in the vulva. If penetration feels painful, it could be due to the penis hitting the cervix, which often happens when the woman hasn't received enough stimulation to make her fully aroused. However, it is also possible that pain is caused from emotional pain felt as a result of past experiences, especially relating to childbirth. If a woman has had difficulty relating to childbirth or has had undergone a miscarriage or childbirth has not been positive for her due to psychological, physiological, or other reasons,

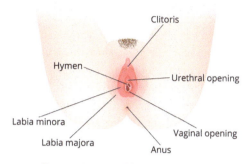

Figure 90: Anatomy of female genital organs

then a lot of trauma can get stored in this area, which can end up blocking her energy flow and impacting the way she can feel orgasm. Likewise, a woman who has had positive and beautiful experiences (even possibly orgasmic) relating to birth could have positive effects on her ability to receive pleasure and become more orgasmic in this area.

Once I worked with a client who had a miscarriage 15 years ago. Over the next five years, she had undergone various kinds of healing, so that all of the emotional pain attached to the miscarriage could be released. However, during our bodywork session, some deeper core of her womb was touched, which brought up all the unreleased emotional pain attached to the miscarriage, an experience that was still stuck inside her on the cellular level. Later on, she revealed the history of her

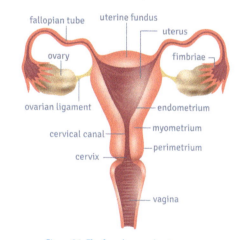

Figure 91: The female reproductive system

miscarriage, which even she had long forgotten about, which is why it wasn't disclosed during our initial consultation. Although she connected with an emotion more than a decade old, it enabled her body to let go off that pain even more, so that she could receive more pleasure and experience deeper orgasms going forward.

Sex and orgasm in general are good during pregnancy (though the latter part of pregnancy might not be that enjoyable) due to increased blood flow to the pelvic region, increased sensitivity which increases the ability to receive more pleasure, the production of oxytocin and other feel-good hormones, as well as increased lubrication.

Male Reproductive System

When we talk about the male reproductive system, it is most important to talk about sperm and how it is made, since this is critical to understanding ejaculation. (We will discuss the practice of sperm retention in more detail in Part II.)

In the human reproductive process, two kinds of sex cells (also known as gametes) are involved: the sperm (male gamete) and egg or ovum (female gamete). The characteristics of the parents are passed onto the child through the genes carried by the gametes.

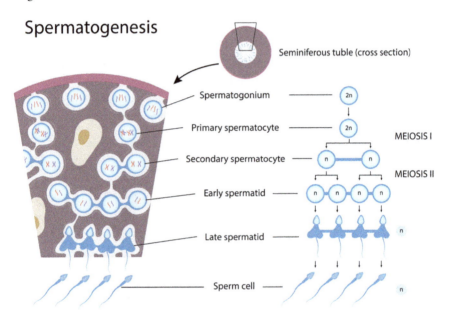

Figure 92: Formation of sperm through the process of spermatogenesis

Once boys attain puberty, the testes start producing and storing millions of sperm each day. They are extremely small (0.05mm long) and they develop in a system of tiny tubes called seminiferous tubules. During puberty, testosterone and other hormones cause the simple round cells to transform into sperm cells.

The cells divide until they have a head, the acrosome, a cap-like structure to cover most of the nucleus which contains genes and whose main role is to penetrate the outer layers of the ovum. They also have a short tail, the flagellum, which is a long, whip-like cellular appendage that pushes them into the epididymis, a process which takes four to six weeks. The sperm then move to the sperm duct (vas deferens).

When men are sexually stimulated, the seminal vesicles, Cowper's gland, and prostate glands produce seminal fluid. This milky fluid combines with sperm to make semen. When the penis is stimulated during erection, the muscles around the reproductive organs force the semen through the duct system and push it out through the urethra, which is referred to as ejaculation (climax). Each ejaculate can contain up to 500 million very active sperm. At an energetic level, men may feel uncomfortable if they do not ejaculate, often experienced as an itchy and painful sensation.

Millions of sperm (about 1,500 per second) are produced every day. However, a full regeneration cycle, known as spermatogenesis, takes about two-and-a-half months, or roughly 74 days. This cycle starts in the brain, where the hypothalamus constantly monitors testosterone levels. If it falls, the hypothalamus starts secreting GnRH (gonadotropin-releasing hormone), which flows to the pituitary gland and results in the production of luteinising hormone (LH) and follicle-stimulating hormone (FSH). LH then goes to the testicles, where it stimulates the production of testosterone, resulting in the production of sperm.

Figure 93: Each sperm is made up of a smooth and oval head which contains a nucleus and midpiece which contains mitochondria that provides energy and a tail that helps in mobility.

Sperm can live for about three weeks inside the body, at which point they die and get reabsorbed by the body. Sperm health is measured by the number of sperm, the movement of sperm (motility, which is measured by how many sperm are moving), and the shape of the sperm.

Sperm remain alive only in a narrow range of temperature, and as such, when exposed to air, die quickly. If ejaculated inside the uterus, they can live for up to five days due to the protective effects of cervical mucus and cervical crypts. Extreme temperatures, drugs, smoking, diet and unhealthy lifestyles can all impact the quality of sperm.

Digestive System

This system includes the organs which transform substances we eat into other elements that can be used in the body for energy, growth, wear and tear. Once the food has been broken down by various chemical processes and nutrients removed, the rest is excreted as waste. There are four stages of digestion – mouth, stomach, small intestine, and large intestine.

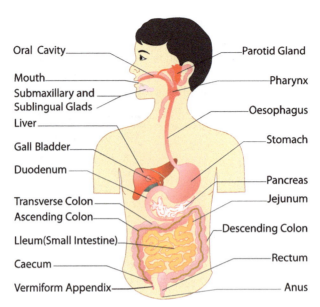

Figure 94: The digestive system contains the gut which contains bacteria responsible for producing hormones, enzymes, and neurotransmitters which are essential for sexual well-being.

A healthy gut is considered to be crucial for orgasm. When we speak about the gut, we are actually referring to the gastrointestinal tract, which starts with the mouth. Saliva also contains special chemicals that help to stop germs (bacteria) from causing infections. And, it is because of these special chemicals that saliva feels so amazing during kissing and sex.

Known as the enteric nervous system, the gut is lined by millions of nerve cells that allow it to communicate with the brain 24/7.[40,41] The amount of saliva released is controlled by your nervous system. The gut contains billions of bacteria which function together in a complex network (hence the gut is referred to as a 'second brain'). These bacteria are responsible for producing hormones, enzymes, and neurotransmitters such as serotonin which are essential for sexual health.[42] Gamma-Aminobutyric acid, also known as GABA, which controls feelings of anxiety, depression, fear, chronic stress and insomnia, is thought to play a role in gut health where it may support gut motility, regulate inflammation, boost the immune system, and regulate hormonal activity.[43]

Figure 95: Chemical composition of GABA

Disorders of the gut include acid refluxes, various kinds of cancer (liver, stomach, bowel,

122

pancreas, stomach), constipation, diarrhoea, hernias, etc. A lot of digestive diseases can get in the way of feeling sexual arousal and orgasms. A better diet can lead to better sex and more orgasms, which in turn can contribute to a healthier gut. When one is in orgasmic states, the circulation of blood increases, which helps to distribute nutrients and hormones where they are needed.

If you have experienced stomach aches after sex, it could be due to gas, deep penetration, tense abdominal muscles, or other forms of gastrointestinal distress. If the gut isn't healthy, excess hormones can be left unused and recycled in the body, which can increase the quantity of oestrogens in women. This can result in feeling pain around the breasts, heavier periods, or increased weight.

EXERCISE: Checking in with Your Gut

Respiratory System

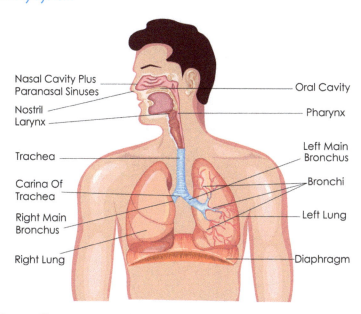

Figure 96: The respiratory system helps to circulate the air in our body. The deeper we are able to breathe naturally, the more pleasure and intense orgasmic contractions we will be able to experience.

This system consists of the nose, lungs, diaphragm, and the air passages such as the trachea which connect them. It takes substances from outside the body, circulates them through the body to cells and tissues, then discharges the excess and waste. Oxygen is considered to be food of the respiratory system and carbon dioxide is considered to be the waste. Breathing is automatic and not automatic at the same time.

Our breath often changes as we pass through various stages of orgasm – mainly due to the wide range of emotions we experience such as nervousness, excitement, or fear, as well as body movements and sexual responses. The more we hold our breath during sex and in orgasmic states, the more we are limiting the amount of new oxygen flowing into our body, which is in turn limiting us from feeling even more orgasmic. Aim to have deeper, longer, slower, and conscious breath during each love-making session. One can also play around with different kinds of breathing or practise rhythmic breathing and see how this alters one's orgasmic states and feeling of sensations in the body. When we breathe slowly and deeply, we begin to feel more and come alive. Breathing is key to different kinds of orgasmic pleasure and to prolong the whole experience of love-making. (We will cover breathing in more detail in Part II.)

EXERCISE: Becoming Aware of Breath

Urinary System

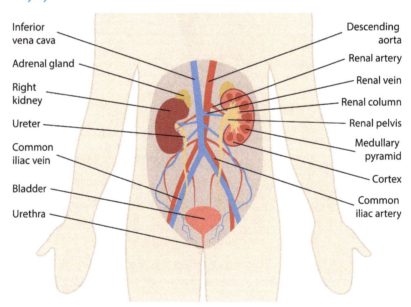

Inferior vena cava
Adrenal gland
Right kidney
Ureter
Common iliac vein
Bladder
Urethra

Descending aorta
Renal artery
Renal vein
Renal column
Renal pelvis
Medullary pyramid
Cortex
Common iliac artery

Figure 97: The urinary system holds the waste substances as such the muscles relating to this system which often are held up as tense and contracted which reduces the flow of energy. Efforts should be made as much as possible to relax these muscles.

This is one of the human body's waste disposal systems and it is composed of kidneys, ureters, bladder, and urethra. This system helps to empty harmful waste substances such as urea and alcohol through filtration and excretion processes. The urinary tract in men consists of the kidneys, bladder, urethra (waterpipe), and prostate gland. For women the urinary tract consists of the kidneys, bladder, and a shorter urethra. The main muscles responsible for holding the urine in when a person doesn't want to urinate are the pelvic floor muscles.

Urinary symptoms, erectile dysfunction, ejaculation problems, fertility problems, as well as reduced arousal, desire, and ability to have orgasms are some of the problems that can be caused due to dysfunctions in the urinary system.

EXERCISE: Urinary Tract Health

Integumentary System

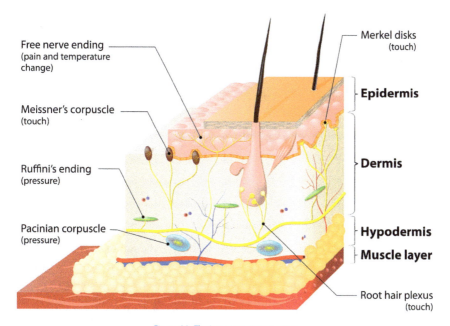

Figure 98: The integumentary system

The integumentary system consists of skin, hair, nails, and exocrine glands. Skin, which is the largest organ in the body, protects the body from disease, physical damage, wind, water, UV radiation, chemicals, and invasion from other external stimuli. The exocrine glands produce sweat, oil, and wax to regulate body temperature and to keep the skin moisturised. The epidermis is the most superficial layer which is visible to our eyes and is arranged into five distinct layers.

The dermis, which is the layer underneath epidermis is made up of irregular connective tissues and is connected to the nerves, blood, and lymph supply. The dermis contains these main types of structures: specialised cells, nerve endings, sweat glands (eccrine and apocrine), hair follicles, sebaceous glands, lymphatic capillaries, and papilla.

Hair and nails are the accessory organs of the skin and each play a part in creating arousal and pleasure during physical intimacy. Examples include caressing the hair or scratching and teasing with the nails. Eccrine sweat glands are found in every region of the skin while apocrine glands are found mainly in axillary and pubic regions of the body.

Caressing, touching, and kissing the skin leads to arousal because the skin contains specialised sensory nerve structures that transmit information to the central nervous system. The integumentary system regulates body temperature due to its connection with the sympathetic nervous system which is continuously monitoring body temperature and initiating appropriate motor responses.

Orgasm results in a rise in body temperature and metabolism and also helps the skin to glow due to an increased rate of oxygenated blood flow as a result of expanded blood vessels which boosts collagen production which stimulates and repairs the skin. Pheromone (axillary steroids), the chemical molecules which play a role in excitement during sexual encounters, are also produced by the apocrine glands.

EXERCISE: Becoming Familiar with the Integumentary System

Erogenous Zones

An erogenous zone is an area with increased sensitivity, the stimulation of which can alter the state of feeling and generate a sexual response – such as a feeling of mild, gentle, or intense sexual arousal, sexual desire, sexual fantasies, and even orgasm.

The human body is highly sensitive to touch due to many erogenous zones, but during physical intimacy we often have a tendency to rush into the stimulation of genitals. However, every single area of the body is connected. We should therefore be spending time with the less-explored parts of the body. It not only activates the energy in that area, which is important for whole body orgasms, but it also helps us break away from routine and predictable patterns of touching during physical intimacy.

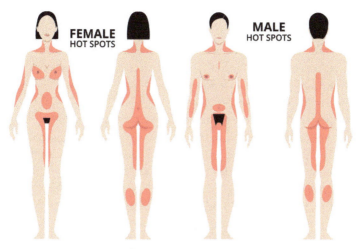

Figure 99: Erogenous zones

We are multi-orgasmic and one of the reasons that make us so is the existence of erogenous zones. The level of sensitivity in each varies due to different levels of concentration of nerve endings, the flow of blood and energy, and even the way our mind has come to understand these areas through fantasies or past experiences of pleasure or trauma. In regards to touch, Professor Valeria Gazzola explains: "Intuitively, we all believe that when we are touched by someone, we first objectively perceive the physical properties of the touch – its speed, its gentleness, the roughness of the skin. Only thereafter, in a separable second step based on who touched us, do we believe we value this touch more or less."[44]

Blood contains electrolytes which have electrical charges. It is this charge which is felt like electric current during orgasm. So the more the blood is able to flow throughout the body, the more one will be able to feel orgasm. Likewise, increased blood flow is associated with erogenous zones, particularly when they are stimulated.

In addition, medical procedures, medications, age, and injuries can alter the sensitivity of these regions. Thus, although we can learn a general map of these zones for women and men, individual differences are always a factor and can change over time.

Erogenous zones are divided into two categories:

- **Specific Zones**: These zones have a high density of innervation, have the capacity to stimulate cerebral arousal, and are associated with sexual response. They include areas such as the genitals, lips, and nipples.
- **Non-specific Zones**: These are zones which have a high density of nerve endings and generally produce an anticipatory response when touched or tickled. Examples include the sides and back of the neck, inner thighs, inner arms, and the sides of the thorax.

These zones can be stimulated by caressing, kissing, licking, biting, gentle whispering, tickling, breathing, and exhaling softly. They can be stimulated by hands, fingers, toes, mouth, lips, tongues, and external objects. Stimulation often produces a pleasurable experience for one or both the partners involved. Please note that the list below is not exhaustive, nor does it apply to every individual. Rather than seeing the erogenous zones as a kind of checklist on the way to orgasm, it is better to approach them as a map which offers some guidance on a journey of exploration.

You may notice from the image that these zones are very similar in both male and female bodies. In regards to erogenous zones between women and men, neuropsychologist Oliver Turnbull explains: "We're actually pretty stable across all humans, as regards the main erogenous zones. There are modest differences between men and women, but they have – I believe – been exaggerated."[45]

EXERCISE: Getting Curious About E-Zones

Hair and Scalp

Playing with hair can work wonders because the nerves on the scalp are known to heighten pleasure. Running the fingers through a partner's hair can give them sensual pleasure, while also expressing tenderness and care.

Forehead

Figure 100: Touching and caressing of the hair and scalp feels so good. Have you ever wondered why?

Massaging the area from hairline to eyebrows can trigger the release of dopamine and serotonin, causing good feelings. One must be careful in kissing the forehead however, as it can trigger emotions relating to love and care offered by mom or dad during childhood. So, depending on how someone's relationship with their parents may have been, touches on the forehead can feel pleasurable or trigger negative feelings.

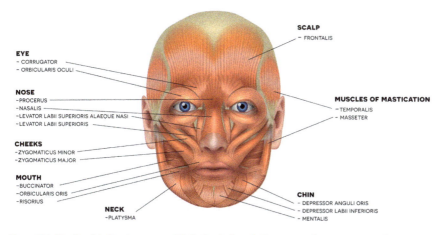

EYE
~ CORRUGATOR
~ ORBICULARIS OCULI

NOSE
~PROCERUS
~NASALIS
~LEVATOR LABII SUPERIORIS ALAEQUE NASI
~LEVATOR LABII SUPERIORIS

CHEEKS
~ZYGOMATICUS MINOR
~ZYGOMATICUS MAJOR

MOUTH
~BUCCINATOR
~ORBICULARIS ORIS
~RISORIUS

NECK
~PLATYSMA

SCALP
~ FRONTALIS

MUSCLES OF MASTICATION
~ TEMPORALIS
~ MASSETER

CHIN
~ DEPRESSOR ANGULI ORIS
~ DEPRESSOR LABII INFERIORIS
~ MENTALIS

Figure 101: Muscles of the head are responsible for headaches which many people can experience after orgasm. This happens due to the build-up of sexual excitement which causes the muscles to contract and become tense.

Mouth, Lips, and Tongue

Prolonged kissing without genital contact at the get-go can result in better orgasms because kissing activates neurotransmitters which flow through our bodies and brain, boosting the level of dopamine, and releasing oxytocin. The mucous membranes and very thin skin that comprise the lips bring a dense supply of nerve endings closer to the surface, making them more responsive to stimulation. The erotic power of the mouth is almost equal for both women and men. However, instead of rushing the kisses every time, we should develop a practice of paying attention to each kiss given and received and the impact they have caused, including noticing the kinds of sensations arising in the body.

Cheek and Chin

It may be surprising to learn that the cheek and chin are zones that are considered to be

Figure 102: Kissing is very arousing due to the release of endorphins and oxytocin and due to large numbers of nerve endings in the lips.

Figure 103: A kiss on the cheek feels so good and assuring, especially the soft, light and gentle ones

erogenous. The chin is often associated with dominance, self-confidence, courage, self-contentedness, and it links to testosterone, hence kissing on the chin can have a subtle sexual effect due to the prominence it holds.

EXERCISE: Kissing

Neck

This area is very sensitive as stimulation of the neck area sends signals to the circulatory system, increasing blood flow. Care should be taken during biting as it can result in the formation of love bites and not everyone will be happy with that! Many women rank kisses on the nape of the neck as more arousing than those offered on the breasts and nipples.

Ears

The ears are an erogenous zone for many, especially the area behind the earlobe. In the case of men, touching the ears is considered extremely arousing for some. Although the uricologenital reflex (stimulation of the nerve inside the ear canal) can bring a person to orgasm, it is recommended to have a conversation about putting the tongue in the ear as not everyone will appreciate this form of touch.

Figure 104: Biting, nibbling, licking, sucking, whispering, or breathing into the ears feel good and can send sensations down the spine.

Eyes and Eyelids

Generally men tend to be more visual than women in terms of feeling arousal i.e. men can be extremely aroused by seeing the naked female body while for women, eyes tend to be more about trust. Just looking in the eyes of your partner can create sexual pleasure and sensations. When we are aroused, our pupils dilate, which makes the other person more attractive to

Figure 105: Every person's eyes have stories to tell. Looking into the eyes can be deeply intimate and vulnerable at the same time.

us and vice versa. The longer the eye contact between two people, the deeper the level of intimacy. Caressing and kissing on these areas, especially the eyelids, can arouse the feelings of being deeply cared for and loved. Notice how if there has been a conflict with your partner, sometimes it becomes difficult to look each other in the eyes. You may have also experienced how just the sight of your lover can evoke emotions relating to love, care, and even sexual feelings.

We often spend so much time keeping ourselves distracted, but one of the easiest ways to create intimacy is by looking at each other in the eyes without any distractions.

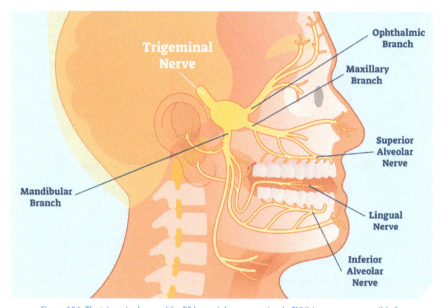

Figure 106: The trigeminal nerve (the fifth cranial nerve, or simply CNV) is a nerve responsible for sensation in the face and motor functions such as biting and chewing.

EXERCISE: Gazing into Our Lover's Eyes

Arms and Armpits

These areas are particularly sensitive, especially at the softer skin of the inner arms and the skin covering the ventral side of the elbow. The existence of pheromones in this region can activate our sense of smell and connect us with the sexuality of our partner through these potent neuro-activating chemicals.

Hand Reflexology Chart

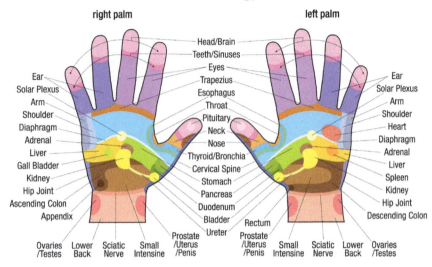

Figure 107: The science of Hand Reflexology is based on various reflex points on the palms and around the hand.

Our hands, and particularly our fingers, have many nerve endings which can be ticklish and are responsive to a very light touch like scratching, biting, and caressing. Reflexology shows that the palms are connected to various organs of the body and are very rich in nerve receptors so touching them generates a great deal of pleasure. Walking hand in hand also feels soothing, and is a reminder of our bond. Care should be taken in sucking the fingers, as not every person likes that. However, for those that do, sucking on the partner's fingers and massaging them with the tongue sends signals to the reward centres of the brain, just like sex.

EXERCISE: Getting to Know Hands as E-Zones

Inner Wrist

This area of the body has thin skin and many nerve endings. It is right at the radial pulse point, so touching at this place can help create a good vibe for intimacy.

Bums and Anal

Bums are an area of excitement for many lovers. Holding, squeezing, grabbing, spanking, stroking, teasing around the bum area can be very exciting.

Make sure that the glutes are as relaxed as possible and that you have a conversation and her consent before you touch this area as it can trigger lot of emotions related to past experiences. When touching the areas around and inside the anus, great care should be taken and progress should be slow.

Figure 108: The touching of bums during sexual activity can be very arousing but care should be taken as it can also be triggering for some.

EXERCISE: Reflecting on Attitudes and Beliefs About Anal Stimulation

Chest, Nipples, and Breasts

The erogenous power of nipples is quite reduced for many men but very high for many women. In women, the areola and nipple contain concentrations of nerve tissue in the area of the ducts. The kidney meridian passes through the breasts and when the nipples are stimulated, the kidney and bladder get stimulated too, which in turn activates sexual glands resulting in the arousal of the whole genital area.[46]

When nipples are stimulated intensely, it results in the activation of the genital sensory cortex (the same area which is aroused by vaginal or clitoral stimulation) and the production of oxytocin and prolactin, which causes arousal in the genitals and may lead to orgasm. Nipples can be twisted and pulled to great effect, but extreme care should be taken in terms of pressure as they are very sensitive. One should not go directly at the nipples but instead build up the excitement by warming up the areas around them first. Do not pounce at them or squeeze them hard, but instead be gentle and observe how her body is reacting to every move.

It is highly recommended to have a conversation and her consent before touching the breasts and the nipples, as powerful emotions can be stored here. Many women can experience nipple orgasms (and some men too) if stimulated continuously and the sensations can be felt throughout the body. Breast sensitivity and arousal can increase during menstruation due to hormonal changes. We will be touching in detail on the role menstruation plays in orgasm in Part II of the book. The harder the nipple becomes, the more sensitive it will be to direct stimulation.

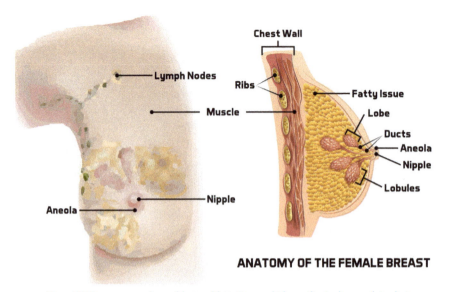

Figure 109: Breasts are made up of duct and fatty tissues which can alter in shape and size during sexual activity due to changes in the blood circulation.

Figure 110: Stimulation of breasts can be very arousing due to the nipple that has hundreds of nerve endings which makes them very sensitive to touch

EXERCISE: Exploring Nipple Play

Centre of the Chest

Men and women love being touched on the chest. Men often associate manliness with reference to chest size while for women it is more connected with intimacy. As the solar plexus energy centre is situated at this position, men who have not worked on activating this centre may be operating from a place of ego, so touching and kissing this area will help them feel their ego being caressed and massaged. Women who have issues with intimacy may find touching in this area to be quite painful or they may feel very vulnerable.

Figure 111: Touching the centre of the chest can be very comforting, boosting confidence, and making one feel vulnerable.

Lungs

People often mistake the erogenous zones to include only areas on the outside of our bodies. Inhaling and exhaling deeply can help our partner feel relaxed, grounded, present and can even help in feeling pleasure from sensations inside the lungs.[47] It can be very arousing if both partners are inhaling and exhaling together. Pay attention to the air that is inhaled and see if you can breathe all the way down to the lower belly and even to the genitals. Intentional breathing techniques can even lead to orgasmic sensations.

Figure 112: Breathing together can be very arousing but care should be taken not to breathe out into each other but rather breathe together, slower, and deeper.

Abdomen and Navel

These areas are close to the pubic region and the aorta and sexual pulse passes through this area. Stimulation of this area results in blood flow to the pelvis, creating sexual tension. The abdomen can be a place of vulnerability, especially for women, so although this area is very exciting for many women it can also be triggering for many.

Upper and Lower Back

The upper back is not directly related to the erogenous zones in terms of arousal, but the upper back and shoulders store a lot of stress, especially for women. So, providing a massage or helping to relax this area along with the lower back can help your partner feel relaxed and create space for arousal.

Sacrum

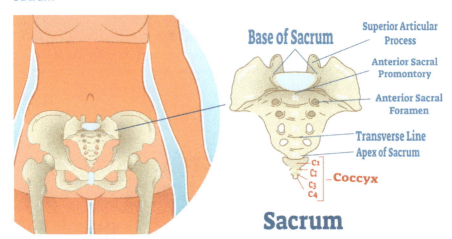

Figure 113: The sacrum, a small triangle shaped bone, can be very comforting and arousing if touched and massaged with right pressure.

This is a small triangle-shaped bone which is found at the base of the spine, between the hips. The nerves in the sacrum are linked to the genitals, so stimulation of this area triggers the parasympathetic nervous system which can result in orgasms for women. In bodywork sessions, we often place emphasis on this part of the body because of the importance it holds. Many of my clients have felt amazing sensations and orgasmic energy when the energy from the sacrum is moved and cleared.

> **EXERCISE: Identifying the Sacrum**

Genitals

These are the most obvious erogenous areas. Please refer to Chapter Five, as we have covered these in detail there.

Behind the Knee

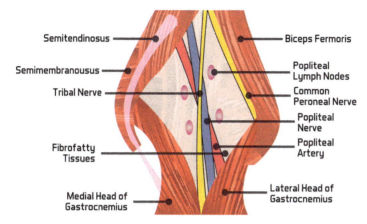

Figure 114: The popliteal artery behind the knee makes this area arousing or ticklish for some.

For many, this is a ticklish spot, but it can also be a pleasure spot, especially for men due to smoother skin and less hair than other places on many male bodies. It can help in building great sexual tension due to the popliteal artery which passes through this point and the popliteal lymph nodes located in this area.

EXERCISE: Identifying the Popliteal Lymph Node

Inner Thighs & Calves

These areas are so sensitive and so close to the ultimate erogenous zones (the genitals) that even a light touch can get the partner in the mood. Meanwhile, although the calves are often ignored, they can be really arousing, especially for women.

Feet and Toes

The feet are found to be extremely erogenous (and also ticklish) by some and not at all erogenous by others. A research study showed that nerve endings in the feet and toes stimulate the brain in close proximity to those dealing with sensations from the genitals.[48] Some studies have denied the findings of this research. We all know that people either love or hate getting their feet touched.

Reflexology, which is a kind of massage based on the premise that different body parts are connected to organs like the feet, palms, ears, through various meridians and by applying various pressures and massaging these meridians, can help to improve well-being and provide various health benefits. For example, reflexology shows us that the inside and outside of ankles are directly connected to the vagina, penis, uterus, prostate, and other organs of the body.[49] The reflex areas located below the ankle bones correspond to the ovaries and testicles. Thus, you may not be surprised to learn that stimulation here can play a role in improving libido and sexual performance. The middle and upper region of the soles correspond to the chest. Stimulation here can send waves of sexual energy to the erogenous zones of the breasts and nipples.[50]

Although there is no doubt that feet are highly touch-sensitive and ticklish, whether or not they are erogenous is up to an individual to decide. During my bodywork sessions, I have found that for some clients, pressure on the feet feels very grounding, some feel it as arousing, and for some it doesn't affect them at all.

Foot Reflexology Chart

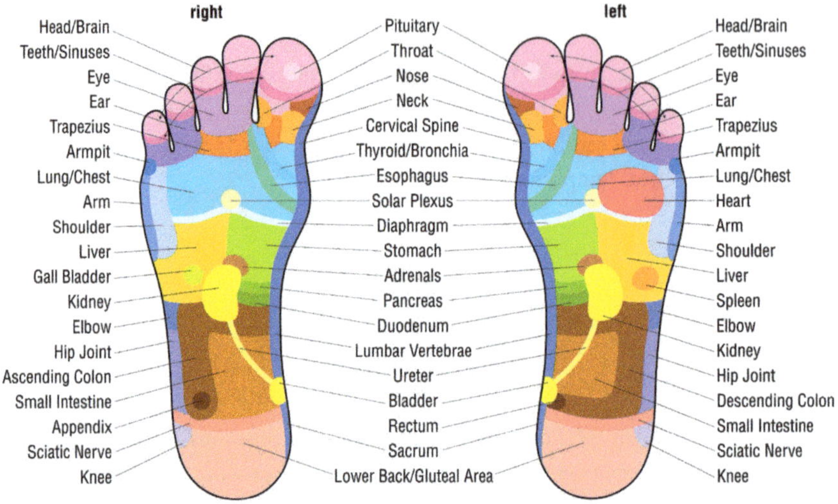

right

Head/Brain
Teeth/Sinuses
Eye
Ear
Trapezius
Armpit
Lung/Chest
Arm
Shoulder
Liver
Gall Bladder
Kidney
Elbow
Hip Joint
Ascending Colon
Small Intestine
Appendix
Sciatic Nerve
Knee

Pituitary
Throat
Nose
Neck
Cervical Spine
Thyroid/Bronchia
Esophagus
Solar Plexus
Diaphragm
Stomach
Adrenals
Pancreas
Duodenum
Lumbar Vertebrae
Ureter
Bladder
Rectum
Sacrum
Lower Back/Gluteal Area

left

Head/Brain
Teeth/Sinuses
Eye
Ear
Trapezius
Armpit
Lung/Chest
Heart
Arm
Shoulder
Liver
Spleen
Elbow
Kidney
Hip Joint
Descending Colon
Small Intestine
Sciatic Nerve
Knee

Figure 115: Similar to hand reflexology, foot reflexology focuses on reflex points on the foot which are linked to various organs of the body.

Brain and Mind

Since we covered the brain in great detail in Chapter Two, we don't need to cover it in detail again here. Except to say that the brain and the mind play a pivotal role in receiving, processing, and making meaning out of our sexual experiences. In this way, they should not be overlooked as erogenous zones that warrant our attention on the Path of Amplified Orgasm.

Body Mapping

As you can see from above, touch is a very powerful way to connect and be intimate with someone and there are several areas on the physical body that can bring arousal and heightened sensitivity. Attention to these areas can help you and your partner experience deeper orgasmic states. However, it is important to note that even though these are particularly sensitive spots on the body, our embodied experience includes much more than simply the physical body. So, there could be an interplay of the mental, energetic, emotional, and spiritual layers of the body as we stimulate these areas, each of which will be unique to each person.

During sexual intimacy, don't assume that a particular area or spot on the body is supposed to be an erogenous zone or that an area which was "hot" before will necessarily be again. Rather, take it slow, feel the response and signals your partner and his/her body is giving you, move from least to most stimulating gradually, and be patient. Needless to say, when in doubt, it is always best to check-in with your partner. In bodywork sessions, I spend a considerable amount of time mapping the client's body so that I can identify various areas/spots that require energy awakening. We will be discussing this topic and more advanced body talk in detail in Part II.

EXERCISE: Mapping Your Partner's E-Zones

The Physical Body and Orgasm

I started this chapter encouraging you to develop a better relationship with your body and that of your partner. When we approach understanding and exploring the physical body with a mindset of curiosity instead of judgement, we can build that relationship without shame. Along the way, many of you may find that there are entire biological systems that you never realised were connected to orgasm at all! And, you may have also learned that you have so many areas of the body still left to explore that you had been ignoring all of these years. Such an exciting path ahead!

In this chapter, I also showed you some of the ways in which emotion and energy are not independent of the physical body, but in fact, deeply connected and integrated into this amazing machine. As you become more aware and in tune with your physical body, you will not only become more aware of sensations, but also the energy and emotion that lives and moves within it as well as between your partner during physical intimacy.

Of course, now that we have arrived at the end of the chapter on the physical body, you may be wondering about something important I seem to have left out. "Michael, how can you write a whole chapter about the physical body and not even discuss the genitals?" Good point! In fact, I think genitals are so important to amplified orgasm that they deserve their very own chapter, which we turn to next.

Chapter Four Summary:

- It is important to develop a positive relationship with your body and that of your partners. To do this, cultivate an attitude of curiosity, exploration, and hunger for knowledge about the amazing human body.
- Knowledge about how the various biological systems play a role in orgasm leads to direct ways to improve the frequency, intensity, and amplification of orgasm.
- Both energy and emotion are stored in the physical body at the cellular level and can create blockages that must be released in order to create better energy flow on the Path of Amplified Orgasm.
- Erogenous zones are areas of the body that are extremely sensitive and can lead to a rise in feelings of arousal when stimulated. Rather than approaching them as a checklist, instead use erogenous zones as a kind of map for exploring the body and adding new dimensions to exploring sensation as well.

CHAPTER FIVE

GENITALS

*Genitals are for seeking pleasure and not something to be ashamed about.
Ironically, we might have a healthy relationship with our bodies everywhere
except with our genitals.*
Michael Charming

What is your attitude towards and relationship with your own genitals? Do you know that there are knots and tangles present in the genitals which can hinder the flow of orgasmic energy? Do you know what is the most important factor for arousal in our genitals?

What is the relationship between energetic imprints in different layers of our subtle bodies and our genitals? Does the size of a cock really matter for women to experience orgasm?

In this chapter, my focus is to spread awareness around our genitals. Talking about orgasm and sex would be incomplete without talking and getting to know the genitals, wouldn't you agree? Genitals play a pivotal role in orgasm. And yet, many people have only a cursory understanding of them. Worse, what people do seem to know about the genitals is often limited to the physical dimension, and often incorrect or incomplete.

Although it is important to have a basic map of the anatomical structure of genitals, it is only the beginning of the story. It turns out that these sensitive areas of the body are also located near the sexual energy centre. Learning to harness this power is key to experiencing whole body orgasms. The energy aspect of the genitals also offers the key to becoming multi-orgasmic for both women and men. We will discuss this fun topic in this chapter as well.

The genitals are also important for the emotional body. People who have had negative sexual experiences, trauma, abuse, body shame, and other unfortunate events in their lives often store emotional memory in their genitals. In this chapter we will explore how and why that happens, how to release these emotions and unblock the energy in these areas, laying the groundwork for better flow and amplified orgasm.

In my bodywork sessions, I find it helpful to guide clients towards developing a deeper and more intimate relationship with their genitals, and yes, those of their partner as well. Take a moment to reflect on what it would be like to have a relationship with your genitals and those of your lover which was based on trust, curiosity, pleasure, and joy. If you are not there yet, this chapter is definitely for you!

Just like any other relationship, it helps to understand the emotional and energetic layers as well as the physical. This chapter will hopefully provide the reader with some new insights on how these amazing organs work, and how to identify new ways to enjoy your partner's (or your own!) genitals.

What's in a Name?

Talking about genitals is a very sensitive topic. As we will explore later in this chapter, there are a lot of emotions, memories, and experiences that become attached to our genitals on multiple levels (physical, emotional, energetic, mental, spiritual). So before we dive in to the subject, it is important to make a few things clear to help you in case if you are triggered or if something starts feeling uncomfortable.

There are many ways to name our genitals and I will be making use of many of them. This is because I believe that they can all have their place, contained within healthy narratives about sex and sexuality.

For example, the word "cunt" is often used as a derogatory statement referring to female genitalia, however, some women and some men experience a sexual turn-on when using these words. They are not necessarily "wrong" or "unhealthy" for doing so. Two consenting adults may experience great pleasure from the "dirtiness" of this particular word, and they may be able to use this word without damaging each other in the process because they both understand it is about experiencing a certain fantasy, and not about the reality of women's genitalia or a statement about inherent female inferiority. In other words, this word "cunt" can be used within a form of role play that can be a fun exploration, without carrying the implications of the fantasy beyond the moment the lovers are enjoying the role play.

If you are triggered by certain words, that is also OK. Many of us have had experiences that give words a certain charge. Sometimes this charge may be extremely pleasurable, in other cases, it may feel extremely uncomfortable even to the point of becoming painful and traumatic.

If you find yourself triggered by certain words I use to name genitalia in this chapter, please first simply make a note of it. Please use this opportunity to self-reflect, slow down, feel all the emotions and sensations that arise within you, go back in time or memory when you first felt triggered and then breathe out through your nose slowly and deeply. Try a little journaling so you can make a note of your observations. The good thing about identifying triggers is they offer great insight into the potential blockages that are between you and the Path of Amplified Orgasm. Knowing your triggers is absolutely a good thing, even though going through the experience of them is very uncomfortable.

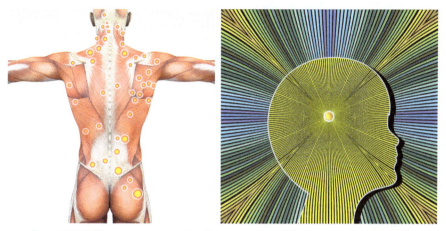

Figure 116-117: Triggers can occur at various layers of our energetic bodies or at various parts of the physical body. Left hand photo shows triggers on the muscles while right hand shows triggers at the mental level.

The second thing you can do when you are triggered by a word in this chapter is to simply note that I am referring to a body part, that my intention is to be inclusive of the various frameworks people can use to experience their genitals, and to simply note that anatomical part, and move on. That is, please find a way not to get stuck on the word itself. Notice that you have your favourite words, as do others, and including only some would, in fact, be exclusionary.

Finally, I ask that you are also sensitive with your lover. When it comes to how to name genitals, rather than assume and use a word during love-making that might be negatively coded for him or her, have a conversation about what words you both already enjoy. And, simply be open to the idea that a word you don't like or know well now may one day be a word that you have come to experience as pleasurable within the right framework.

We will return to the idea of how energy, experiences, and emotions are stored in our genitalia, and how we can overcome blocks that have happened as a result of negative experiences or ideas about sexuality, such as shame. However, first, let's turn to anatomy so that we can share some basic understanding and terminology before moving on to more complex ideas.

Anatomy of the Genitals

Before we dive in, I would like you to understand that I am only offering a basic primer on the anatomy of the genitals. This subject is already covered in great detail elsewhere. While it is a great journey of exploration, I want to focus on ways of understanding the genitals that go beyond the physical. Thus, this is not by any means a comprehensive look at the physical nuances of genitalia. It is, however, enough to lay the groundwork for a more interesting conversation about genitals and orgasm.

The below diagram shows different parts relating to the anatomy of the genitals. Although some readers will be more familiar with the anatomy of genitals than others, I have found that many women and men don't really have a good knowledge about these important body parts.

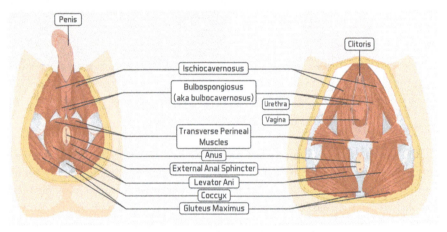

Figure 118: Anatomy of male and female genitals

EXERCISE: Getting Curious About Genitals

Female Genitals

When I started my journey of orgasm, I took a class that was focused on stroking the clitoris. My girlfriend lived in Paris at that time and I decided to take the class so I could use what I had learned to please her. So there I found myself, with a woman who was a stranger to me as my clit-stroking partner.

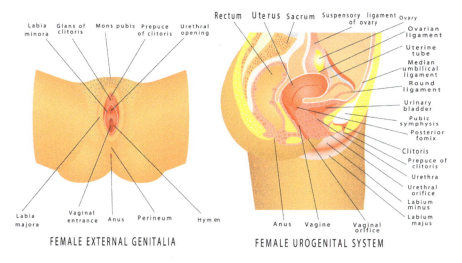

Labia minora   Glans of clitoris   Mons pubis   Prepuce of clitoris   Urethral opening

Rectum   Uterus   Sacrum   Suspensory ligament of ovary   Ovary

Ovarian ligament
Uterine tube
Median umbilical ligament
Round ligament
Urinary bladder
Pubic symphysis
Posterior fornix
Clitoris
Prepuce of clitoris
Urethra
Urethral orifice
Labium minus
Labium majus

Labia majora   Vaginal entrance   Anus   Perineum   Hymen

Anus   Vagine   Vaginal orifice

FEMALE EXTERNAL GENITALIA   FEMALE UROGENITAL SYSTEM

Figure 119: Detailed anatomy of female genitals

She laid down, naked below the waist, and I was sitting next to her, ready to stroke her clit as guided by the instructors. I had my gloves on, lube on the left-hand index finger, and soon it began. The instructor said, "Now open her lips, pull her hood back and then slowly stroke her clit." I was really sweating! I opened her lips, I pulled the hood back too, but where the heck was this clitoris? Deep inside I was worried that this woman was probably thinking I don't know anything about women's anatomy, a fear which made me feel incompetent.

I thought, *I have to show her that I am the best man in the world who can give her the best orgasm. But only if I can find this clitoris!* The instructor came over and assisted me in showing me that sweet spot. There it is! I thought, and then it slipped. And it slipped again and again and again. Now my new anxiety was, *How do I keep hold of this thing?* I looked around. There were 12-15 pairs in the room. I took a glance at the faces of the men and more than 70% of them were in a similar or worse situation than me. Panting, sweating, nervous, and shaking!

After the practice was over, I not only knew where the clitoris is, but also had a realisation that when I am fingering her down there, what I am actually stroking is her clitoris, which is what is making her feel so aroused and turned-on. Ah, now I understand.

By the way, that amazing lady who was my partner, after I finished stroking, was crying with tears of joy, kissing me on my cheeks, hugging me as she mentioned this was one of the best experiences she ever had. I felt puzzled and confused but I hugged her back. Deep inside I was thinking, *What is this? I was struggling to even keep hold of this spot and she felt like that!* This was another reason that made me want to explore this spot even more, which I did for many years after that with several hundred women as I went deeper into this practice.

And, not only did my knowledge of the clitoris grow over time, I also learned much more about other female genitalia and how they are related to female orgasm. So, let's dive in to female genitalia, starting with that most elusive of organs, the clitoris.

Clitoris

I wear a hood, I hide and blush with shyness. To tame me you have to approach me delicately. My name is Clitoris.
Author Unknown

The pearl, the clam-hat, the little bud, the gristle, the jelly bean, the knob, the panic button, the love button, the sweet spot, the jewel, etc. Yes, I am talking about the clitoris! An organ which has been taboo and mysterious for a long time, and in many cultures. An organ which is not so easy to locate or easy to hold. It is very sensitive, yet also the most neglected part of women's genitalia. The clitoris has been the subject of focus by sexologists, medical, researchers, psychologists and the centre of heated debates including topics such as anatomical accuracy, female genital mutilation, and gender inequality.

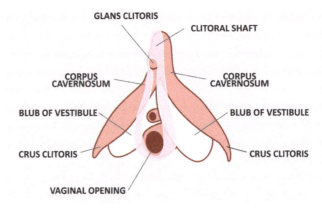

Figure 120: The structure of the clitoris, which is more than just the tiny spot we have known to exist.

The clitoris is a complex structure composed of erectile tissue which is attached to the urethra, vagina, and to the pubic arch via extensive supporting tissues to the mons pubis and labia. The external glans is the only visible part of the organ, although it represents only one-fifth of the size of the entire clitoral structure. The body of the clitoris is composed of two erectile structures known as the corpora cavernosa. It grows in size and hardens during sexual stimulation as blood fills the hollow chambers of these tissues. The clitoris also has two crura, also known as the legs, which extend on either side like brackets from the glans clitoris and deep into the tissue of the vulva, which support the exterior structures of the clitoris and attach it to the underlying tissues.

The clitoris may be as long as seven centimetres in length and the glans makes up only about four to seven millimetres of the whole structure. The clitoral neurovascular bundles ascend along the ischiopubic rami to meet each other. This pea-shaped and sized organ is estimated to have about 8,000 sensory nerve endings, making it a most complex structure, yet the most accessible sensitive erogenous zone on the female body. Though controversial, it is estimated that the penis has 4,000 nerve endings, suggesting the clitoris is as much as twice as sensitive.

Nerve endings in the glans and body are sensitive to stimulation caused by direct pressure and touch from the outside of the body, while the nerve endings of the crus are sensitive to stimulation from within the vagina. This tiny erogenous zone spreads this stimulation to 15,000 other nerves in the pelvis, which is why, if stimulated correctly, women can experience gazillions of sensations throughout their bodies as a result of clitoris stimulation and have OMG, over-the-clouds moments. It is no wonder the practice of Amplified Orgasmic Method works wonders for women. We will be sharing more about this practice in Part II of this book.

During sexual arousal, vasocongestion happens. This means that the clitoris and other genitalia become enlarged due to erectile tissues filling up with blood, and the female experiences vaginal contraction. This process triggers a muscular reflex which expels the blood from the surrounding tissues, resulting in an orgasm. As shared in Chapter Four, blood movement is important for anyone to experience an orgasm so that the more the blood is able to move, the more intense and electrifying an orgasm she can experience.

Clitoral erection happens due to the glans filling up with blood. The ischiocavernosus and bulbocavernosus muscles contract and compress the vein, called the dorsal vein, and the blood continues to flow but it has no way to drain out. It fills the spaces until they become congested and there is no more space to move, further leading to clitoral erection. Unlike the penis, which shrinks quickly when not aroused, the clit can stay engorged for a much longer time, sometimes even for hours, thus making some women feel uncomfortable after stimulation.

The size and shape of each woman's clitoris is different. Size doesn't matter from the perspective of her ability to feel an orgasm, just like size of penis doesn't matter from men's ability to feel orgasm. However, it does matter in terms of pressure, ease of holding, intensity, and the size of the area which can be stimulated, which means that each woman's response to different kinds of stimulation is different as well.

In addition, women who are sensitive to other people's energies and feelings may feel clitoral sensitivity even when you are not touching her clit physically. The energetics of your finger or your body can make an impact on how her clit will feel and respond.

Some of the conditions and issues related to the clitoris which can make pleasure and/or orgasm in this area more challenging or impossible include:

- **Persistent Genital Arousal Disorder (PGAD)**: Like clitoral priapism or clitorism; spontaneous, persistent, unstoppable and uncontrollable genital arousal in women, not connected with any feelings of sexual desire
- **Clitoromegaly**: Clitoris becomes abnormally enlarged
- **Congenital Adrenal Hyperplasia**: Swelling due to hormonal imbalance mainly due to excess of any androgen
- **Vulva Inflammation**: Also called vulvitis or vulvovaginitis
- **Clitoroplasty**: Surgical procedure to reduce the size of the clitoris
- **Loss of Sensation**: Clitoral piercings gone wrong, numbing of clitoris due to heavy pressure or sex toys with extreme pressure
- **Female Circumcision (female genital mutilation or FGM)**: Removal of the clitoris to prevent the woman from feeling sexual pleasure
- **Sore or swollen clitoris**: Too much or too intense stimulation
- **Itchy Clitoris**: Thrush or reaction to soaps, or sensitivity to latex condoms, fungal or bacterial infections.

EXERCISE: Clitography

Stimulating the Clitoris

The clitoris can be stimulated directly through touching the glans, hood, or shaft or indirectly through penis-vagina friction or stimulation as the sensory nerves all connect to the pudendal nerve.

Men often make the mistake of assuming that direct and intense stimulation of the clitoris will be pleasurable for a woman. However, due to the extremely high concentration of nerve endings found here, it can easily be overstimulated, which can cause discomfort or pain. This is why men need to pay attention to the signals their partner is sending, and women need to help them with clear communication in the moment if they can, or have a discussion about it before or after the sexual connection. They may find that softer touch such as licking, or indirect stimulation near the clit but not directly on it, may help their female partner experience more pleasure and be able to relax into the sensations. In addition, tuning in to each other on an emotional and energetic level is also critical to learning to navigate this most pleasurable and sensitive organ.

I have also come across many female clients who have shared with me that they have used sex toys on their clit for masturbation. Unfortunately, few are aware of how much damage this kind of pressure can do to the sensitivity of this amazing organ. A few clients have shared that no matter who they are with, no matter how attractive their partner is, no matter if they are with someone with whom they are deeply in love, they have never been able to experience clitoral orgasms. This mainly happens due to numbness and loss of sensitivity of the clit.

However, after working with me on various AOM and bodywork sessions, they started to experience pleasure through touching of their own clit and they began to experience orgasms, which had become a distant memory for them. We will be talking in more detail about the proper use sex toys in Part II.

EXERCISE: How to Touch a Clit

Female Pelvis

The female pelvis is the lower part of the torso which is located between the abdomen and the thighs and consists of three bones: hip bone, sacrum, and coccyx. It contains the bladder and reproductive organs and provides support for the intestines. It also includes the pelvic floor and perineum.

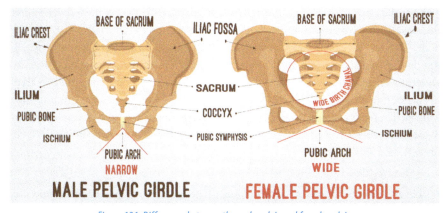

Figure 121: Differences between the male pelvis and female pelvis.

The two female reproductive organs located in the pelvis are ovaries (which produce and release eggs and secrete the female sex hormones oestrogen and progesterone) and the womb (which is the lower, narrow part of the uterus located between the bladder and the rectum). The uterus is a pelvic organ which is hollow and pear-shaped, located in a woman's lower abdomen, between the bladder and the rectum. The walls of the uterus consist of three layers of fascial and muscle tissue as well as a lining. The skeleton of the pelvis is responsible for holding and transferring the weight of the body from the axial skeleton to the lower appendicular skeleton. It is also responsible for protecting the pelvic area and providing attachment to external reproductive organs and associated muscles.

The cervix forms a canal that opens into the vagina and allows the sperm to pass into the uterus. It produces a thick mucus that helps to prevent the bacteria from reaching the uterus itself. This canal, also referred to as the birth canal, is like a tunnel that connects the cervix and the vulva and allows for the fluid to be passed out of the body, especially during menstruation. The female pelvis is generally wider and broader than the male pelvis to provide space for a baby to develop and pass through the birth canal. The bones of the female pelvis are lighter and thinner than the male pelvis and have a round or oval shape as compared with the heart-shaped male pelvis.

The pelvic girdle is the part of the pelvis that contains the two hip bones, each on either side of the body. The sacrum helps in connecting the hip bones to the upper part of the skeleton. Each hip bone is made of three smaller bones that join together: ilium (the broad, fan-shaped, and largest part of hip bone), pubis (connect each hip bone to the other at a joint called the pubis symphysis) and ischium (also known as the sit bones as it supports the weight of the body when one sits down). All these bones join together to form the acetabulum and attach to the femur (the head of the thigh bone).

The sacrum, which is made up of five fused vertebral bones, joins the pelvis between the crests of the ilium. Sacral plexus, which is a collection of nerves, sits behind the sacrum and connects the pelvic area, genitals, buttocks, and lower parts of the body. The coccyx, also known as the tailbone, is made up of four vertebrae which fuse into a triangular shape and connect to the bottom of the sacrum supported by several ligaments. Besides the clitoris, G-spot, and the cervix, the network of nerves in the sacrum plays a big part in triggering genital orgasm and sexual pleasure for women. These nerves and erectile tissues are directly linked with the glandular system of the brain. The pelvic region also contains several digestive organs including the large intestine and small intestine.

There are three major muscle layers:

- **Layer 1**: Bulbo Spongeas (Cavernosus): These form a figure eight around the urethral, vaginal, and anal sphincters
- **Layer 2**: Superficial Transverse Perineal: These muscles connect the "sitting bones"
- **Layer 3**: Levator Ani: This is the group of muscles that lift the bum and attach to the sacrum. This muscle is considered to be the home of the sacral energy centre.

The levator ani muscles are the largest group of muscles in the pelvis and consist of three separate muscles: puborectalis (for holding urine and faeces which relaxes once excreted), pubococcygeus (originates at the pubis bone and connects to the coccyx) and iliococcygeus (serves to lift the pelvic floor and anal canal). Coccygeus is a small pelvic floor muscle which originates from the ischium and connects to the sacrum and coccyx. The uterus, fallopian tubes, and ovaries are supported by ligaments that extend to both sides of the pelvic wall.

Oxygenated blood that travels down the chest through the thoracic aorta branches and becomes the abdominal aorta. The superior mesenteric artery, which is the abdominal aorta's largest branch, supplies blood to the small and large intestines. The second half of the large intestine's blood supply is handled by the inferior mesenteric artery. The paired ovarian arteries branch off from the abdominal aorta and supply blood to the reproductive organs, such as the ovaries, fallopian tubes, and uterus.

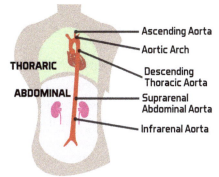

Figure 122: Aorta segments branching from the thoracic aorta to the abdominal aorta

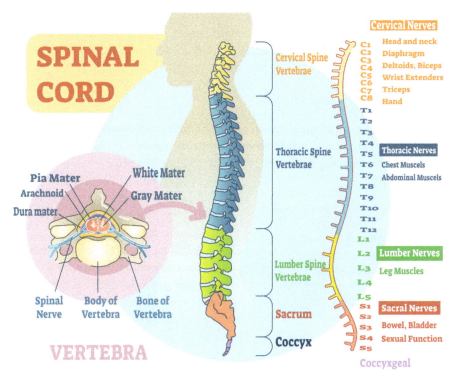

Figure 123: Nerves from the spinal cord are categorised into four categories. The sacral nerves between S2 and S4 result in reflex erections from stimulation.

151

Nerves from the spinal column branch into three categories: autonomic nerves (control involuntary or partially voluntary actions), motor nerves (indicates muscles to move) and sensory nerves (communicate sensory information pain, pleasure, warmth). The sciatic nerve, which is the largest and longest spinal nerve, originates from the sacral plexus and provides sensation to the lower leg and foot.

As there are a large number of organs, bones, ligaments, and muscles involved in the pelvis, so many conditions can affect the entire pelvis or parts within it, affecting a woman's ability to feel orgasm. Some of which include:

- **Pelvic Inflammatory Disease (PID)**: caused due to infection
- **Pelvic Organ Prolapse**: Inability of muscles in the pelvis to support its organs
- **Endometriosis**: Tissue that lines the inside walls of the uterus begins to grow outside of the uterus
- **Pelvic Pain**: Chronic irritation of nerves in the pelvis, menstrual cramps, etc
- **Dysmenorrhoea**: Pain during menstruation, cramps
- **Premenstrual Syndrome (PMS) and Premenstrual Dysphoric Disorder (PMDD)**
- **Pelvic Congestion Syndrome**: Enlarged veins around uterus and ovaries can result in pelvic pain
- **Others**: Enlarged Spleen, Pelvic Floor Muscle Spasm, Gynaecologic cancers, Miscarriage, Ovarian cyst or (adnexal) Torsion, Uterine Fibroids, Placental Abruption, Urinary Tract Infection (UTI), Urinary Incontinence.

The Pelvic Floor and Orgasm

The pelvic floor plays a crucial role in a woman's ability to feel orgasmic. The pelvic floor is the root of a woman's body, her nervous system, her sexuality, her core muscular system, and her reproductive system. It is also the place of storage for emotions and a source of spiritual and sexual energies. The Taoist often refer to this area as the "Cauldron of Desire" because of the functions it serves.

Figure 124: Jade eggs are considered to be beneficial for harmonising the sexual energies for women.

It is often said that if you want to have pain-free sex, easier menstruation, or if you want to process grief, trauma, or any other emotion stored in the body, if you want to get rid of any abdominal pain, or want to have healthy functioning organs like the bladder or digestive tract, then it is the pelvic floor that needs attention.

The strengthening of the pelvic floor muscles is very important for amplified orgasms as weaknesses in these muscles can lead to incontinence or prolapse. Pelvic floor muscles can suffer as a result of intense exercise, constipation, menopause, childbirth, and obesity. Voluntary contraction and squeezing by doing certain exercises like Kegels are recommended for women to strengthen their pelvic floor muscles and for experiencing sexual arousal and sensations. Use of a Jade Egg is also recommended to bring the energy into harmony in the genital area, although I don't recommend using eggs for extended periods of time and instead the focus should be on strengthening the muscles through contraction and expansion. Weakness in the pelvic floor muscles can also be caused by too much tension or too much or lack of toning (clenching inner thighs, keeping the belly tucked in) or from physical/emotional trauma like anxiety, sexual abuse, and unprocessed emotions.

EXERCISE: Kegel Exercises

The Pelvic Floor and the Energetic Body

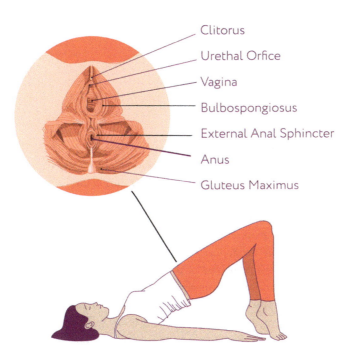

Clitorus

Urethal Orfice

Vagina

Bulbospongiosus

External Anal Sphincter

Anus

Gluteus Maximus

Figure 125: Pelvic floor exercises help to improve sexual health and pleasure by providing relaxation to vaginal muscles and improving blood circulation to the genitals.

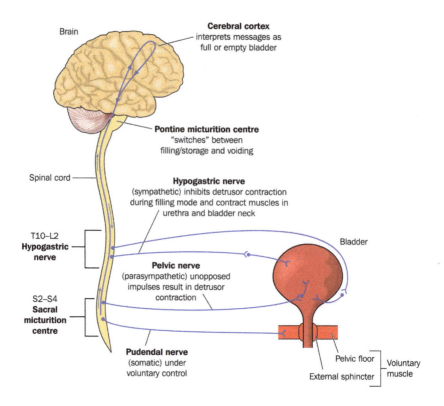

Brain

Cerebral cortex
interprets messages as
full or empty bladder

Pontine micturition centre
"switches" between
filling/storage and voiding

Spinal cord

Hypogastric nerve
(sympathetic) inhibits detrusor contraction
during filling mode and contract muscles in
urethra and bladder neck

T10–L2
**Hypogastric
nerve**

Bladder

Pelvic nerve
(parasympathetic) unopposed
impulses result in detrusor
contraction

S2–S4
**Sacral
micturition
centre**

Pudendal nerve
(somatic) under
voluntary control

Pelvic floor
External sphincter
Voluntary
muscle

Figure 126: The pelvic floor and its impact on the bladder and other muscles. The pudental, pelvic, hypogastric, intercostal and vagus nerves all play an important role in creating female orgasm.

The sacral energy centre is associated with the pelvic floor, so having a strong and awakened sacral energy centre provides strength to the pelvic area. The inter-exchange between the physical and energetic world, especially during love-making, can result in experiencing orgasms and pleasure in a way never experienced before. As we have seen in Chapter Three, a balanced sacral energy centre contributes to feelings of happiness, joy, creativity, sexual desire, pleasure in life, and sexuality. So, an out-of-balance centre will result in feelings of unhappiness, violence, dissatisfaction, and uncontrollable emotional needs. The first two layers of the pelvic floor are associated with the root energy centre, while the third layer onwards is associated with the sacral energy centre.

Strong pelvic floor muscles help to improve sexual performance, act as a lymphatic pump for the whole pelvis, and help better flowing of energy between the physical body and the sacral energy centre which fires up creativity and sexuality. The stronger the second energy centre, the more one will be able to define one's boundaries and express them or ensure that they are being adhered to. A weakened energy centre will make you prone to lower back pain and issues relating to vaginal tension and dryness.

We often clench our pelvic floor muscles on hearing bad or fearful news or anything that affects our sense of safety and results in fight-or-flight reactions. Any burying of emotions will affect the second energy centre and often result in pelvic pain, painful sex, and/or period dysfunction.

I have found the pelvic floor of most women I have worked with to be often too tight, mainly due to fear, tension, and stress stored in the body. During bodywork sessions, I devote a section of the session to massaging the sacrum, which helps to release any blockages, triggers, energy, or pain being held in this place. Once the blockages are released, it helps the flow of energy and blood in this region, which helps lead women to experience multi-orgasms. We also work on creating new neural pathways by reinforcing a new pattern while letting go of old patterns and blocked energy.

G-Spot

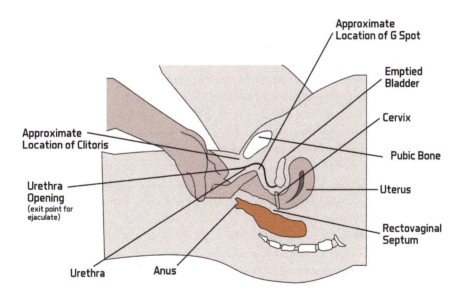

Figure 127: Location of the mysterious G-spot

The Gräfenberg spot, or G-spot, named after the German-born physician Ernst Gräfenberg, has been a topic of much controversy and argument for many decades. It is considered to be one of the most elusive spots of female anatomy.

There's a common joke about the G-spot: "The difference between a G-spot and a Golf Ball is that a guy will actually search for the ball and will be back in 20 minutes with a ball in his hand." Or you might have also heard this one: "A newly opened stripper bar called 'The G Spot' closed down after one month because none of the guys could find it." Joking aside, it is not surprising that we have a multimillion-dollar industry that has focused on developing various sex toys, vibrators, tools, and even G-spot augmentation, G-spotplasty or even the G-shot injections to help women achieve G-spot orgasms.

Research done by Pierre Foldès and Odile Buisson in 2009 found that G-spot is actually the end of the clit's legs (the vestibular tubes surrounding the urethra canal), thus answering the controversial question of whether or not the G-spot is real.[51,52] It turns out that this pea-sized nub, or the bean-shaped area of the vagina, is actually located just in the front wall of the vagina, about two-and-a-half to three inches in, directly below the urethra. It can be found by having a partner insert a middle finger and curl it towards themselves in a 'come hither' motion until it senses a nickel-size circle of dimpled flesh.

Given that the G-spot is an extended portion of the clitoris, most women enjoy a little clitoral foreplay before being stimulated on to the G-spot. The combination of both clitoral and G-spot stimulation can produce a strong, satisfying orgasm or multi-orgasms, and for some women, can even result in female ejaculation, more commonly known as "squirting." Sometimes, women can get a feeling of wanting to pee, which is because the bladder is located right beside the G-spot. So, when the G-spot is being pressed, whether with fingers or with a penis, it is going to put some pressure on the bladder, which can cause a sensation of needing to urinate.

Sometimes women feel that they are unable to find the G-spot and, funnily enough, some even begin to think that they were born without one. One of the reasons why it can be difficult to find the G-spot is because it needs to be aroused to be able to make it protrude enough to find. The G-spot lies under the area called the urethral sponge, which contains a gland called the Skene's gland which gets filled with fluid when aroused. As this gland swells and expands more and more, it causes the G-spot to become more sensitive and protruding.

As we have seen in the clitoris section above, the clit's legs are made up of vestibular bulbs, so when these get aroused, it results in contraction of these bulbs, which creates orgasm for women. Women's bodies are completely different from one another and are also different at different times for the same woman. Some women are more sensitive at the internal shafts of the clitoris, which is why for some women vaginal penetration feels more arousing than it does for others. Since the G-spot is made up of erectile tissue if it is not aroused, then touching it can be unpleasurable and it will also be very hard to locate.

This sacred spot is often called mysterious because the G-spot is an erectile tissue which only appears when women get aroused, so men need to have patience while stimulating the front side of the vagina before the G-spot can be felt and seen. All women can have G-spot orgasms unless there is a medical condition or damage to the vagina or unless there are emotional blockages due to past bad experiences. Some women's G-spot is located closer to the entrance while for others it may be either midway or further back by the cervix. It is on the roof of the vagina at 12 o'clock when a woman is lying on her back.

Different women have different feelings associated with this spot. Some feel a lot of pleasure, or even overwhelming sensations. Some feel pain, discomfort, electric or scratchy sensations. These sensations can vary within the same woman depending on the time of day, emotional state, or the sense of connection and feelings of trust with her partner.

G-Spot and the Energetic and Emotional Bodies

Since the G-spot is a point where a lot of sexual and emotional abuse is held, part of bodywork sessions include working through releasing the emotional trauma held in the cellular memory of this sacred place. Any unexpressed feelings will be stored in the form of energy in our body which will either result as tension in the muscle fibres or will end up forming knots/tangles causing blockages. The G-spot is a sensitive spot that tends to accumulate these repressed feelings and tension.

For women, the unexpressed feelings can be anything ranging from not sharing her desires, being touched non-consensually, rape, sexual and domestic abuse, and so forth. Also, any pleasure or pain associated with birth experiences, besides in the womb, are also likely to be held up here as well.

As a result of the knots/tangles or energy blockages, this part of the body can lose sensation and get numbed out. Many women lose sensitivity in their G-spots due to hard, fast, and rough sex or due to some childhood trauma. Even those who have had these experiences have felt arousal, sexual desire, and experienced multi-orgasms after bodywork sessions.

> *EXERCISE: Finding and Stimulating the G-Spot*

Other Genital Parts

The other parts of the genitalia which are equally important are the vagina, perineum, labias (minora and majora), anus, pubic hair, and various spots such as the A-spot, U-spot and other spots around the cervix. (Several of these will be discussed in more detail in Chapter Seven) Attention should be given to exploring each of these areas, as every part of the genitalia is capable of giving pleasure and contributing towards orgasmic feelings if stimulated correctly.

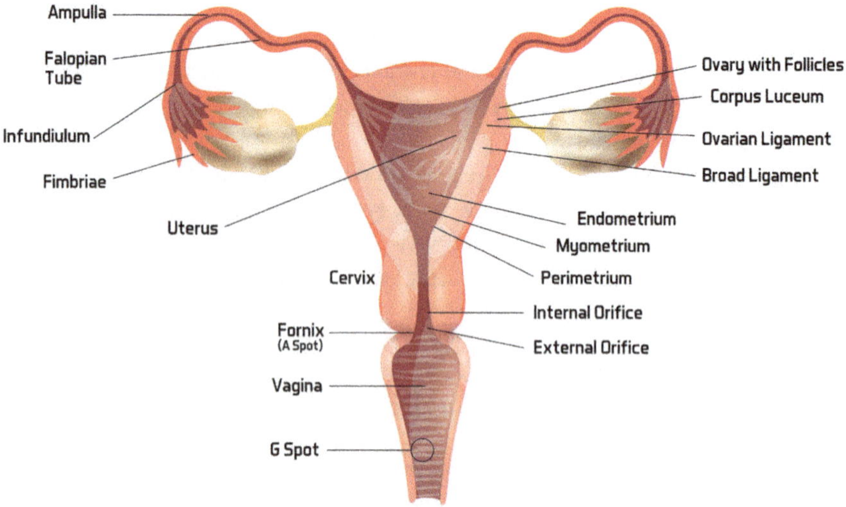

Ampulla
Falopian Tube
Infundiulum
Fimbriae
Uterus
Cervix
Fornix
(A Spot)
Vagina
G Spot
Ovary with Follicles
Corpus Luceum
Ovarian Ligament
Broad Ligament
Endometrium
Myometrium
Perimetrium
Internal Orifice
External Orifice

Figure 128: Other parts of women's genitalia

Genital Massage

The organs in our body generally become blocked either due to sedimentation as a result of physical toxins (food, drink, smoke) resulting in blocked capillaries or as a result of emotional toxins caused by stress and trauma resulting in knots and tangles.[53] So, depending on the woman's lifestyle, her past experiences, and the kinds of emotions held, these areas can be pleasurable, emotional, painful, or numb. In full body de-armouring session, I spend about 60-90 minutes giving a genital massage. During this massage, my aim is to find knots and tangles in this area, especially in the deeper parts of the vagina, G-spot, and the lips to help release emotions by untangling these knots. During this process, a lot of emotions can come up and it can also be a very painful experience. For instance, once I worked with a client who had a tiny spot just at the entrance of the vaginal opening. When I worked on that point, a lot of fear and pain came up which was related to her first experience of sex which was very painful. As a result of this trauma, she had had a lifelong fear of sex and anything to do with touching her vagina. The bodywork sessions helped her develop a more positive relationship with this area of her body.

I have also worked with a few clients who have undergone labiaplasty to have their labia shortened. Such clients have generally been shamed by a partner or the expectations of pornography. Similarly, many women keep this area of their bodies shaved, even if they do not really want to. All these experiences can develop an unhealthy and disconnected relationship with the genital parts and cause the storing of emotional pain and feelings of shame.

Another example of how past experiences can change the way we experience our genitals comes from a client who was in several narcissistic relationships and all of her lovers wanted to have hard and fast sex. As such, she was so used to hard and fast stimulation that anything slow would not make her feel aroused and her genitals felt completely numb. In a session I worked on releasing that numbness and by the end of the session, she only desired slow and gentle finger strokes as they felt so pleasurable and soothing to her.

Muscle Fibers of a Trigger Point up close

Contracted knot in muscle fiber stops the blood flow. It makes the tissue deficient in oxygen and nutrients. This area results in pain, tension and spasm due to metabolic waste and toxins that begins to accumulate.

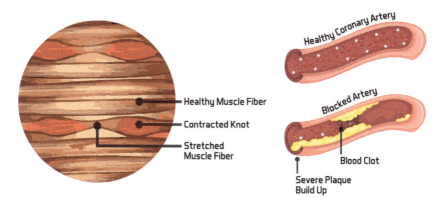

Healthy Coronary Artery

Healthy Muscle Fiber

Contracted Knot

Blocked Artery

Stretched Muscle Fiber

Blood Clot

Severe Plaque Build Up

Figure 129-130: Left: Different muscle fibers based on how triggered a particular muscle fibre is. Right: Difference between blocked artery and healthy artery.

In a genital massage session, as knots and tangles get smoothed out, and as emotional pain and trauma begins to release, clients tend to experience joy, happiness, pleasure, orgasmic waves, and develop more positive attitude towards their own genitals, sex, relationships, and life in general. As per Taoism, different parts (pressure points) of the vagina are also connected to different organs of the body so, depending on the consultation and client needs, I also focus on working on these points to assist with different healing of different organs.

EXERCISE: Exploring Other Female Genital Parts

Male Genitals

The male genitals are often just as misunderstood as women's. In fact, while most people know a little bit about the penis and scrotum, much of their knowledge stops there. Few know of the secret spots for male pleasure such as the Million Dollar Point. Curious yet? Read on!

Penis or Lingam

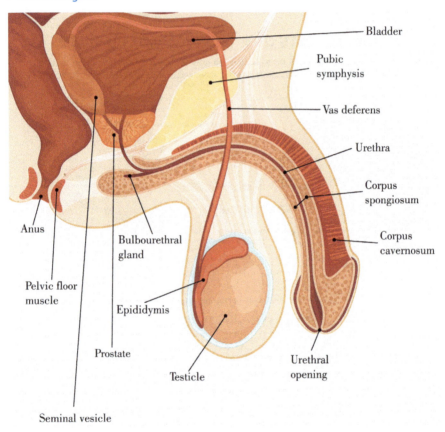

Figure 131: Anatomy of the penis

If you ask men, generally speaking, the term sex usually involves their penis. That being said, few know much about this amazing sexual organ. Most of them are concerned with the size of their penis as they believe that in order to have great, mind-blowing sex, having a large penis is important. We will explore this myth a little later in this chapter. For now, let's get a closer look at the physical processes related to the penis.

160

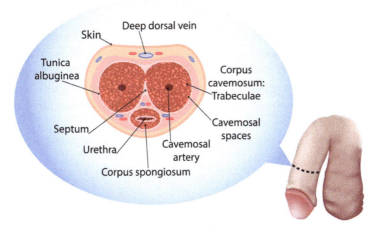

Figure 132: Internal anatomy of the penis at the shaft

The penis consists of two continuous areas, each made up of several parts. The shaft, also referred to as the body of the penis or the external portion (often known as the hanging part), is the first part. The second is the root which is the internal portion. The shaft is cylindrical when flaccid but it takes on a triangular shape in cross section when erect.

The glans, also known as the head or tip of the penis, is a mushroom-shaped structure. It is covered with pink, moist tissue called mucosa and the beginning of the glans is covered by a circular fold of skin, referred to as foreskin (prepuce) in uncircumcised/uncut men. In circumcised/cut men, this foreskin is surgically removed and mucosa transforms into dry skin. This is a very sensitive part of the penis and men with their foreskin intact tend to be much more sensitive in this area.[54]

The corpus cavernosum are two columns of tissue that consist of muscles, fibrous protein, and elastic fibres which run along the sides of the penis. During sexual stimulation these areas get expanded by blood that flows into the tissue and fills the empty spaces. When erections happen the extra blood is temporarily trapped in the penis by the constriction of blood vessels. The blood pressure makes the penis enlarged, hard, and erect.

The corpora are surrounded by a hard membrane called the tunica which limits the amount the corpora can expand. After ejaculation, the signals from the brain change rapidly and dramatically resulting in the flow of blood out of the corpora, causing the erection to quickly subside. It is worth noting that not all kinds of erections are due to sexual arousal. Erections fall into three categories: psychogenic (due to a visual or mental image), reflexive (due to physical stimulation), or nocturnal (during sleep).

All of these involve different bodily systems: muscles, nerves, blood vessels, brain, hormones, emotions, energetics, etc.

The corpus spongiosum is a column of sponge-like tissue which runs along the front of the penis and ends at the glans. This keeps the urethra open and also gets filled with a constant flow of blood during erections. The urethra, which runs through the centre of the corpus spongiosum, carries pre-ejaculation (precum), semen (cum), and urine. The frenulum is where the foreskin meets the underside of the penis. It looks like a small V and is also a very sensitive area.

It is worth noting here that the penis can be desensitised through excessive or rough masturbation.

EXERCISE: Cock Massage

There are several conditions associated with the penis that can affect men's ability to perform during sex and to experience orgasm (ejaculation). Here are some of the more common issues:

- **Erectile dysfunction**: Lack of sufficient hardness of penis mainly due to damage to arteries
- **Premature ejaculation**: Excreting semen much earlier, before or immediately after penetration
- **Priapism**: Continuous erection several hours after stimulation has stopped
- **Balanitis**: Inflammation of the glans
- **Urethritis**: Inflammation or bacterial infection of the urethra mainly due to gonorrhoea or chlamydia
- **Syphilis and herpes**: Types of STIs (sexually transmitted infections)
- **Penis warts**: From human papillomavirus.

Scrotum and Testes (Balls)

Next, we will look at testicles, which are sometimes called balls, scrotum, fondlers, hanging loops, etc. When you think of balls, what are the first thoughts that come to your mind? It is more than likely that at least once in your lifetime, you would have probably made a ridiculous comment about balls.

Figure 133: The balls are elastic and can be stretched a lot.

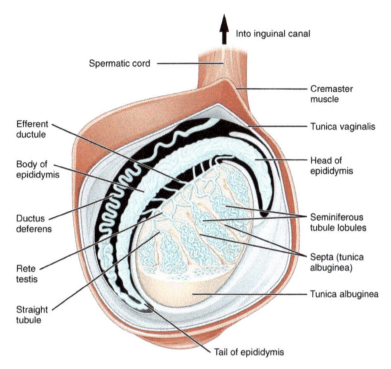

Into inguinal canal

Spermatic cord

Cremaster
muscle

Efferent
ductule

Tunica vaginalis

Body of
epididymis

Head of
epididymis

Ductus
deferens

Seminiferous
tubule lobules

Rete
testis

Septa (tunica
albuginea)

Straight
tubule

Tunica albuginea

Tail of epididymis

Figure 134: Anatomy of the balls. (Credit: OpenStax College - Anatomy & Physiology, Connexions Web site. http://cnx.org/content/col11496/1.6/, Jun 19, 2013., CC BY 3.0.)

The phrase, *I'm going to kick your balls!* is often used when we are angry or when we want to threaten someone or make fun of the other person. Certainly, when you look at a naked man's body you will see that the balls are hanging there possibly thinking that they serve no real purpose. A friend of mine once commented, "When God created man, balls were added as an afterthought from the leftover portion of clay. Not knowing what to do with that, he struck them there as two hanging sacs." I laughed when she said that.

The scrotum, one of the very sensitive parts of male genitalia, is a thin external sac of skin which forms an expansion of the perineum. It is divided into two compartments by a middle ridge called the perineal raphe. Each compartment contains one of the two testes and epididymides where the sperm is stored. Internally, the raphe is connected to a muscular partition, the septum. The skin contains hair, pigments, sebaceous (oil-producing) glands, and sweat glands. The function of the scrotum is to protect the testes, blood vessels, and tubes that release sperm into the penis. It also regulates temperature to optimise sperm production by drawing testes close or away from the body as needed.

Each testicle is covered by strong, fibrous layers of tissue (tunica) and is divided into lobules which contain tiny and very fine U-shaped tubes called seminiferous tubules (roughly 800 in number) which are tightly coiled within each testicle. These tubules are further connected by ducts in the epididymis, which joins to the vas deferens. Lymph fluid travels through vessels in the spermatic cord (which holds the testicle in the scrotum) and drains from the testicles into several groups of lymph nodes called the retroperitoneal lymph nodes. These nodes help germ cells make sperm.

The most common conditions affecting the scrotum, its contents, and men's ability to feel healthier/happier orgasms include:

- **Inguinal hernia**: Part of the small intestine penetrates through an opening in the abdominal wall into the scrotum
- **Epididymitis**: An infection or inflammation in the epididymis which occurs mainly as a result of STIs
- **Testicular cancer**: Cells abnormally multiply within the tissue of the testicles forming tumours
- **Testicular trauma**: Impact on the testes is not absorbed by the spongy material of the scrotum
- **Hypogonadism**: The inadequate production of testosterone
- **Infertility**: The absence or reduction of sperm production or sperm produced that do not function normally
- **Others** include hydrocele, spermatocele, testicular torsion, scrotal mosses.

Although men often worry about testicles of different sizes, it is normal for one of the testicles to be a bit bigger than the other and hang a little lower than the other within the scrotum. Other men express a sense of great vulnerability about their balls and may be hesitant to explore sensation there out of shame, guilt, or fear of this vulnerability. Often bodywork with these men includes creating a safe space to be able to identify their first memories or bad experiences around their own balls, help them release different kinds of emotions held in this sensitive region, have them feel pleasure through gentle massaging of the balls, and learning to channel the energy around the genitalia. After a few sessions, men often fall in love, or at least develop a better relationship, with their balls. When men are getting penis massaged during the session, the request to get balls massaged too, is not so unheard of. Massaging of the balls is important for good circulation of energy, especially when someone starts experiencing blue balls, which we will explore more in Part II.

In my coaching sessions, women often share with me that they have some sort of worry, anxiety, or nervousness about touching the balls due to the fear of causing pain. I often stress that as long as they are not causing pressure and they have the consent of their partner, they can play with them for as long as they desire. You can gently stretch, kiss, lick, and even softly twist the sac and it won't feel painful to men. Gentle pulling of the sac can actually be very pleasurable and exciting for men and can also help in delaying ejaculation.

Now that you have a little bit more knowledge about balls, let's take a moment to enjoy them as one of the more sensitive and sexually stimulating areas of a man's body!

Benefits of balls stimulation and massage include:

• Improved blood circulation resulting in improving the quality of erections
• Identify any irregularities such as lumps which can be early signs of testicular cancer
• Encourage lower hanging testicles to help boost sperm count and strength
• Increase testosterone levels by stimulating hormone production.

Prostate

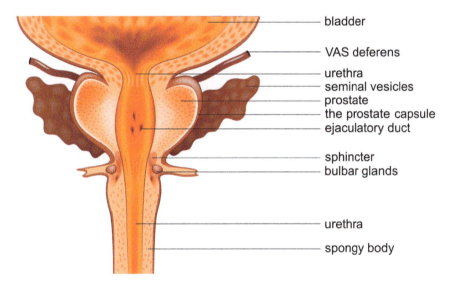

Figure 135: Anatomy of the prostate

Many men are fine talking about their cock, even maybe their balls. But the prostate, it seems, is another matter. Shrouded in mystery and often conflated with homosexuality, many men who identify as straight are not even aware of just how pleasurable this male part of the body can be. I invite you to bring an open mind to this section, and at least be open to learning more about this pleasure-generating organ.

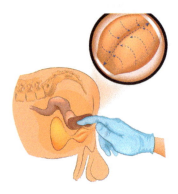

Figure 136: Examination of the prostate before prostate massage.

The prostate is a walnut-sized gland that is just above the perineum, in the middle of the pelvis, and in front of the rectum. It surrounds the upper part of the urethra tube just below the prostatic urethra and controls the flow of both urine and ejaculation via two muscles called sphincters.

The prostate secretes slightly acidic, alkaline and milky fluid (prostatic fluid) that nourishes and protects sperm and helps them live longer and be more mobile. The fluid contains a number of ingredients including enzymes, zinc, sodium, potassium, calcium and citric acid. The two ejaculatory ducts, along with ducts from Vas deferens and seminal vesicle, carry sperm from the testes to the seminal vesicles which contribute fluid to semen during ejaculation. The prostate then squeezes this fluid into the urethra during ejaculation and, with the help of smooth muscles, it expels the fluid along with the sperm.

The urethra runs through the centre of prostate. It is very sensitive, and is often referred to as the male G-spot. Yes, men can have orgasms through prostate stimulation. In fact, quite powerful ones!

The prostate gland is responsible for erections too due to prostate erection nerves which stimulate and activate the penis to enlarge by filling it with blood. This is the reason why many prostate procedures can have unwanted side effects including impotence or erectile difficulties. It is due to the role of these sphincter muscles that Kegel exercises are often recommended to men who want to have better control of their ejaculation and want to become multi-orgasmic.

In order to function properly, the prostate needs male hormones (androgens like testosterone produced by the testicles) and dihydrotestosterone (DHT). If you are lacking in these hormones, it is affecting the ability of your prostate to function.[55] Accumulation of toxins in the prostate affect the production of enzymes, which often results in reduced sex drive.

Prostate cancer is very common in men, which can affect their sex life on many levels: mind (anxiety, low self-esteem), body (medications, therapies and treatment can damage nerves and blood supply necessary for erections) and relationships (insecurity, sexual relationships with your partners).[56]

The Prostate and Pleasure

On the Path of Amplified Orgasm, the more relaxed and sensitive the prostate would be, the more arousal and sensitivity a man will feel in his body, which will lead to him experiencing full-body orgasms and a better connection with his partner.

I am sure the majority of men would find it shocking to learn that men don't even need an erection to enjoy pleasurable orgasms! There are many ways for men to experience orgasms and prostate stimulation is one of them. And, that different zone will stimulate a different kind of orgasm, opening men to the idea of exploring different kinds of feelings that are associated with orgasms, rather than just those feelings that come with ejaculation.

Our bodies are designed to experience pleasure, our sexual organs exist to experience joy, so don't you think we should actually question the stigmas and resistance found in beliefs that have been formed without us even trying to experience what it could be like? We deny ourselves pleasure, which in turn results in us causing ourselves pain and more suffering.

Unless we try, we never know what it is like for us and, more often than not, we form judgements based on other people's opinions and reactions without even allowing ourselves to fully feel the effect of a new experience in our own body.

At an energetic level, we know that the prostate and genitals are associated with the second energy centre which is associated with money, sex, control, power, and greed. So, any dysfunction in any of these areas of life (financial loss, sexual abuse, rape, abandonment, deception) will create negative and disharmonising energy in this centre.

Prostate massage has many potential benefits, including on the physical and energetic layers. However, because it must be approached with great care and sensitivity, we will explore this practice more in Part II of this book (as well as briefly in Chapter Seven of Part I).

There are many diseases associated with the prostate which can interfere with accessing pleasure and orgasm in this area:

- **Prostatitis**: Inflammation of the prostate
- **Benign Prostatic Hyperplasia**: Prostate gland enlargement
- **Prostate Cancer**

Perineum

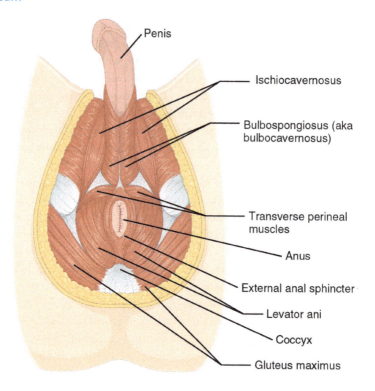

Figure 137: Anatomy of the perineum

Taoists call the perineum "The Gate of Life and Death" due to the role it plays in preventing ejaculation. Many men have a deep desire to prolong their ejaculation so that they can pleasure their partner more. They may try different methods such as drugs, lubricants, or taking their attention off their partner during sex. However, few know that squeezing the perineum offers a safe way to prevent ejaculation. And, the so-called "Million Dollar Point," a hot spot for sexual pleasure in men, is found on the perineum as well. So, let's get to know more about this part of male genitalia to learn more secrets about how it functions and the role it plays in sexual pleasure.

The perineum is an anatomical region in the pelvis which is located between the thighs, between the pubic symphysis and the coccyx. It is separated from the pelvic cavity by the pelvic floor. The region containing the perineal muscles contains structures that support the urogenital and gastrointestinal systems. In clinical practice, it is used to describe the area between the external genitalia and the anus while in anatomical terms, when legs are abducted, it forms a diamond-shaped structure. It consists of the pubic symphysis, the tip of coccyx, the pelvic floor, skin, fascia and the inferior pubic rami, inferior ischial rami and sacrotuberous ligament. The theoretical line that subdivides ischial tuberosities splits it into anterior urogenital and posterior anal triangles.

The anal triangle includes the anal aperture (opening of the anus), external and sphincter muscles (voluntary muscles for opening and closing the anus), ischioanal fossae on either side (fat and connective tissues for the expansion of the anal canal) and pudenal nerve (supplies perineum with somatic fibres). The urogenital triangle, which is associated with the external genitalia and the urethra, is bounded by pubic symphysis and the ischiopubic rami, a theoretical line between the two ischial tuberosities and additional layer of strong deep fascial called perineal membrane. Layers of the urogenital triangle consist of the deep perineal pouch (bulbourethral glands and deep transverse perineal muscles), the perineal membrane (attachment for muscles of external genitalia and is perforated by the urethra), the superficial perineal pouch (erectile tissue that forms penis and three muscles), the perineal fascia (consisting of deep fascia and superficial fascia) and skin (urethral orifice). The perineal body (or central tendon of the perineum) consists of skeletal muscle, smooth muscle, and collagenous and elastic fibres. It connects muscle fibres from the pelvic floor and the perineum itself.

The perineum is an important part of the genitals, as it supplies the urinary tract and genitals with blood and nerve signals. So, any injury to the perineal muscles can impact erections and can result in:

- **Bladder control problems**: Nerves carry signals from the bladder to the spinal cord and the brain and also to the pelvic floor muscles controlling urine
- **Bowel control or sexual problems**: Relating to damaged blood vessels resulting in erectile dysfunction or inability to maintain firm erections
- **UTIs**: Urinary tract infections
- **Perineal injury**: Sexual abuse, straddle injuries, impalement, and perineal surgery (prostatectomy, urethroplasty, colorectal), can result in perineal injuries.

Perineum Massage

Again we return to the idea, familiar by now, that our ability to feel amplified orgasms depends on the generation and free flow of blood and energy throughout our body. Any excess tension, contractions, knots, or tangles will result in blocking this flow, thus diminishing our orgasmic potential and vitality.

The perineum is the most underrated and neglected pleasure point, as we have a tendency to focus on the parts of the body that we are most used to associating with pleasure. Hence most often people stroke the penis, as it has the most nerve endings. Because of the familiar pathway to orgasm, stimulating the penis has become essential for many men to feel orgasm. However, this is more of a habit and a mindset than it is a biological constraint.

Perineum massage and stimulation will facilitate a better flow of energy and the feeling of more sensations, which will assist in orgasmic amplification. Stimulating the perineum also plays a part in improving prostate health. It is so sensitive that men can even orgasm from stimulation of perineum alone, particularly if they have not desensitised themselves or made themselves numb. Be careful to avoid perineal muscle strain.

At an energetic level, the perineum is the central point of the Root energy centre, so stroking this part helps in activating the energy of this centre. At first, it will feel very arousing and difficult to deal with the sensations. However, over time and through regular practice, when the energy of this centre starts integrating, a man will start feeling grounded and more in his body during sexual experiences.

EXERCISE: Perineum Massage

The Million Dollar Point

The Million Dollar Point (MDP) is a small spot located on the perineum. It is referred to as the Million Dollar Point because of the kind of sensations it produces, and because it helps in stopping ejaculation for men.[57]

In Taoism, the "three-finger lock" technique introduced by Mantak Chia is used to prevent ejaculation even when it has passed the moment of testicular release, a.k.a. "the point of no return." I disagree with this technique in the sense that I do not believe we should be using any kind of force to suppress ejaculation because force will often result in pain and other side-effects. Michael Winn, co-author of the book Taoist Secrets of Love, also warns against using pressure on the MDP as it can result in other kinds of sexual dysfunctions (erectile dysfunction, poor prostate health, blue balls, pelvic floor pain, etc).[58]

In order to avoid any physical or/and energetic complications, I recommend to my clients to massage the spot and the area around it instead of applying direct or forceful pressure to help circulate the energy internally and to open the energy pathways. For amplification of our orgasm, we should be aiming for subliming and transmuting our sexual energy rather than suppressing it through any kind of force. Anything that causes congestion of energy can result in pain (a slight discomfort is OK) and many unintended side-effects. So, our focus throughout the Path of Amplified Orgasm should be to move and channel the energy rather than trying to block it. In order to avoid the tendency of using pressure, massaging the spot before and after ejaculation is recommended.

It is important to note that if the other channels are not opened for the energy to move freely, the energy can get stuck in this area, resulting in a lot of discomfort, restlessness, and frustration, or erupt like an explosion coming out of your penis. Working on this point will take time, so listen to your body and carry on practising either alone or with your partner and resist the temptation of finding a quick fix or getting there quickly. Instead observe, remain curious, feel and continue your practices. Remember the feeling-over-

Avoid putting the pressure or force

Figure 138: Quite contrary to belief, we should actually avoid putting pressure or force on the perineum spot but rather massage the spot and the area gently.

doing formula (discussed in the introduction) and listen and respond to your body's sensations.

I was not aware of this spot until one day when I was exploring myself and happened to touch this spot, which produced lot of sensations which were very different and unexpected. I became curious so I decided to explore more. The more I explored, the more I found this spot to be amazing, very energising, and also very overwhelming. With other practices and techniques, I was able to circulate the sexual energy from this spot into deeper parts of my genitalia, which opened doors to even newer sensations. It was after a few weeks and months of exploring that I decided to do some research when I came to learn about the MDP. Apparently, I was not the first to know about this amazing area of the male body!

Please note that when massaging the MDP, it is possible that you might feel highly electric charges in your seminal fluid and if you get to a point of needing to ejaculate because it becomes uncomfortable or blocked, my recommendation is to ejaculate rather than try to hold back. Then work (massage, genitals, breathing techniques) on this area at some other time so that during sexual arousal you can develop more ability to hold higher levels of energy and sensations in your body.

Often performing MDP massage can result in Retrograde Ejaculation in which semen which has been released from the testicles but not ejaculated, goes into the bladder, and comes out with urine the next time you pee (which can also be noticed as mistiness in the urine).

EXERCISE: Massaging the Million Dollar Point

Other Genital Parts

The other parts of male genitalia which are important and should be explored are the anus, pelvic floor area, and pubic hair. As mentioned in the prostate section, many men tend to have an unhealthy attitude towards their other genital parts with the exception of an erect penis which they consider as proof of masculinity. Men often view the anus either as dirty or associate anal pleasure with being gay, not realising that many heterosexual men enjoy getting the anus and the areas around it stimulated.

From an energetic point of view, Kundalini energy is considered to be at the base of the spine and connects to the coccyx via three loops at the anal sphincter in both women and men, but men often do not explore the possibilities around their own anal area as much as women. The flow of Kundalini is completely interdependent upon the capacity to relax the anal sphincters, so the more one is able to open and relax these muscles, the more it will allow the flow of Ida, Pingala and Sushumna.

Just like women, men should also work on strengthening their pubococcygeus (PC) muscles, which will not only help them have better control over their sexual muscles helping them connect with energetic orgasms, but it will also help with premature ejaculation, urinary incontinence, overactive bladder, erectile dysfunction, etc. Performing Kegel exercises is part of my daily/weekly routine.

Emotional and energetic blockages which can impact the feeling of orgasm happen for men too, though the reason for such blockages are often different from those women typically experience. My male clients have found bodywork sessions to be helpful in dealing with depression, developing a stronger connection with their genitals, helping them to become multi-orgasmic by learning to channel their sexual energy from their cocks to different parts of their body, gaining a sense of trust and confidence in themselves, prolonging ejaculation, etc.

EXERCISE: Strengthening the PC Muscles

Genitals in the Energetic Body

As we have seen, it is important to spend some time getting to know genitals beyond the physical or biological sense, that is, as important areas of the energetic body and the flow of sexual energy in the course of love-making and orgasm.

In fact, a significant portion of Part II of this book will explore specific energetic practices such as female ejaculation, male sperm retention, prostate massage, edge play, and more. Since these practices take some dedication to master, they are somewhat advanced. However, learning to become skilled at these energetic practices is an important part of the Path of Amplified Orgasm.

For now, it is important to simply work on expanding your awareness of energy moving through your energetic body, noticing how stimulation of different genitals changes that energy movement and to simply notice those genital areas that seem to create energy flow, verses potential areas of energy blockage. As you progress on the Path of Amplified Orgasm, having a sense for this basic information about your genitals and energy flow will come in handy for the advanced practices shared in Part II of this book.

EXERCISE: Mapping the Genitals on the Energetic Body

The Importance of Checking in With Your Partner

Before we begin taking the next steps on the Path of Amplified Orgasm, it is important to emphasise, again, that communication and trust are at the heart of creating intimacy and a safe space to be vulnerable. Without this foundation, it is impossible to release the blockages that the genitals can create at an energetic level. To improve energy flow, we must first be sure there is a good flow of communication. We will be sharing about how to create a better flow of communication with your partner, especially during uncomfortable situations, in Part II of the book.

As we are turning now from theory to practice, take the time to learn more about where your partner is in regards to being willing to explore the genital energy centres, if they have limits or boundaries you will need to respect, and if they are open to exploring the areas you are ready to. Rather than focus on what is "off limits," start by focusing on what is on the table. In time, by respecting each other's boundaries without question, you will find that trust builds, and usually we become willing to face and address blockages with our partner that may have previously seemed impossible or frightening.

Genitals in the Emotional Body

Let us now turn to yet another layer in understanding genitals and getting further along on the Path of Amplified Orgasm. As I discussed briefly at the beginning of this chapter, our genitals can store memory of both incredibly positive experiences, as well as those that are painful and traumatic (often stored in knots or tangles which can be relieved through bodywork). Understanding how this happens gives you the power you have to change and unblock these areas of your body.

In this section I will draw on ideas explored in previous chapters of the book on the emotion and the mind. To refresh your memory, modern neuroscience tells us that the neural pathways that tie sensation, memory, and emotional responses together through experience, are not set in stone. They build over time, and with intentionality, we can rebuild them to suit our goals, such as becoming our best self and even having more satisfying orgasms.

Naming Genitals

Notice for a moment that there are many names for genitals, Here are just a few:

- Vagina
- Penis
- Pussy
- Cock
- Cunt
- Shaft
- Fondlers.

As we discussed briefly in the introduction to this chapter, these different ways of naming genitals are themselves embedded in different cultural narratives about sexuality, gender, and morality. And, we all have our own unique position relative to these narratives, and the extent to which we choose to buy into them as real, based on our individual life experiences and the degree to which we are self-aware.

For some, these words may be associated with degradation and even past trauma. For others, the same words may conjure perfectly healthy "hot" fantasies between consenting adults. On the Path of Amplified Orgasm, you will want to explore your own relationship to these names, the stories they are associated with, and identify those that cause you excitement or trigger you in negative ways.

One way to explore the relationship between genital names and the narratives that contain them is by way of example. In tantra, pussy and cock are often referred to as *Yoni* and *Lingam*, and they are considered to be sacred. In this paradigm, the genitals are the organs that empower you, the organs that liberate you, the organs that provide you with an abundant source of deep, electric energy, and the organs that have the capacity to provide you with ecstatic bliss and pleasure. In addition, Yoni and Lingam are considered the source responsible for the creation of all human beings. That is a pretty major honour!

When people choose to use these terms to refer to genitals, they are tapping into this larger story about love, energetic bliss, and creation. Thus, it would be nonsensical to associate Yoni and Lingam with shame, guilt, fear, or trauma.

In addition, those that have trauma associated with certain ways of naming genitals may find it helpful to start using new terms, such as Yoni and Lingam, as a way to start a new relationship with their genitals that is not fraught with the emotional baggage of other terms.

It is not about choosing the "correct" or "superior" terms for genitals in the abstract. Rather, your journey on the Path of Amplified Orgasm will require that you and your partner have some agreed-upon terms that conjure meanings that are in line with your journey of exploration and open the door to both people feeling comfortable with naming these vital areas of the energetic and orgasmic body.

No matter what terms you land on as a couple, for a deeper level of intimacy, it is all about shifting intention to bring sacredness, love, warmth, heart-connection and desire to connect with one another in an authentic and most vulnerable way. I often hear about people going on retreats, sacred places, doing workshops in nature to experience deeper levels of orgasms. No doubt that being away in nature, away from the daily hullabaloo of life and with the right teachers, tools, and techniques, is bound to lend itself to deeper understanding and growth. However, in my view, what is even more important is your own self. It is not a matter of running away from something or someone or somewhere, but it is a matter of owning oneself, owning one's feelings, and facing what comes up both internally and externally.

Cunt, pussy, or vagina can bring the same level of turn-on, sexiness, juiciness, connection, energetic feeling just like Yoni and Lingam would do, as long as we are willing to drop deeper into our own heart, become aware of each other's energetic bodies and sensations within our bodies, and as long as we have the right intention, right mindset, and a deeper level of awareness and openness.

We may also find that if we are honest with ourselves, we can all stand to become more aware of how we use words referring to genitalia as insults. In fact, doing so doesn't just damage those we use them against, but it also can damage our own relationship to ourselves and our pussies and cocks on an emotional level. We often shame others, calling them names like cunt, dick, tiny cock, or pussy, but in reality, there is a lot of hurt, pain, insecurity, or other forms of triggers stored underneath, as a result of past experiences, within the person who is calling such names.

For example, when a man calls a woman a "cunt," the reason could go back to his own deep hurt from a previous relationship or frustration that he cannot get what he wants in the romance department. This does not justify this kind of abusive behaviour, however it does give us insight into the fact that choosing this route is not helping him in the long run. In fact, it is further creating distance between him and what he truly desires: intimacy with women.

In addition to becoming more in touch with the words we like to use for genitals with our partners, we must also participate in using these words in positive ways outside the bedroom, or at least avoid further associating them with negative emotional charges by way of using them as insults.

EXERCISE: What's in a Name?

175

Porn and Media: Objectification and Performance

Figure 139: Men who get addicted to porn can often find it difficult to relate with their partner in real life and it can deeply influence their sexual behaviour.

In our society, the porn industry, with an over-emphasis on female objectification and male performance, has degraded the beauty of the connection that emerges from two naked human bodies connecting in deep intimacy. The images, fantasies, and superficial preferences can easily get in the way of experiencing deeper orgasm. For instance, men who watch porn get the idea that sex needs to be harder and faster, and women get the idea that they need to look sexy and moan and cry out. Thus, trying to compete with an arbitrary standard set by adult film-makers, we lose sight of our authentic feelings of desire, and indeed even the sensations of the moment can be lost to this ritual of performing to porn standards.

Women are often brainwashed by media and advertisements that wearing a certain kind of underwear, attaining a certain body size, or showing themselves off in a certain way will make them look sexy. Even if she manages to attain these often-unrealistic standards, it doesn't necessarily mean that she will feel sexy from inside. And more often than not, men often buy into that superficial sexiness and act upon it, which propels this damaging cycle even further, creating a never-ending circle. Then one day she feels awakened and realises this is all bullshit. She may then feel resentful against these men, against the media, and possibly against herself too. If she gets stuck in this place of rage, it can create a major block to the ability to experience any sexual pleasure.

Although these issues do seem to do much more damage to women, there has been a profound rise in the rates of psychological conditions such as body dysmorphia, anorexia, and bulimia among the younger generation of men, suggesting shifts in society have begun to focus on making men insecure about their bodies in ways previously reserved for women (alongside a marked increase in consumer products aimed at male beautification).[59,60] In addition, these same stories create problems for many men by exacerbating performance anxiety.

While we can certainly say that the change needs to take place at the larger level of society, and I would not argue with this position, we must also recognise our own individual power to liberate ourselves from these damaging narratives about "the right" kind of sexiness or sexual experiences.

This process begins by first identifying sexual narratives that you have bought into. Then, decide if these narratives are serving your journey, or creating discord or disconnect during your sexual experiences. Finally, it requires finding new stories about sexuality that open up the pathways for exploration, help you recognise your intrinsic sexual power, and free you from shame, guilt, and fear.

For many, this is a long journey that is greatly benefited with the help of a bodywork specialist or orgasm coach. Such bodywork sessions are generally intense as there is a lot of rage, resentment, hurt, and pain stored in the body. However, once these are cleared, clients feel so much love for themselves and others, past and present, who have shared their journey in life.

EXERCISE: How Has Porn Influenced Your Sex Life?

Does Size Matter?

One of the persistent issues that I have addressed with men during my bodywork sessions and work as an orgasm coach is the issue of penis size. In part, this may relate back to porn, with many larger-than-average penises making the cut for male porn

Figure 140: Penises come in all shapes, sizes, and forms. Its size matters mostly in men's heads. The focus should ideally be placed on increasing the width of the penis rather than the length.

actors. In addition, however, it is a common myth that is constantly circulated in our culture by way of stories, hurtful jokes, movies, etc.

Many men can become so focused on the size of their penis that it can even start to feed into performance anxiety. The stress from these factors combined can then lead to real problems with having or maintaining an erection in the presence of a partner, ultimately leading to a lack of desire for intimacy, which can become associated with a humiliating experience.

The truth is that the size of the penis is not as relevant to a woman's pleasure as the art and skill of love-making. In some cases, having a large penis definitely helps, but not in all cases. Large penis can definitely help in accessing certain parts within her vagina or can help to move certain energies by accessing those parts, but it is not true that only a large penis can help achieve the state of orgasm. For example, fingers and toys can also be integrated into our sexual experiences in ways that enhance the experience for both

177

partners. Large penises can at times also result in pain, particularly if they end up being too deep during penetration and love-making.

Some men resort to unhealthy options to address insecurity about penis size. For example, taking medicines to lengthen their penis, plastic surgeries, penis extenders, and penis stretches, penile implants, and so forth. All of these methods can be really dangerous and can create scars both at the emotional and physical levels.

What men need to understand is that women's sexual pleasure and orgasm is more a function of intimacy, love, and other psychological and energetic factors than any sort of specific technique or penis size. For example, a man's ability to show emotional vulnerability is likely a much more important aspect of satisfying a female lover than cock size. Men need to remember that there is more to physical intimacy than penis in vagina!

When men become vulnerable with their genitals, it creates a deeper sense of connection and trust in women which is essential for nourishing orgasms. "Cocks have feelings!" I often tell my male clients, which often comes as a big surprise, shock, and also amusement to them.

EXERCISE: Cocks Have Feelings!

So, let's not worry too much about the size of the penis and also remember that we have different bodies which go beyond the physical. In fact, we have the energetic penis for which there is no size limit. It can be as small as a pea and as large as the whole human body or even larger. And if you end up having sex with your partner with an energetic penis, it can penetrate all the way up to the brain, or shall I say, at least she will feel it that way.

EXERCISE: The Energetic Penis

Genitals and Sexual Trauma

Rape, sexual trauma, abuse, non-consensual touching, victim shaming, emotional abuse, and all other forms of trauma upon any of our layered bodies stays in the cellular memory, especially in the genitalia. It can block the flow of each of the energy centres and prevent us from experiencing sexual pleasure, sexual desire, and of course, orgasm.

Sexual abuse, whether physical, verbal, emotional, mental, or energetic, results in injury to one or all of our energetic bodies in the following ways:

- **The Physical Body**: These might include the inability to feel arousal and orgasm, pain and numbness in different parts of the body, especially genitalia and erogenous zones, disturbing sleep patterns, digestion and metabolism problems, eating disorders

- **The Mental Body**: These may include depression and anxiety disorders, PTSD, panic attacks, disruption in thought processes, decreased decision making, poor judgement, confusion, suicidal thoughts, inability to focus
- **The Emotional Body**: These may include feelings of shame, terror, guilt, fear, sadness, denial, blame, lack of sexual confidence, disconnection from sex and sexual feelings, other sexual dysfunctions, feelings of hopelessness, lack of self-worth, chronic fears, fear of abandonment, personality disruptions, issues relating to intimacy, attachment and non-attachment issues, drug, alcohol and other addictions, nightmares, insomnia
- **The Energetic Body**: This may manifest as lack of energy, hypersensitivity to the energy of others, feeling vulnerable to the energy of others, pain which is not related to the physical body
- **The Spiritual Body**: Survivors may experience a loss of faith in God, loss of connection with the universe, loss of faith in the goodness of humanity, a deep urge to withdraw from people and community.

Figure 141: Sexual trauma is more than just the assault and it deeply impacts the person's overall well-being.

Often survivors of sexual trauma experience mental health issues including PTSD, depression, anxiety, and substance abuse, among other serious conditions. Survivors may need medical care to recover from injuries as well as ongoing mental health care to recover emotionally.

In addition, survivors of sexual abuse benefit from having loving and compassionate partners who are knowledgeable about the abuse and the specific needs of their survivor partner. For example, seemingly irrational reactions to common events need to be approached with patience and compassion. Gentle probing questions to help the victim identify their fears and holding space for them to allow them to be comforted, validated, and heard is important. Dismissing or gaslighting the fears of survivors can actually retraumatise them, and worsen the damage of the original abuse.

Survivors of sexual abuse need to understand that all of the feelings that may come up during the recovery process are valid. Suppressing them or denying them will not make hard feelings go away, and in fact, may manifest in self-destructive behaviours down the road. Instead, survivors need to build a community of support that may include their partners, trusted friends, therapists, or spiritual teachers in order to safely feel and process the complex emotions and feelings that can come up even decades after the abuse occurred.

In addition, to address the emotions and energy that can and often do get stuck in the body, I recommend emotional detoxing and body de-armouring with a certified bodyworker with experience of helping survivors deal with trauma in the body. In my practice, I have helped many clients work through the effects of trauma on the body, and am happy to report that recovery is possible. Many survivors of trauma find that they can more fully access pleasure in their body, including sexual pleasure, and experience orgasms that they thought were beyond their reach.

The Shadow Self

Although we will be exploring the notion of the shadow self in more detail in Part II of this book, it is worth mentioning the concept now. This is especially the case since

Figure 142: We should be embracing our shadow self for us to be able to work it through.

many readers may want to continue their growth with the help of experts and teachers, a practice I am very supportive of. However, understanding a little bit of the shadow self provides important safety information for those looking to expand themselves with the help of a guide or teacher in this realm.

What I refer to as the shadow self can be understood as those aspects of ourselves, often born of past traumas or pain in our own lives, that can manifest as damaging subconscious beliefs, addictions, judgements, behaviours, and emotions (particularly guilt, shame, repressed desires, etc). A prime example of how we can see this pattern play out is when victims of childhood sexual abuse sometimes grow up to become sexual abusers themselves. Although this is of course not always the case, nor even the majority of the cases, the victim-to-perpetrator cycle has been documented.[61 – 63] And, sometimes, our shadow selves, because they are largely subconscious, appear in covert ways. For example, substance abuse following sexual trauma is one way some people process the trauma. This self-destructive behaviour may be the shadow self trying to protect the victim from the unmanageable and extremely painful emotions of sexual trauma, particularly if the victim does not face and seek treatment to process the experience.[64]

However, it is important to understand that all of us have shadow selves, not just overtly abusive people or those with addiction problems. How intense and destructive we allow them to become is, of course, highly variable. What we need to understand is that usually the shadow self emerges first as a protective mechanism and, if allowed to, often takes on a life of its own through the suppression of emotions and desires, not dealing with fear, feeding addictions, following compulsions, ignoring our shadow self, etc.

Acknowledging and addressing our shadow selves is hard work and is almost always emotionally painful. So, there is an incentive to ignore this part of ourselves, precisely the condition it needs to grow in terms of its destructive force on both our own spirit and those whose lives we impact. In Part II, we will be exploring this process in more depth.

For now, it is important to recognise that as you explore your unique Path of Amplified Orgasm, you are making every effort to get enthusiastic consent from your partners. Also, understand that consent cannot be given by people who are inebriated or are potentially coerced by power dynamics. If you do not have enthusiastic, sane, sober, and uncoerced consent from your partner, the odds that you may do harm to them dramatically increase. Get consent explicitly rather than assuming it, or reading some non-verbal signal as implicit consent. This is imperative. It should go without saying, but I feel compelled to say it all the same, that minors and animals are not able to give consent for sexual touching of any kind, under any circumstances.

In addition to making sure your own shadow self is not causing harm to yourself or others, it is particularly important to make sure that your advisors and teachers are not operating from their shadow selves. This is important because people who are abusive often seek out such positions of power in order to feed their shadow self's need for power, manipulation, and abuse. So, we do see more than the average number of people operating from this spiritually damaging place among leaders, and as such, we need to learn to identify and avoid them.

Time and again we often hear the news of sex cults, sexual predators, abusive leaders, tantra teachers, priests, ministers, yoga teachers and spiritual gurus engaging in rape, sexual assault, aggression, manipulation, hypnosis, mind-control, emotional and other sorts of blackmailing, seduction, zero tolerance for criticism, and using other brainwashing tactics. We see this in various communities in the name of modern spirituality, healing, and enlightenment. Even in medical fields, some doctors, psychologists, and therapists resort to such behaviours. Such people shouldn't be trusted with your emotional, physical, mental, and/or spiritual well-being. They end up using power or position to their advantage, keeping things secret or asking others to keep them secret and using threats, manipulative language, and abusive tactics to maintain a stranglehold on their power in their community.

I have worked with so many clients who have been abused by various sexual and spiritual teachers, gurus, leaders, doctors and at times it has been heartbreaking to hear their stories. If you are starting on the journey of personal development, especially relating to sexuality, make sure that you take the following steps to save yourself from the detrimental effects caused by people operating knowingly or unknowingly from overdeveloped shadow selves:

- Enquire and research about the person's history from multiple sources (online research, current students, former students, etc).
- Find out their history and credentials. Where did they study? Who did they study under? What makes them an "expert"?
- Ensure that you and the person who you are working with fully understand and respect boundaries, consent, and rights to privacy. Consent should be a community-held priority among any group of people exploring sexuality together, first and foremost embodied by its leaders.
- Notice whether the person is providing you with tools that aim at empowering you. If you sense that you are being disempowered or told that the only path to what you seek is through this or that advisor, this is a red flag.
- Make well-informed decisions about your journey when you are grounded, rather than responding when you are overwhelmed with emotions. If you sense that you are being pressured to decide or take action while under emotional duress, this is a red flag.
- Notice whether they are using shameful, fear-based, manipulative language or whether they are using positive, uplifting, and empowering language. Anyone seeking to "break you down before building you up" is employing brainwashing techniques and should be avoided.
- Notice whether they are shifting the focus or pressuring you towards private sessions which could be a precursor to sexually intimidating activities.
- Have a close buddy with whom you can share your experiences but also with whom you can speak with honesty to provide a self-reflection on how they see things and your transformation.
- If someone says they can heal you or make you sexually enlightened then please treat that as a warning sign, because no one can guarantee these things. Enlightenment is a process which depends on how much work someone puts in and the teacher should only be there to facilitate and guide.

Sexual healing doesn't need to be abusive. However, due to the vulnerability of people seeking it, the terrain is ripe for scam artists, narcissists, and abusive cult-like leaders seeking only personal fulfilment of ego rather than a true mission to help people self-actualise their own potential (a.k.a. personal empowerment).

In addition to cautioning potential students and followers of this or that practice, I also encourage the leaders in these communities to become more aware of their own shadow selves and to engage, confront, and process these parts of themselves to help prevent damaging those who come to you for help, guidance, and healing.

Genitals and Orgasm

In this chapter we explored the genitals in great depth. Although anatomical information about our genitals is very important, and certainly most people can benefit from more of it, this physical dimension is not the only aspect of getting to know your genitals that matters on the Path of Amplified Orgasm. In fact, hopefully it is clear now, the genitals are also important areas of the energetic, emotional, and even mental body as well.

On an energetic level, the genitals are seated near the sexual energy centre, perhaps the most critical energy centre for the experience of mind-blowing, full-body orgasms. We have also explored how the genitals can store memory of trauma, shame, and negative experiences from our past. On the emotional layer of the body, these organs of extreme intimacy can become blocked from such experiences, although healing is always possible through emotional detoxification and de-armouring bodywork.

Figure 143: Once the trauma is released from the genitals, the sexual energy begins to flow allowing the person to become orgasmic and start experiencing different kinds of orgasms, including whole body orgasms.

Last but not least, the genitals also have a place in the mental body. Our brain processes the input from sensation-producing neurochemicals that can build the sexual experience through arousal. Neural pathways form as we touch our genitals in certain ways and in certain contexts, leading to habitual patterns that can become unhealthy and get in the way of the Path of Amplified Orgasm. And, the mind, as it makes sense of our genitals through fantasy, core beliefs, and even social scripts, comes to project meaning onto these sacred places, sometimes in ways that limit us and sometimes in ways that empower us to more fully enjoy them.

As you may remember, the goal of this chapter is to help you to develop a better relationship with your genitals and those of your partner. If you already enjoy your genitals, then hopefully you have learned some ways to deepen your relationship through curious exploration and energetic practices. If you have been blocked from fully enjoying your genitals, then hopefully this chapter will have given you some insight into why that might be, and what avenues to explore on your journey of healing. And noticing where those blockages are is actually very important to discovering your true desires and which fears are associated with them, a topic we will explore in the next chapter.

Chapter Five Summary:

- Genitals go by many names. The pleasure or displeasure you feel by the use of certain words for genitals is often related to your life experience and belief system. Noticing that certain words bother you is a helpful exercise, as further probing about why may help you identify emotional blockages related to the flow of sexual energy.

- Many people lack detailed and accurate information about the genitals. Finding the clitoris, the G-spot, the Million Dollar Point or other particularly sensitive areas is best approached with a sense of curiosity and exploration, rather than under pressure or judgement.

- Sensitive areas such as the clitoris and the tip of the penis have a large amount of nerve endings. Care should be taken to avoid overstimulating them as this can desensitise these areas which play a critical role in sexual pleasure and orgasm.

- Since the genitals are near the sexual energy centre, they can unlock tremendous energy explosions and also become the centre of sexual dysfunction. Energetic practices such as female ejaculation and semen retention can be explored to further one's path towards becoming multi-orgasmic, and indeed, on the Path of Amplified Orgasm.

- Sometimes, limiting beliefs can cause emotions such as shame in relation to our genitals. Learning to recognise and replace them with empowering beliefs is one avenue to developing a better relationship with your genitals.

- Trauma from abuse can also be stored in the genitals for many years. Working with an experienced and certified bodywork coach is one way to heal the body from such trauma and open up new doors to experiencing orgasm.

CHAPTER SIX

THE SPIRITUAL BODY: DESIRE AND FEAR

Life is found in the dance between your deepest desire and your greatest fear.
Tony Robbins

When it comes to our connection to the divine, there are many paths and languages to make sense of a spiritual journey. Christianity, Hinduism, Buddhism, Judaism, Islam, Shintoism, are but a few of the ways to understand and connect to something larger than ourselves, a force beyond our immediate control, that drives the creation of all that is beautiful in our world. The fact is that our spiritual journey is a highly personal one, and is often deeply shaped by our cultural heritage and life experiences.

When choosing how to teach about the spiritual body, I have found that it is critical to respect these different paths to a connection to the divine among my clients and students. I do not propose that one is more valid than another. However, I do believe that a connection with a higher power, a force greater than ourselves as individual human beings, is important for our overall health and well-being. I do believe that connecting with our higher life purpose is central to a spiritual journey. Regardless of the specific faith you hold, feeding and nourishing the spiritual body is very much on the Path of Amplified Orgasm.

In my work with clients and students over the years, I have found that regardless of the specific religion, faith, or language used to describe a connection to something greater than ourselves, two key concepts pop up over and over in terms of the spiritual body: desire and fear. I have chosen to focus this chapter on these concepts because they require no specific faith, and yet, they are universal to developing greater spiritual health on the Path of Amplified Orgasm.

Desire and fear are by no means the be-all and end-all of the spiritual body. In fact, we will be discussing many more aspects, such as the role relationships, practices, values, and transcendental love making play in developing and nurturing the spiritual body in Part II. However, these two foundational concepts, desire and fear, are good starting points.

Desire, at its core, is about the spiritual body trying to show us the way to fulfil our life's higher purpose. As we will see, properly identifying and connecting with your true desires is complicated in our modern world full of conveniences, addictions, and distractions. Still, only by allowing our true desires to become our guide can we connect with our higher life's purpose.

Fear, on the other hand, is also common to the human experience regardless of the faith we practice. And, it has a very special relationship with desire. Where true desires emerge, so too will fear, always trying to block us from our path of spiritual growth. Identifying, facing, processing, and releasing fear is thus central to learning to trust and strengthen our spiritual body, again, regardless of the specific religious tradition we use to make sense of our connection to the divine.

Desire

"What is your desire Michael?" One of my teachers asked this question when I started my journey of orgasm. I responded, "I want to have a girlfriend who is similar to my previous ex-girlfriend."

Figure 144: Our real desires are hot, fiery, and passionate.

She asked again, "What is your desire Michael?" I felt confused and surprised as I thought I had just answered her question.

Seeing me confused and surprised she said, "What you want is not necessarily what you desire." She went on to explain the difference.

From that conversation I came to understand that what I desired was a lover who could deeply relate with me and understand me. I deeply desired to be in a meaningful, loving, and intimate relationship. The "want" was only on the surface. The desire beneath it was from a deeper place. It was also a more accurate picture of what I truly needed to experience next in my love life.

This was the first time in my life that I had the realisation that most of my life, I had actually been driven by wants. By, confusing wants for desires, it had not occurred to me that my wants had not really been deeply nourishing for me. That is, by chasing my wants, I was missing the opportunity to fulfil my desires. I was wasting time and energy by failing to seek to satisfy these true desires that were calling from a deeper place.

What does "desire" mean for you? In my coaching sessions, I often find that people are not familiar with what this word really means. In fact, asking them to name their real desires may even be overwhelming. We live in a world full of moment-to-moment distractions, advertisements everywhere we turn telling us to buy this or that product, and opportunities to satisfy almost any want with a single, instantaneous click. We are being trained by the conditions of the modern material world to exist in a constant flow of wants. So much so that many of us have lost touch with our true desires.

In order to develop a stronger understanding of desire, we must take the time to clarify the concept by learning about what it really is, and also what it isn't. We will start by investigating the meaning of some similar feelings: cravings, urges, impulses, etc. Then we will dive into how chasing these urges can cost us dearly in terms of progress towards the true desires that live at the core of our life's purpose. And, we will learn about the damage done by trying to repress desires.

Finally, we will turn to the principles of desire, a practical guide to learning how to hear and respond to your true core desires, and those of your partner. And, we will see how desire plays a critical role on the Path of Amplified Orgasm.

What is Desire?

Figure 145: Confusion around desires, wants, needs, cravings, etc. is normal

Desire arises from deep within us. It is connected to fulfilling a larger purpose in our lives; it is persistent, and it demands fulfilment from us. When we are in tune with our true desires, we can use them to help guide our life journey, to show us what we need to learn next, and to give us direction in terms of personal growth, spiritual fulfilment, or the achievement of great things.

We often discuss desire as if it pertains only to love or sex, but in reality, desire can apply to a broad range of life experiences, including our careers, our family, our desire to travel and see the world, and so on. What makes desires special is that they are tied to our sense of self, are highly individual, and if ignored they cause damage to our well-being without us realising the damage being done. When our sexual and orgasmic desires are suppressed, denied, or ignored, it has negative impacts on our relationships, our ability to access sexual pleasure, and indeed, our orgasmic potential.

As we shall see, it is easy to confuse desire with similar feelings such as wanting, wishing, or yearning. In some cases, these feelings can help us identify our deepest desires. However, in other cases they may distract us from our deepest desires, keeping us stuck and lost in cycles of addiction, self-destructive, or counterproductive behaviours. For example, being in a relationship with a narcissistic person, continuing to keep having sex on drugs or alcohol, or other destructive and repetitive patterns that don't feel good at all on a deeper level.

Let's take a closer look at some of the feelings that may feel similar to desire:

Wants

Wants reflect wanting something that we do not have. They tend to be somewhat generic: *I want a car. I want a new hairstyle.* They are subject to change frequently, and are often caused from seeing what others have or are driven by a sense of insecurity. Advertising works on the principle of want: It aims to tell you a story about how you are "less than" unless you have this new gadget or a certain body type which will make you feel better, gain respect, or show others that you are important.

Wants are superficial by nature. Wants can often be achieved through action. However, if you pay attention, you will realise that when you satisfy a want, the sense of accomplishment is soon replaced by yet another want. Generally, we don't gain deep satisfaction from the fulfilment of wants, which is one of the characteristics that separates it from desire. *I want to have sex vs I desire to have sex.* Do you feel the difference?

Wishes

Wishes are a largely powerless or passive expression of either a desire, or merely a want. What distinguishes wishes from other types of feelings is that they usually carry no real intent for action on our part: I wish you a great day. I wish I had more time. I wish I had more sex.

Needs

Needs, in contrast to wants or wishes, are essential to our well-being. Although people tend to think of food, water, and shelter as our only needs, in fact, this is too limited a view.

In 1943, psychologist Abraham Maslow developed what is known as the hierarchy of needs, which remains influential in the field of psychology to this day.[65] As you can see, the physical needs are only the most primitive level of human need. In addition, in order to self-actualise, that is, reach our human potential, our needs extend to include companionship, freedom, health, self-esteem, and more.

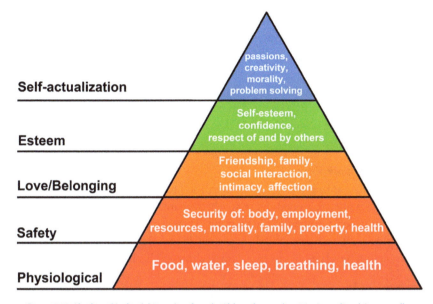

Figure 146: Abraham Maslow's hierarchy of needs. Although sexual activity is not listed, I personally believe that some form of sexual connection is needed at all these levels.

Impulses

An impulse is a sudden, unconsidered, and often irrational urge that is immediately followed by an action. Impulses are usually unrelated to our true desires. They are usually triggered by some stimulus in our immediate environment that is tied to a strong emotion. Acting on an impulse is thus reactive rather than thoughtful or mindful. A good example is buying that candy bar as you stand in line at the grocery store. It may be that you reacted to the emotion of comfort or that of hunger, but either way, the satisfaction will not last. Another example might be if you end up having sex with someone you don't really like and later on end up regretting it. It may be that you acted on sexual urge or didn't take the time to think and feel it through.

In some cases, acting on impulse can be self-destructive. In other cases, impulse can create spontaneity. Learning to identify impulsive urges and becoming thoughtful before reacting is an important aspect of becoming more mindful and intentional. And, learning to identify sexual impulses and becoming more intentional about our responses can also enhance our sex lives, lead to deeper and more trusting connections with our partner, and help us to sort out our true sexual desires from these fleeting impulses.

Compulsions

Compulsions are impulses that are so powerful that they feel impossible to resist. For example, people suffering from obsessive compulsive disorder may have certain rituals that they are compelled to perform, over and over, despite a lack of rational support for those activities. Compulsions feel beyond our control and they can take up a great deal of time that would be better devoted to activities that will bring forth our true desires instead.

Compulsions can become part of addictive and self-destructive behaviour, such as risky and frequent sex with strangers. Likewise, porn addiction can include compulsive behaviours which can ultimately erode our orgasmic potential with real-life partners and damage our relationships.

Longings and Yearnings

Longing includes strong feelings of missing the presence of someone or something deeply, which is often sustained and relatively constant. When longing pertains to love, relationships or sex, we often call it yearning. These feelings are often associated with sadness and loss. We can often feel them as a pull in the solar plexus. Sometimes longing or yearning can be related to our true desires, although this is not always the case.

Cravings

Craving is a physical longing felt within the body. For example, if you have not had sex for a while, you might have a craving to go and meet your ex and may even consider rekindling the relationship. As a result of the cravings, you may do things you didn't really want to in the first place, like calling your ex, browsing through his/her social media feeds, or having sex with strangers.

It is important to understand that not all cravings are bad. Only those unhealthy and unfulfilling cravings are detrimental. Ideally, if we are in tune with our body's wisdom, we are actually going to crave healthier sex and deeper orgasms. Nothing wrong with that!

EXERCISE: Learning to Identify Desire

Compensatory Desires

Compensatory desires are those that we think will make us feel satisfied, and they may be easier to achieve than our real desires in the short term, but they ultimately do not compensate for the real thing. Real desires cannot be felt as long as compensatory desires are running the show. Real desires are only felt when we are willing to sit in the discomfort of not having them met.

Figure 147: We constantly run after our desires, some of which are not even satisfying or fulfilling.

Figure 148: Overconsumption, which is detrimental to our overall well-being, is mainly due to lack of consciousness, presence, and awareness.

In our society, where we are full of overconsumption and hectic schedules, we often run from one thing to the next without a pause, or even do several things at once, such as driving and eating, or talking while browsing on the phone. When one desire is fulfilled, instead of really allowing ourselves to feel the pleasure of it within our bodies, we start running after the next compensatory desire.

Sometimes, before one desire is even fulfilled, our attention has already jumped to the next one. We don't allow the fulfilled desire to really bring a sense of satisfaction, completion, and fullness. For example, when we are engaged in and enjoying oral sex, let us fully feel the experience and pleasure of this part of the engagement before jumping to the next part of the experience, such as physical penetration.

There is nothing wrong with running after other desires as long as it is done by allowing enough time for fulfilment of that desire to create the impact it was supposed to create within you.

Sometimes we end up following a chain of compensatory desires to such an extent that we end up becoming victims of desire rather than having it act as part of the fuel which is meant to ignite us. First we think we want a new car, then we get that and think we need a new house. We get a new house but now we think we need a bigger house. Unsure what is driving these compensatory desires, pretty soon half of our life is spent chasing them. Then one day we pause and realise that what we really desired all along was to be loved and accepted on a deep level. Having a nice car or a big house might have gained us some status, we might even have surrounded ourselves with people impressed by these accomplishments, but these things would never have addressed our true desire and these people may not be capable of seeing us beyond our material possessions. Instead, we should have been putting our energy into learning more about intimacy, vulnerability, how to give and receive love, and finding the kind of person ready to take a journey of deep love and acceptance with us. Chasing compensatory desires can keep us from our deeper life's purpose.

Just like feelings, desires are there to be felt. Whether they make us feel happy or satisfied, or make us feel our worth or not, or whether they are there to bring something to our attention, desires are all part of us. And we need to recognise whether those desires are leading us into compulsion or providing deeper nourishment which will ultimately lead us to our life's higher purpose.

On the other hand, we often have the tendency to kill our desires through logic. Many of us may have the tendency to shoot down our desires before they are even fully felt: *I can't have that. This is so not me. I shouldn't want that. This desire is not mine.* When we do this, we are denying a part of us and also shutting down the opportunity to really explore and see what that particular desire is trying to tell us to explore. As we will see, shame plays a major role in this pattern.

EXERCISE: Reflecting on Compensatory Desires

Desire vs Greed

It is often important to ensure that we are not ruled by greed, as greed makes us follow an endless quest for something which may not necessarily be important for our overall growth. In addition to our own personal greed, we should be aware of the greed of other influencers in our social worlds and how they can impact our desires. We need to pay attention to how desires emerge within us, as desires can cloud our thinking and make us feel that they are ours, while in reality they could be merely the result of distraction caused by media, social networks, and our surroundings.

Figure 149: Many humans tend to portray the qualities of hungry ghosts often driven by intense emotional needs, small necks, large and empty bellies, which signifies that they are often seeking things externally to satisfy their insatiable hunger just for a temporary relief. Quite often we are not aware of our needs. hence making us stay hungry.

When desires take the form of greed, they encourage us to want more and more but with no real satisfaction. It is like eating fast food which does fill up the stomach and satisfy our hunger temporarily, but in reality doesn't provide any real nutrients. Thus, the body's true hunger for nutrition grows greater, even as the stomach is full, creating a cycle of over-eating that leads to many health problems.

One example of how this can apply to our sex lives is when we focus on only the physical dimensions of sex, with climax as a goal of our sexual interactions. Because this layer of the sexual experience is so limited, there can be a tendency to want more and more sex, and this is particularly true if our true desire is for emotional and/or energetic connection. Thus, a kind of greed encourages us to want more and more sex, and meanwhile, our real needs are not being met no matter how much climax-oriented sex we are having.

EXERCISE: Identifying Greed in Our Lives

Types of Desires

Different philosophers, theologians, and researchers have identified different types of desires and expressed different views relating to them – some supporting the existence of desires and some calling them sinful. I am a big supporter of desires. In fact, I think

Figure 150: Three types of desires

desires are so important that we need to develop some language to better understand the role desire plays in our lives. Let's start with talking about three types of desires: small desires, big desires, and core desires.

Small Desires

Small desires are those that will enable you to get to big desires. The small desires are all about minute details, qualities, and experiences that impact the way you relate to and experience life. Small desires can be a desire to take a five-minute break and have a cup of tea and relax, have a bath, or enjoy 15 mins of sex.

The smaller and more specific the desire, the easier it is to feel when the desire has been fulfilled. Likewise, when you are able to be specific and communicate your small desires to your lover, they are better able to satisfy those desires.

Big Desires

These are the desires that have much higher intensity, those which relate to our life's purpose. When we get distracted in life, it is these big desires that can bring us back on track.

Examples of big desires include: having a healthy and supportive relationship, a fulfilling job, a deeper sexual connection, or experiencing deeper states of orgasms. Big desires are not as much about specificity but more about the overall feeling, whether be it in a relationship, life in general, or sex. They help us to align with our life's purpose by guiding us to grow and learn in these ways.

Core Desires

These are the desires which don't change easily, are intense, and are so deeply rooted that they are not fulfilled easily. However, if fulfilled, these desires can bring about deep nourishment and bliss to our spirit. These desires are generally the essence of your soul, so deeply ingrained that you will know when they are fulfilled because they will bring significant personal transformation. Examples may include a desire to be touched in a way that you have never been touched, a desire to feel connected on a deep spiritual level, or the desire to immerse yourself into orgasmic bliss so deeply that you become one with the universe.

We should allow ourselves to be in touch with all three of these desires: small, big and core desires. Denying one of them or fulfilment of just one without the fulfilment of the others over a long period of time will not be conducive to our overall well-being.

The nature of each of these desires will vary from person to person depending on where one is in their orgasmic journey.

Figure 151: People are often shamed for their desires, especially sexual desires.

EXERCISE: Identifying Small, Big, and Core Desires

Desire and Shame

No desire is shameful at an individual level. If there is a desire that is present and you feel it is shameful, then it is important to inquire within to find out where it comes from and the feelings associated with it. Only then can we let go of shame, a necessary step on the Path of Amplified Orgasm.

In lot of families, cultures, and traditions, there is shame around touching, kissing, sex, and orgasm. In some religions, some of these forms of intimacy and affection are even considered to be sinful. As we have discussed in Chapter Two, these can be the basis of limiting core beliefs if internalised.

When one feels sexual shame, it means considering one's sexual being as wrong, inhuman, broken, or even fundamentally bad. The notion of "fixing" oneself can also develop as a result of shame. Shame can be felt for having sexual desires, the kind of sexual partners one prefers, the gender identity one identifies with, the type of position one likes, the kinds of sexual fantasies, or the type of sexual activities they enjoy.

Notice whether you or your partner feel that having too much pleasure is bad or unhealthy for you or if you both fully support pleasure and sexual activities. Notice whether you have shame around sexual and orgasmic desires as a result of your family upbringing, culture, traditions, or from social media, past trauma, inappropriate messages, harassment, or abuse. If one has sexual shame, it will impact one's ability to feel sexual pleasure, intimacy, love, and deeper orgasms.

By not talking about shame, you are not dealing with shame but instead hiding it even more.

As seen from previous chapters, anything not expressed will start getting accumulated in our muscles, energy centres, or subtle bodies, which will hinder the flow of blood and orgasmic energy. In order for one to have amplified orgasms, shame needs to be let go of so that desires can emerge fully.

One of my clients had shame around the way she looked and as a result there were a few areas on her body she didn't like to look at or have touched. This meant that during every love-making session, part of her mind's consciousness was always working on ensuring that these parts were not seen, touched, or caressed. She had never experienced orgasms and she and her lover had tried everything they possibly could.

After the consultation, when we had a bodywork session, we worked on addressing her shame. A big emotional release happened, after which she felt happier, more confident, and had a very positive attitude towards her body. During the session she also felt a glimpse of what an orgasm actually is for the first time in her life.

Our desires are also shamed in our society, especially if they tend to diverge from the norm. Shaming a desire results in collapsed desire, loss of life force, fear, denial of desire, and ultimately the repression of our dreams. This can also result in a lack of creative force, lack of drive, negative attitude towards life, and may end up creating limiting beliefs (explored in Chapter Two). All of these will hinder one's ability to amplify their orgasm.

EXERCISE: Identifying and Releasing Shame

Figure 152: Repressed desires result in one feeling collapsed.

Repressed Desires

Desire drives us no matter how hard we try to repress it. If a desire is coming up, it means it is present in our body, in our subconscious mind, and it needs to be dealt with. When we repress desire, it comes out in distorted ways. We cannot eliminate it, for it has a life force of its own. It seeks expression and fulfilment and will always be present in one form or the other. What we deny ourselves will hold even greater allure and will serve to control us.

I often have clients who have repressed their desires for a long time, telling themselves all sorts of stories along the way. If a desire, especially a sexual desire, has been constantly knocking within you for a consistent period of time, it is important to listen to it rather than suppressing it or completely dismissing or not hearing it. We often have a tendency to sabotage our desires by telling ourselves stories such as:

- *My desire is wrong.*
- *What will my friends and family think?*
- *It is so selfish of me to desire this.*
- *I cannot fulfil this desire.*
- *What if I change my mind during the course of seeking this desire to be fulfilled?*
- *Who would I become as a result of this desire being fulfilled?*

Women and men tend to have different kinds of conditioning around desires that have been shaped by gender norms in our culture. Men tend to believe they know what they want, but in reality, it is not what they really want most of the time at a deeper level. Generally, if men do know what they want, they go for it rather than sitting and reflecting deep to see if there is something more that they truly desire. If men really want to get on the Path of Amplified Orgasm, the growth for men in this area of desires is first to get to know what desires are, to learn how to express their feelings and desires rather than repress them, and to develop healthier attitudes towards women's often-fluctuating, never-ending, and erratic desires.

Women, on the other hand, might know what they desire but they often don't give themselves the permission to have them fulfilled. Females are conditioned to be "good girls" and are often told that showing or expressing their sexual desires is bad for them and will get them in trouble. From an early age they may learn to say 'No' to their desires.

Another conditioning factor for many women is the push to put the needs of others before their own. Hardly ever does a woman get to speak her sexual and orgasmic desires and even then, hardly ever does she put her desires ahead of her lover. Just like men, if women want to experience amplified orgasms for themselves and their partner, they need to learn to express their desires and ensure that some of them, if not all, get fulfilled.

EXERCISE: Identifying Repressed Desires

Willpower and Desire

The stronger the desire, the more planning and willpower will be needed to have it fulfilled. For example, if a man desires to control his ejaculation, he will need a plan that will enable him to fulfil this desire. And on top of that plan, he will need the willpower to be able to take action to work on that plan.

In order to bring your desires into being, it is important to balance both the intensity of the desire and your willpower to take the actions necessary to achieve it. Dr Napoleon Hill, noted self-help author, said: "The starting point of all achievement is desire. Keep this constantly in mind. Weak desire brings weak results, just as a small fire makes a small amount of heat. When your desires are strong enough, you will appear to possess superhuman powers to achieve it."[66] As this quote points out, desire and willpower are thus intertwined.

The Push and Pull of Desire

It is important to note whether your desire is leading to more pleasure or avoidance of pain and whether you are doing the right thing for the sake of doing the right thing. Desire is intimately connected to pleasure and pain. The pleasurable things, such as sex and sugar, are wired to be desirable, whereas the painful things like experiencing vulnerability and intimacy after being deeply hurt, are wired to be undesirable.

The real desires lie deep within our subconscious mind and it takes a bit of work to have them surface into our consciousness. But before desires come into our consciousness, they compete with a number of conflicting desires and we need to be able to spend time and energy to find out what our true and real desires are. During a coaching session, I asked a client what she desired and she said, "I desire to settle down but I desire to remain free. I desire to travel but I desire to save money and buy a house. I desire to have many lovers but I desire to be with a man who is committed to me. I desire to experience multiple orgasms but I don't want to let go of control."

Figure 153: The push and pull of various desires sometimes can make it very difficult for us to move forward.

It is important to note whether your intellect is rebelling against your emotions and suppressing your core desires. Sometimes we use intellectual debate as resistance to deny or suppress the intense desire we have and this results in an internal push-and-pull state. In such a case, if it feels really right, the best thing to do is to follow the desire and plan on how to have that desire fulfilled. When this happens, it is said that one is surrendering to one's desire in a healthier way.

Have you ever come across a time when you thought to yourself, *Should I have sex or should I not have sex? Should I invite him/her for dinner or should I not invite him/her for dinner?* When that happens, what do you do? Do you sit and inquire to see what is it that you really desire, or do you use logic, try to rationalise and come to conclusion, or do you use a combination of both desire and logic? The next exercise can help you learn to navigate this common experience.

EXERCISE: Getting to Know the Push and Pull of Desire

Collapsed Desire

Quite often, just like we might have a habit of sabotaging ourselves or our relationship, sometimes, in the same way, we may sabotage our own desire, known as a collapsed desire. Collapsed desire can occur either due to our own actions or lack of actions (often subdued by one's own rationalisation or too much thinking) or due to the action or lack of action of others. For example, suppose a woman asked her partner to come home early on a particular day as she has a surprise for him. While he originally agreed to come home early, for whatever reason, he did not. The woman, who has been so happy, excited, and desirous of him throughout that day, would have her desire crushed in the evening, irrespective of whatever his reason might be. Rationalising is no substitute to compensate for a desire that has collapsed.

Desire as Our Fuel

How would you feel if I were to remind you that your own existence began with the desire of two people? That is, you were someone's desire that manifested into the form of you.

How ecstatic is it that two people's desire, when backed by actions and willpower, have the ability to create a marvellous living being? Such is the force of desire!

The most interesting thing about desires is that they constantly arise within us whether we are conscious of them or not. When one desire finishes, or gets fulfilled, or gets repressed, then another one arises. Desires constantly fluctuates in a cyclic and spiral manner, constantly rising and falling, ebbing and flowing, sometimes linear, sometimes with no sense of direction. It is this desire that moves us and gives our life direction and purpose, consciously or subconsciously.

Figure 154: When desire is used as a fuel, one begins to fly or rise in life quickly.

Desire drives us and determines our decisions. If we repress our desires, especially sexual desires, they are still determining the course we take. However, we may seek fulfilment through other avenues in covert ways. For example, a woman who represses her sexuality may have deep cravings for food. Eating could be a substitute for her sexuality. Another example is when a man whose desire for sexual experiences with women is replaced through pornography. When true desires are repressed or ignored, then wants, cravings, and urges will drive our actions, usually in detrimental ways.

It is also possible that if we are not honest and aware of our deep desire for attention, we may come to manifest this desire by chasing tangential wants that are actually counterproductive and even harmful. For example, self-destructive patterns such as addiction to drugs, alcohol, or nicotine sometimes begin as a form of attention-seeking behaviour among teenagers.

Desire is the fuel and ignition that can drive us towards the happiness when used correctly. But it can result in us having collapsed desires or bring out the unwanted parts of us.

Desire as Emergent

When your partner tells you they desire to have sex or have an orgasm, what are the thoughts that come to your mind? Do you have a conversation asking them how they would like their desire to be met?

More often than not, when a woman expresses a desire for sex, men often go with the idea that she wants to have a good fuck or that she wants to have an orgasm. As a result, throughout the sexual session, most of the time his mind will be occupied with giving her that best orgasm or that good fuck. In other words, the focus is on the end result, a predetermined goal, rather than on desires as they emerge. After all, he wants to prove he is the best lover in the world! This can actually prevent both partners from being emotionally present, aligned, and connected.

Tuning into desire as it emerges throughout your love-making session is the key to staying aligned on this level. Pay attention to your partner. Perhaps there is a desire to be touched, kissed, or caressed in a certain way. Perhaps different parts of the body want to be touched with different intensity and pressure. When exactly during the sex act does her body really desire to be penetrated and with what intensity, pressure, how many strokes? What kinds of penetrative movements does her body desire? Is her body ready for deeper and more orgasms and, if so, what does she and her body need for that to happen? Needless to say, the same attention to emergent desire during sex applies to the pleasure of men as well.

As we will discuss in more detail in Chapter Seven, female orgasm is different from male orgasm and the ways to achieve orgasms for both are also different. In the same way, the sexual and orgasmic desires for each of the genders will vary, so regular check-ins are important to achieve amplified orgasms together.

The relation between sexual desire and amplified orgasm is that of a never-ending loop if used in the right way, as this diagram shows. The sexual desire rises, which generates arousal and desire for even more arousal, which will create the desire of wanting to be more intimate and find a deeper connection. Now, instead of acting upon the arousal, instead of rushing into sex, connect with your desires, connect with each other's arousals. The couple can use this cycle to build on desire. When you are both ready, then you can connect at the various layers (physical, emotional, energetic, mental, spiritual), which will bring immense satisfaction and lead to more sexual desires at a deeper and more intense level. And this loop will continue until one of you have peaked. See if both of you can peak at the same time and then carry on with the rest of the stages of orgasm together.

EXERCISE: Understanding Desire as a Feedback Loop

The Principles of Desire

Now that you have a better understanding of desire, what it is and what it isn't, and the role it plays in helping to guide us on the Path of Amplified Orgasm, it is time to move on to what I like to call the Principles of Desire. These practical tips are designed to help you learn to speak your desires, effectively respond to the desires of others, and get comfortable with the process of how intimacy involves the exchange and often evolution of desire.

1. Stay connected with your desires.
Wants, greed, and compulsions can become distractions from your true desires. Take the time to understand your core desires to make sure you are not simply being distracted.

Whatever sexual connections you have engaged in life, how in touch have you been with your sexual and orgasmic desires in those engagements? Having sex while drunk or high, or having one-night stands or with complete strangers – how many of these were actually driven by your real desires and how many of these were driven by a lack of consciousness about your relationship with your own desires, or were driven due to desires of your friends, people, or the culture around you? And what impact have those encounters had on your relationships currently?

The more we are in connection with our own sexual and orgasmic desires, the healthier the relationship we have with those desires, and the more our real desires will be fulfilled. Fulfilment of each sexual desire leads us further on the Path of Amplified Orgasm.

EXERCISE: Connect with Your Desires

2. Use your desire as a compass.

Sexual desires have a push-and-pull effect which can be felt not only in our physical body, but in our energetic bodies as well. A desire that is being pushed can get repressed, which over time builds and leads to resentment and disconnection with the self. How many times have you denied yourself that sexual connection with a person you were attracted to or in love with even though your body knew it was the right thing to do? How many times have such desires been repressed by someone else, and what impact has that caused?

Figure 155: Instead of curbing our desires, we should be using desire as a compass to navigate through life.

A desire that is being pulled can makes us feel overwhelmed, which can end up making us feel powerless. Have you ever experienced a time when your desire to experience orgasm was so strong that you were willing to do whatever it takes to get it?

Fulfilment of true desires will require a greater level of discipline to ensure that other small desires don't end up distracting you. The greater the desire, the greater the force of it, and the bigger the anchor you will need to plug into so that the force of your desire can be met with steadiness. Once these are in place, the key to fulfilling your desires is having the courage to move in the direction of them. That's it. Move in their direction and eventually you will get there.

The more we are able to navigate through the push-and-pull forces of desire and use desire as a compass, the more we will be able to engage and do things that feel right rather than what sounds right. In deeper states of orgasms, where it might not be possible to communicate with words, sounds, or signals, it is this compass of desire and ability to feel what is the right thing to do in that moment that will guide the lovers further on this journey.

3. Understand the alchemy of desire.

Your external reality is a reflection of your internal reality, and your internal reality is a product of your past external experiences. Thus, it is helpful to understand that desire is created through a process of iteration between the two that is ever evolving and shifting.

If you have been attracted to someone but you know that deep down that they are not what you really desire, then the questions to explore could be: What is deep inside you that is making you not really desire that despite feelings of attraction? What beliefs have you established around the qualities this person holds that might be understood through your past experiences (external) or beliefs (internal)? What is it about that person which is causing that attraction? How are your genitals feelings towards that person?

In the process of alchemy, it is important to look at both internal and external drivers to identify those desires that are true to our journey, and those that may be driven instead by impulses, compulsions, greed, or simply transitory wants. To achieve deeper states of orgasm, alchemy alignment is important not only for you, but for your partner as well. In desire coaching, we go deeper to explore what is it that you really desire, what kind of stories you tell yourself, what beliefs you have chosen, and what it is that stops you from having what you really desire.

4. Express desire clearly, directly, and authentically.

Desire is direct, positive, clear and succinct. If you are not clear about what your desire is, then take the time you need to reflect until you have clarity. Learn to state your desire in a positive tone, without apologising, and with as much specificity as you can. Expressing desire need not be toned down from fear of non-fulfilment or the effect it might create as a result of the expression.

If you are not authentic about communicating your desires, you leave your partner and the people who love you powerless to help you manifest your true desires. A common example of where this occurs during sexual experiences is when women "fake" orgasm. Although often done in an attempt to appease their male partner and prevent hurt feelings, the problem is that, ultimately, it will prevent her partner from learning the truth of her desires, and unlocking her orgasmic state. Both partners are denied a deep and honest connection, even though in the short term it may be less painful to face.

5. Express your desire without shame or guilt.
This may be challenging, however, if you are unable to express your desires without shame or guilt, then it is a sign you still have shame or guilt to release. This requires some additional work you will need to do before having any desire fulfilled. Desire needs to be expressed without feeling shame or guilt for having them.

6. Find healthy ways to explore taboo desires.
Desires have their roots deep in your being and cause harm if they are repressed or denied. Find healthy and safe ways to explore your desires, even those that may be kinky or different from the norm. As long as your practices are with other consenting adults who are not being harmed, and you are not engaging in harmful compulsions or self-destructive behaviours, you can explore sexual taboos without shame and guilt.

7. Hear communicated desires as an invitation to play.
It may sound obvious, but it is important to learn to notice when your partner has communicated a desire. Remember that it requires vulnerability and courage to speak a desire, so try to be sensitive and open-minded. Remember, you need not act upon a desire straightaway, or even at all. You can simply say thank you. You are not required to justify your reply, but if you do explain the reason, it will facilitate more connection.

You can choose to consider this as an invitation to play and use it to pull out more desires from the other person. Receiving someone else's desire is not easy because of the magnitude of force/intensity it carries for that person. The more one is able to receive someone's desire, the bigger is the capacity of receptivity of that person.

8. Expect desires to change over time.
Desires are not static. As we experience having our desires fulfilled, they will often change and evolve. In addition, our desires are often influenced by those of our partner and vice versa. In this way, we can understand desire as having its own evolution, unique to you and your partner and working in conjunction as well.

Try to get comfortable with the idea that desires can change over time, and often do. Rather than feeling threatened by changes, try to adopt a mindset that is about taking a journey together. How fun would a holiday be if you kept going around in the same neighbourhood or having sex in a similar fashion without navigating each other's desires at times before the sexual intimacy? Change and variety keeps things interesting and exciting. When you both trust one another, you can experience the journey of changing desires together, which can help amplify your orgasms.

9. Start exploring small desires and build from there.

Learning to navigate desire from the moment it is first felt to the moment it is fulfilled benefits from practising. Starting with small, well-defined, easy-to-fulfil desires allows both partners to build trust, learn to fully experience the sensations of fulfilment, and develop the skills to explore larger desires together.

Sometimes, when we are very close to success or a big breakthrough, we are not used to having so much pleasure when our desires really get met. We can collapse. In order for that not to happen, it is important to start receiving smaller desires. For example, if you desire to have a beautiful and loving girlfriend, a simple step could be to go out and chat with beautiful girls in the social arena without focusing on the end goal of having them as a girlfriend. First we need to learn how to feel the pleasure of having a desire, then feel the pleasure of moving towards it, and as our desire begins to move towards the sense of fulfilment, we embrace and enjoy every single part of this process.

The same applies to becoming multi-orgasmic. First we need to experience the desire of becoming multi-orgasmic, then experience what an orgasm actually feels like in the body, then take steps that will enable us to share the journey on the Path of Amplified Orgasm.

10. Check in with your partner to verify shared desires.

We will also need to see whether our partner shares the same desire of becoming multi-orgasmic and learn where they are in their journey. Because orgasm happens in connection and in relation to each other, so their desire and their growth in this journey will be impacting our desire and our growth in our journey. The bigger the desires for both the partners involved, the deeper your orgasmic journey will be and the more amplified your orgasms will be.

11. Let energy centres be your guide.

The depth, intensity, and quality of orgasm is often dependent on you and your partner's energy centres and which of these are awakened. For example, if one has a stronger sacral energy centre, then that person will be mostly driven by the desires of sexual impulses, fantasies, and sexuality that may be very primal in nature. However, if one has a stronger heart centre, then that person's sexual desire will be driven by core desires for love, compassion, and kind-heartedness. The level of energy flow and attitude of sexual desires at each of the energy centres will play a role in creating your partnership's Path of Amplified Orgasm. Each journey is unique.

EXERCISE: Practising the Principles of Desire

Please don't suppress your desires.
Just like feelings, they are there for a reason.
Get in touch with your small desires.
Get in touch with your big desires.
And most importantly,
get in touch with your burning desires and do something about them.
Or,
let them burn you to such an extent that you have no other option but to listen to them,
to feel that burn and then to do something about it.
Make them your fuel to power you, to ignite you,
and not the walls or brakes to hinder you, to stop you.
And please, keep your non-supporting beliefs totally out of this game!

Be pulled by these burning desires, or
be pushed by these burning desires.
Most importantly, listen to them.
Don't keep them waiting and knocking within you for that long
that they end up killing themselves,
or feeling completely dismissed and unheard.

Fear

Now that we have thoroughly covered desire, and its importance on the Path of Amplified Orgasm, we turn to fear. At first glance it may seem odd to turn to this subject next. However, as we dive deeper into the concept of fear, we will see that it is central to learning to embody the Principles of Desire, and as a result, fear is also an important aspect of the spiritual body.

Although other emotions such as anger, guilt, shame, and happiness all play a very significant role in terms of our sexuality and orgasmic flow, fear is one of the emotions that should be given special attention, because it will often come up as we develop the intimacy, trust, and connection that we need to develop with our partner in order to experience amplified orgasm.

In addition, as this section will explore, learning to identify and work on fear is a powerful tool on the Path of Amplified Orgasm. In fact, fear is, in a way, a great blessing because it allows us to point directly at areas where we can grow and develop as human beings and open our experience on this earth to the full range of experiences and emotions available to us on this amazing journey of intimate and sexual connection with other human beings. Indeed, fear is a normal and expected part of the process of becoming deeply orgasmic.

Fear and Desire Are Connected

When desire dies, fear is born.
Baltasar Gracian

If you are on the Path of Amplified Orgasm, then you will start connecting with your desires. The more your desires come alive, the more fear will start kicking in just underneath the surface. Every desire will often be met with an equal or even more forceful fear, however, if you stay on the Path of Amplified Orgasm, eventually either fear will make way for desires to outshine them, or you will be able to learn how to alchemise the energy of fear into something that is powerful and supportive. As you have seen in the section relating to desires, when desires start being fulfilled, they start providing nourishment to the spiritual body, which in turn helps the person with orgasmic amplification.

Desire	Fear
I desire connection.	*I have a fear of intimacy.*
I desire sex.	*I have a fear of sexual intimacy, getting an STI, or that I won't be good in bed.*
I desire a fulfilling relationship.	*I have a fear of never being enough or not being able to find someone who will resonate with me.*
I desire to own my sexuality and be completely free.	*I have a fear of being judged, called a slut or whore, and/or not being understood.*
I desire to live long and enjoy cherishable experiences of life.	*I have a fear that I won't live long or won't be healthy enough to enjoy such experiences.*
I desire to have a huge family.	*I have a fear that I will never be able to find a partner who wants to have a huge family; I have a fear that I will not have enough money or time to look after them.*

Where Does Fear Come From?

Fear can come from many sources and it has been studied through a variety of scientific lenses.[67] Psychology tends to focus on fear as a learned phenomenon, often through a conditioning process such as that which we explored in Chapter One of this book.[68] Evolutionary biologists have shown that the capacity of fear indeed seems to have a genetic component.[69] Neuroscientists tend to understand fear as a neurochemical process of related neural pathways, and biochemical transmitters, hormones, and the processes of the central nervous system.[70 – 72] Some ancient traditions believe that fear can be passed from one generation to the next through ancestral connections. And, although it may sound a bit "woo-woo," it turns out that modern research in epigenetics has provided some scientific support for this potential source of fear as well.[73]

Remember a time when you felt fear.

What did it feel like in your body in terms of sensation?

What was your immediate response?

Did you go into fight or flight mode?

Did you become hysterical and start laughing, did you freeze, or become more alive?

Have you ever experienced fear and excitement at the same time?

Fear Lives in the Body

If you remember back to Chapter One, we discussed that emotional states can be understood as "rooted in the body" by which we mean that emotions correspond to certain physical states marked by biological indicators such as pulse, breath, neurochemicals, hormones, etc.

For example, on a biochemical level, fear is a survival mechanism that includes the body signalling on the neural, chemical, and cellular levels to react with "fight or flight." The body's Autonomic Nervous System (ANS) system controls the fight-or-flight response in our body. The sympathetic nervous system activates physiological changes including the release of norepinephrine. When we confront a perceived threat, our bodies respond in specific ways such as sweating, increased heart rate, and high adrenaline levels. These biochemicals make us extremely alert and ready to respond to a potentially life-threatening situation.[74]

After the trigger has passed, the parasympathetic nervous system activates the release of the neurotransmitter acetylcholine and activates the "rest and digest" response and returns the body to homeostasis after the fight-or-flight response.

We also, on the physical level, experience the sensation of fear in our bodies. The body maps below were created from the aggregation of data from participants who were asked to colour images of bodies in relation to certain emotional states. As you can see, people tend to experience the sensation of fear as activated in the chest and head areas more than the lower torso and extremities.[75]

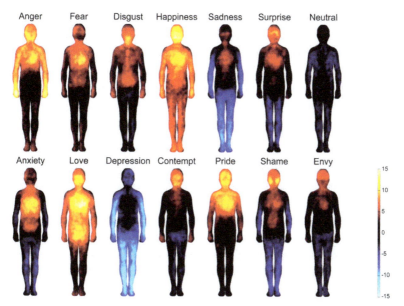

Figure 156: Body map showing emotions felt in different parts of the body when associated with words. Increase in activation denoted by warm colours, decrease in activation denoted by cool colours. (Credit: Proceedings of the National Academies of Sciences. Image taken from https://www.pnas.org/content/pnas/111/2/646.full.pdf).

Fight or Flight: Intimacy and Orgasm

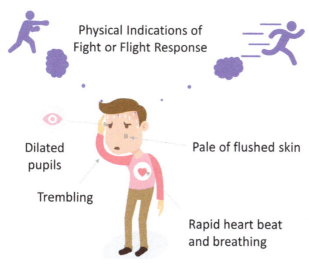

Figure 157: Fear as fight or flight mode

Let's focus for a moment on what happens when fear surfaces during a sexual encounter and either the fight or flight response is triggered. What does this look like? Well the answer is that it can look very different for each individual. Sometimes it is obvious, and other times it isn't. Here are a few examples which are not an exhaustive list, but hopefully they will simply allow you a chance to see what the fight-or-flight response might look like in practice.

Example #1: A Flight Response

A couple is enjoying a sexual encounter when the man begins to run his hands along her sides and belly. This triggers in her a fear of not being attractive because she has recently been trying to lose weight and has a heightened sense of her body "not being good enough." She begins to "pull out" of the sexual experience, dissociating from the pleasure and sensation of it. She becomes less responsive and present in the encounter. She may continue to "go through the motions" but she is no longer enjoying the experience or able to fully connect with her partner. In response to the fear induced by the body shame trigger, she has reacted with flight from her body and her mental, physical, and energetic connection with her partner.

Example #2: A Fight Response

A couple is enjoying a sexual encounter when the woman tells the man that she needs him to "fuck her harder." Her request triggers in the man a deep fear of sexual inadequacy. Rather than hearing her request as a sign of her passion, he hears it as, "You are not giving me enough." In response to his fear that he is not giving enough, his ego engages and he overcompensates by going really hard on her in a kind of fight response. He becomes completely overwhelmed, disconnected from reality, and loses his sense of when to stop until it is too late. That is, either he has ejaculated or his penetration has begun to hurt her. This is an example of a fight response, but it has fear at its root.

We need to learn to recognise fight or flight responses and acknowledge that they are both normal and valid (as long as neither consent is broken or harm induced). As we can see in the second example, fight responses in particular can cause harm to the other. If we can learn to spot these reactions, and take them as evidence that an underlying fear is likely to blame, then we can begin to get to the heart of the matter, that is, identifying the fear. This is a first step in the healing process.

Fear Can Be Exciting Too

While fear is often discussed as provoking only two possible responses (fight or flight), we actually can see there is one other obvious response to fear that some people display: excitement. We see it when we see daredevils walking a high-wire between skyscrapers, in certain sports such as surfing and rock climbing, as well as in our everyday lives, such as the little rush we might experience when driving too fast or having sex in a public place.

Fear, and the heightened feelings of alertness and aliveness that comes with it, is something that most of us have experienced in a positive way at least once in our lives, such as a roller coaster ride. In fact, most of us have enough experience with fear to realise that we are all capable of a flight, fight, or excitement reaction to the emotional state of fear. Rather than being rooted in certain individuals, it may be life experience and context that drive our initial reaction to a fear state in the body.

When orgasm moves through the body, it will at times create a lot of excitement, but at other times it will trigger various emotional spots relating to fear. Sometimes certain sensations could feel itchy or heavy, giving a feeling of suffocation or sometimes a fearful thought can emerge from nowhere. Or, you might be able to sense fear in the auras of yourself or your partner. The more connected you are to your deeper sense and life purpose, the more you will be able to trust this path and your growth, the more you will be able to feel excited about these kinds of fears rather than being taken aback by them or going into fight-or-flight mode.

Becoming aware of how fear can be a source of excitement is one way to explore sexuality and add some new levels of excitement to the bedroom. For example, some people experience fear around exploring deep desires they have only recently allowed to surface. Exploring these with a loving and trusting partner can be a safe way to harness this power of fear to excite and titillate us.

In my coaching sessions, I work with couples to help them explore each other's desires and fears in a safe space which creates a lot of intimacy, turn-on, increased sexual desire, and love for each other. Sometimes, it can also bring out feelings of shame and resentment for not expressing and communicating the things that mattered to each of them, which can take some time to work through. I also work with singles to help them explore their fears, desires, shame and help them find their life purpose. We will explore these subjects around communication and safe space in more detail in Part II.

However, it is also important to note that the endorphins and hormones associated with fear when we experience it as excitement can also lead to addictive and compulsive behaviours such as chronic cheating, frequent risky sex with strangers, or sex addiction.[76]

EXERCISE: Getting Familiar with Fear

Fear and the Energetic Body

At the most basic energetic level, fear exists in the energy centres related to the attribute that each centre offers. For example, fear of sexual connection happens at the sexual energy centre, fear about life occurs at the root energy centre, fear of communication happens in the 5th energy centre, fear of intimacy in the 4th energy centre, etc.

Fear has a very powerful energetic charge which can be used to empower us and help us move ahead in life and achieve our goals. However, the same energy can become overwhelming, disempower us, take us aback, freeze us into paralysis, and drive us to lose control, which results in our inability to move forward.

When the latter happens, there is a tendency for us to fall into victim mode, experience a disconnect and dissociate from present reality, and/or deny us the experience of being fully present for each of life's moments. In addition, fear can limit us from the energetic involuntary state, required for amplified orgasm.

Our most basic fear is survival, which is deeply programmed into our body and energy centres – fear of death, losing our career, war, financial crisis, death of loved ones, climate change, etc. Our body can actually feel like the manifestation of fear on an energetic level. As we discussed in Chapter Three, meridians are a system of energy channels in the body, also called nadis. Nadis are like little streams and rivers flowing through our entire body providing every organ and cell with the necessary life energy. Fear creates contraction in those nadis and if a nadi stays contracted, it breaks the energy flow. The cells and organs associated with those nadis become weak, resulting in disease.

Diet, medicine, movement, massage, and nutrition can help to kill microbes and relieve muscle stress, but the strength of the organ and cells served by nadis blocked with fear will be difficult to recover unless we go to the root cause of the contraction and work on releasing it. If we do not do this, it is only a matter of time before the contraction will set in again. Different healing modalities aim to remove fear from the core, and this is why bodywork is such a powerful tool.

The bodywork sessions that I give are all about working with breath, body movement, sound and release. When we feel fearful, we have a tendency, whether consciously or unconsciously, to clench muscles, lock our jaws, forget to breathe and exhale, and tighten everything else we possibly can.

Individuals or couples who want to experience orgasms, especially deeper states of orgasms, also start doing the same i.e. clenching the pelvic floor and other muscles, jaws, holding things tightly, stopping their breath or making it heavier, etc. In reality, what they should be doing is exactly the opposite. Orgasm is an energy, so we should allow that energy to flow and not hold it back. We should allow the breath to flow through our body in as relaxed a way as possible: relaxing our pelvis, staying present with as many sensations as we can, breathing slowly, deeply and gently into our body, inhaling through the nose and exhaling through the mouth. As we have seen in Chapter Two, the more consciousness, presence and awareness we have of the states we are in, the easier it will be for us to make shifts from our hyper-states to relaxed states.

Fear Is Also in the Mind

Fear is not just in the physical body. It is also a product of the mind. And this is important. In fact, this is critical. Why? Because the mind also offers us a pathway to both construct and deconstruct our fears. It offers us the tools to become conscious, aware, present, and intentional about our fears. It allows us to speak our fears to another, to hold space for each other, to process fear in healthy ways, and to have empathy and compassion when we see others experiencing this emotion.

Sometimes our fears are created out of the beliefs we hold about our value as individuals, as men or women, as sexual beings, as romantic partners, etc. As you may recall from Chapter Two, we spent a good bit of time learning how social scripts (such as: *real men are tough and never show emotion*), cultural traditions (such as: *women should remain chaste before marriage*), and even the influence of other important individuals (such as: parents shaming female sexuality) can be internalised as core beliefs.

Figure 158: Fear in the mind can make us a hostage of our own selves.

In addition, we explored the role of limiting beliefs, which are those that encourage us to place limitations on ourselves, others, or our world, such as "I am never going to be loved," "Homosexuality is immoral," or "Love is always suffering." We explored how when we choose to believe in these limiting beliefs, we tend to see them as true everywhere we look, we limit ourselves in specific ways, we suppress our desires, and we may feel shame. In addition, these kinds of limiting beliefs can create the groundwork for fear to show up in our lives.

Let's look at a few examples. Someone who believes the story that "Only thin people can be attractive" is more likely to experience the fear of being rejected if they themselves do not happen to be thin. A man who believes the story that "Men are rational and women are emotional" may come to fear the emergence of emotions in himself, cutting him off from deep intimacy with another human being. A woman who believes the story "All men are sexual predators" may have a very difficult time feeling safe enough during a sexual encounter with a man to experience any pleasure at all.

Because these social scripts about gender, love, romance, and sex can play such a pivotal role in helping to construct our fears relating to sex, it is not surprising to see certain patterns emerge when it comes to women and men and the kinds of fears they experience. This is not to say these patterns are rooted in the sex of the person, but rather, that the way we come to identify with gendered stories of what it is to be a "good man" or a "good woman" creates some patterns in our fears as well. And, understanding those patterns can offer insight into common relationship dynamics, especially when those dynamics create certain common feedback loops in our relationships.

For example, her fear of abandonment makes her desperate for his attention, which triggers his fear of loss of independence. He responds with withdrawal to get some space, which further triggers her fear of abandonment, and conflict escalates out of control due to this common fear dynamic in heterosexual couples. This is not to say the roles cannot be reversed, and sometimes they are, but the former is certainly a more common pattern in my experience.

To say that the mind may create the context for fear is not to say that those fears do not still manifest in the body. They still do. No matter how big or small, no matter how deep or shallow, no matter if these fears are relating to your sexual experiences or not, the fact that you are experiencing fears that have not been released means that these fears are still existing in your body, in your psyche, in your cellular memories, and in your energy centres, whether you are aware of it or not.

In one of my bodywork sessions there was a great deal of emotional release during a session. A few days later, when the client reflected back on it, she realised she had suffered abuse during her childhood but she had completely forgotten about it for 35 years. She did not even realise that her body had been living in trauma for all of these years. After a few more sessions, not only she was able to begin releasing the memory of the abuse in her body, she also began to feel happy and jovial. Her body began to feel relaxed and calm and she experienced a full-body orgasm for the first time in her life.

Fears can be experienced as an intense physical fear of harm or a more subtle kind of "flight" from the body, or any range in between. Fear is still felt in the body, and often stored in our body tissues and energetic centres, even if it is the mind that helps us come to know certain fears through the lens of our belief system.

Avoiding Fear

Often when we are confronted with fears, we do not want to "go there," we do not want to talk about them, and we are always ready to find many sources of distraction so that we do not have to face them. The reality is that facing our fears is often an uncomfortable process. It is no surprise then that we sometimes avoid facing our fears, or indeed even refuse to acknowledge their existence, to avoid the initial discomfort. We may do this consciously or unconsciously.

However, regardless of why we refuse to face our fears, the damage is the same. While avoiding fears may be more comfortable in the short term, in the long term, unaddressed fears will manifest as blocks to our ability to maintain intimacy, follow our true desires, and from becoming the best version of ourselves more generally speaking. Thus, unaddressed and unreleased fears keep us from progress on our spiritual journey, and thus, negatively impact the spiritual body.

Fear and desire are deeply related concepts. If you are to take seriously the Principles of Desire, then it is important to recognise the role that fear can play in terms of blocking our progress towards connecting with our true desires and allowing them to be our compass in life. And, fear can create a block to true and deep intimacy in our relationships, a requirement on the Path of Amplified Orgasm. In order to clear these blockages, we must become willing to identify, acknowledge, name, and face our fears.

Fear Creates Destructive Patterns in Our Lives

When we do not face and process our fears, they become a destructive force in our lives. Often these repressed fears can influence our subconscious minds, causing us to react in ways that cause repetitive patterns that we continue to keep reliving over and over, despite the fact they are not helping us get closer to fulfilling our true desires in life, both in and out of the bedroom.

Unaddressed fear also keeps us from feeling comfortable enough with vulnerability to become fully open to connections with others. By now it should be very clear that this kind of openness, trust, and willingness to be vulnerable to the touch, emotions, and energy of another human being is required to take the journey of the Path of Amplified Orgasm.

Types of Fears Most Relevant on the Path of Amplified Orgasm

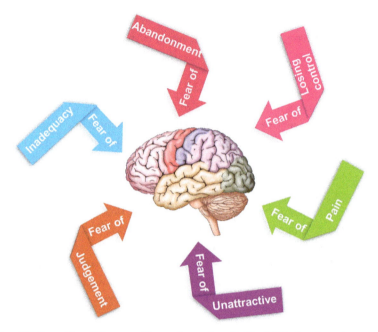

Figure 159: Types of fears. It is not possible to make an exhaustive list of all the fears that exist as every person's experiences and life path is different. Since fear often gets passed through our ancestors, we may sometimes experience fear that is not at all related to us directly. Use this as a guide to self-reflect and see what kind of fears that you identify within yourself at various times.

There are many types of fears that we can experience in our lifetime. However, for the sake of this book, we need to ask the question: what types of fears are related to the Path of Amplified Orgasm? In my experience of doing coaching, bodywork, and AOM with couples, the most common types of fears include the following general types related to love, intimacy, sex, relationships, and the body.

Fear of Lack of Attractiveness

A fear of not being attractive enough to ignite the passion of our lover is one that both men and women can experience, however, it does tend to be more common for women, likely because we place a lot of value on women's looks in our culture. These fears can be general or revolve around a specific body part or genital. Here are a few examples of what this type of fear might look like if it were to be named out loud:

- *My breasts are too small (or too big, or too droopy, or too far apart, or too....) to be sexy.*
- *My cock isn't big enough to turn a woman on.*

- *I am too chubby to be attractive to anyone.*
- *Only men with more muscles than me can attract a beautiful woman.*
- *I don't like to be touched there because it makes me feel unattractive.*
- *I will only have sex with my clothes on because being naked makes me feel too exposed and I am afraid it will be a turn-off for my lover.*
- *I worry a lot during sex with my partner that my pussy just doesn't get very lubricated now that I am post-menopausal.*

Fear of Judgement (Shame)

Ultimately, shame is the fear of not being a good person or the fear of being negatively judged by others. Often tied to social scripts that are about restricting or shaming sexuality, shame is a common fear that comes up when we are dealing with sexuality. For example, "Good girls are xyz." Or "Good Christians should only have sex to procreate." Sometimes we learn to associate certain kinds of sex acts with shame because we are told they are "not normal" by others in our lives or through cultural norms.

Shame can manifest in many ways, but often it involves blocking energetic centres as well as getting trapped in the physical body, often in the genital regions. Of course, shame can also create mental and emotional blocks on the Path of Amplified orgasm.

Some examples of shame, or the fear of not being a good person, include:

- *When I express too much pleasure during sex, it makes me feel like I might look whorish and that makes me feel ashamed.*
- *I am terrified that I might fart when my lover tries to penetrate me in the doggy style position... so I am not able to enjoy it.*
- *I am afraid that if I explore my desire to try prostate stimulation that it means I am a homosexual.*

Fear of Inadequacy

The fear that we are somehow "not enough" for our partner in some way is extremely common, both in relationships as well as during sexual encounters. Sometimes these types of fears are instilled at a young age by demanding parents who did not show their children enough love and acceptance or who were critical of every attempt the child made to please them. In other cases, we come by this fear as a result of life experiences as adults, including a particularly embarrassing moment, abuse, or trauma.

Intimacy is, at its core, the act of exposing our innermost self to another human being with the hope that we will be loved and accepted. It is therefore no surprise to find that the fear of being judged "inadequate" once we make ourselves vulnerable comes up quite often in relationships and sex where intimacy is part of the landscape.

Performance anxiety is a common specific type of fear of inadequacy. It can be made worse by repeated situations in which some aspect of our performance is critiqued or if we simply don't have the biological reaction we would like to have during sex.

Of course, we often talk about performance anxiety in relation to men and erections and/or premature ejaculation, and it is true that this is a form of how fear of inadequacy can manifest. However, less talked about is women's fear of inadequacy. For example, some women become so engaged in "acting like the porn stars" that sex can become a kind of performance for the pleasure of a man, and meanwhile, she can become more and more disconnected from her own authentic sexual pleasure as a result.

The range of fear of inadequacy is very wide and varied. Here are just a few examples to give you a clear picture of this type of fear:

- *I get so exited during sex that I cum very quickly. It is extremely embarrassing and it is such a big fear for me that I am afraid to even approach women for a date.*
- *I don't make very much money. No woman (or man) is going to want to get into a serious relationship with me.*
- *My ex once told me that my vagina didn't taste good and ever since then I have no interest in allowing a man to perform oral sex on me*
- *I am afraid that if I share my feelings with her, she will see me as weak and effeminate and lose respect for me.*

Fear of Abandonment or Loss of Self

At first glance, these two fears seem very different. But because they often operate in relationships as a kind of escalating dynamic, I have chosen to keep them together. It is important to understand that fear of abandonment is not just about physically losing a partner (that is separation, divorce, or moving out). It can also include emotional abandonment or withdrawal.

The fear of loss of self, a role often but not always played by men, is the fear that true emotional intimacy means somehow becoming reliant and/or emotionally dependent on another. It is often accompanied by related fears that he will be controlled or emotionally manipulated by her, ultimately threatening his sense of manhood.

As we have seen in one of the examples shared earlier in this chapter, this can become an extremely toxic relationship dynamic if these fears are not addressed. In addition, both can become barriers to true intimacy, and as such, represent hurdles on the Path of Amplified Orgasm. Examples include:

- *She says she wants to "talk about the relationship" but I feel like she is just trying to manipulate me with emotional blackmail to get her way.*
- *I am afraid that he will leave me if I am not thin enough (smart enough, giving enough, sacrificing enough, etc).*
- *He says he needs some space, but I am afraid he is looking for another woman to replace me.*
- *I fear giving up my independence in a committed relationship. So, I prefer to just keep things casual.*

Fear of Losing Control

Many people associate a feeling of "being in control" with safety. And, for these people, feeling out of control can feel frightening as a result. This may be on the emotional level, such as a fear of "falling in love." Or it may be on the physical level, such as the fear of letting go and relaxing during sexual experiences. Sometimes this fear can manifest in relationships as a need to exert constant control over a partner in order to feel secure in the relationship.

If left to run our lives, the fear of losing control can be extremely damaging both to our own journey of love and orgasm, as well as to those we interact with. It is also deeply tied to our spiritual body, because embracing the divine requires getting comfortable with a universe that goes on largely outside of the domain of our personal control.

For survivors of sexual trauma, PTSD symptoms often include a host of fears related to not being in control. Sometimes these fears may seem highly irrational and with no particular connection to the original trauma. However, survivors and those that love them are encouraged to be patient in the process of naming, processing, and releasing fear as part of a recovery process that has to proceed at its own pace rather than being forced.

Learning to identify this fear is critical if we are to become more able and willing to explore the unknown and grow as human beings. This kind of fear can become a major block not only to sexual energy, but the ability to grow in any area of our lives, because we can be blocked from precisely the kinds of new experiences we need to see the world in new ways.

In addition, since fulfilling our desires often points to experiences we have not yet had, this kind of fear can ultimately get in the way of achieving our desires. In fact, in my Deep Dive Desire coaching, I see the fear of losing control as one of the major hurdles to many people in the pursuit of their true desires and hence their spiritual growth.

- *I only feel comfortable in my home if things are done a certain way. If they are not that way, I get agitated and restless.*
- *I am fine to go on a long holiday, as long as I am behind the wheel of the car. I get very nervous when my partner drives.*
- *I find it difficult to relax during sex because I am afraid to "lose control."*
- *I am able to orgasm from masturbation, but I have never been able to orgasm from my partner's touch.*
- *I have a lot of fears related to the unknowns in life such as death, disease, or events that I can't control or predict. Sometimes I notice that it makes me averse to taking even small risks.*
- *My partner wants to try some new things in the bedroom, but I am afraid to try things that are outside of my comfort zone.*

Fear of Pain

Finally, we turn to the fear of pain. Notice first that of course this can include any of the layers of the body: emotional, mental, energetic, physical or spiritual. We can experience pain at all of these levels, and almost always, more than one level of the body is involved in the hurt caused in the context of sex and intimacy.

Pain from past experiences is perhaps the most common block to intimacy and becoming orgasmic. Although trauma from abuse can certainly apply here, it is not limited to that. Even a healthy relationship can include hurting each other deeply, often without even realising we are doing so.

Negative sexual experiences, even if they were consensual, can also create this fear. For example, we may come to feel that we are simply "not sexual beings" because of the poor sex we experienced in a past relationship. Or we may decide that "love is pain" after we have found ourselves in a string of painful and emotionally toxic relationships. Physically painful sex is also a way that we can come to fear pain, and as a result, become less open to exploring sexual pleasure.

- *I have had too many "failed" relationships. I am just not cut out for love.*
- *The only men I have ever loved have abused me, so I guess I deserved it. Better to just not get involved with men at all.*
- *I was cheated on and lied to by my ex. I just don't trust women anymore and I am not sure I will ever be able to again.*
- *I sometimes experience pain during orgasm. Fear of that pain happening again keeps me from fully relaxing and enjoying the experience.*
- *The closer I get to my lover, the more fear I have that he will break my heart*
- *She gets angry every time we try to have any discussion. Now I find myself afraid to even talk about things because I am afraid of getting yelled at.*

Facing and Healing Fear

Since fear lives in the emotional, mental, energetic, physical, and indeed even the spiritual bodies, the process for confronting and healing fear on the Path of Amplified Orgasm usually involves some combination of these layers of our experience as well.

Once my clients are ready to work through their fears, we make facing and healing fear the focus of our bodywork sessions. Although it can be painful, discomforting, and emotionally draining, once the release happens, then most clients report feeling happy, energised, and have a more positive perspective towards life, sex, and orgasm. Many feel as if they are reborn, their body feels light and they tend to become more sexually energised, orgasmic and are happy to have gone through this journey with me.

I believe that working through fear can happen through many sources: a trusted friend, a therapist, a spiritual leader, and of course, your romantic partner. However, because I also believe that fear can become trapped in the body and the energy centres, I do recommend that people find someone qualified in energetic and bodywork healing to work with, particularly for dealing with fears related to love, sex, and intimacy.

I can help you begin this journey of confronting, facing, and releasing your fears with the strategies below. However, please understand that while these tips are provided to be helpful, it would take an entire book devoted to the subject of releasing fear to fully cover this subject.

Start by Getting in Touch with Your Fears

If you are ready to see the value in facing and confronting your fears, the first step is simply to start identifying your fears. At first it may simply be identifying that you are reacting with fight-or-flight types of reactions, or feeling the sensation of fear in your body. But with practice, you can dive deeper into the root fears that may be triggered.

EXERCISE: Naming Fears Related to Love, Intimacy, Sex, and Orgasm

Share Your Fears with Someone You Trust

After you start to get a sense of what your fears are and are able to name them, then sharing them with a trusted friend or teacher to get some perspective can be helpful. If you feel that your relationship is strong enough and you are both good at working through fears, then taking your fears to your partner is another option.

When we share our fears with people who love and trust us, the healing process truly begins. This is particularly true if we are met with openness, empathy and compassion. If we find ourselves being met with judgement or negativity, then we can simply notice that we have chosen someone not at a place in their journey where they are ready to be helpful to us rather than internalising their judgement. In such cases, it is a sign that we need to invest energy into surrounding ourselves with more supportive, open-minded, and compassionate people. For many, this realisation is the impetus to start building a spiritual community in their lives such as joining a meditation group, volunteering in their community, taking on service responsibilities in their church, or other forms of spiritually driven fellowship.

EXERCISE: Giving and Receiving Trust

Hold Space if Someone Shares/Experiences Fear with You

When you experience your partner in a flight-or-fight reaction from fear, what is your response? Do you become fearful too, or do you provide support to your partner or/ and do you get curious to know what has triggered the fear? Is it a newly created pattern or is it something that is a reappearing of an old pattern? How do you provide support to them?

What do you do when you end up facing your own fear as a result of providing support?

If you find yourself in the position of hearing someone else's fear, try "holding space" for them to express themselves. Try to listen from a place of compassion and empathy and look for a time in your own life when you may have had a similar fear.

"Holding space" means to make room for talk as well as emotional and energetic exchange to process fear. It means listening without judgement, condemnation, or ridicule. It means not dismissing the fear as irrational, but rather probing with gentle and curious questions to help the person find the root cause of their fears.

Holding space also means not taking it personally and honestly; this is the hardest part when we are in an intimate relationship with someone. Hearing someone else name their fears so often can trigger our own fears, so there can be a tendency to react to the naming of a fear with defensiveness.

For instance, she says, "I am afraid that you don't find me attractive" can be heard by him as, "You are not doing a good enough job of making me feel sexy." Sometimes the listening party can have a fear reaction themselves in this moment, and get frustrated or even angry. If that happens, try to own it, and then move back to the original fear at face value. With practice, you can get better at hearing your lover's fears without taking it personally.

> **EXERCISE: Practise Holding Space**

Identify Limiting Beliefs and Transform them into Empowering Beliefs

If you remember, in Chapter Two, we developed the idea of limiting and empowering beliefs and how learning to identify and transform from limiting to empowering beliefs opens you up for personal growth and development in many areas of your life. And, in this chapter, we have discussed how limiting beliefs can also be a source of fear. Sometimes, preparing the ground to release fear is simply a matter of identifying the limiting beliefs that create them.

For example, take the limiting belief: *I have lost every boyfriend I have ever had, and I will lose this one too.* Notice how this limiting belief creates the context for a fear of abandonment. And, if you hold on to this belief, it will likely live in your subconscious, driving you to take action to indeed make this happen. For example, encouraging you to be clingy, emotionally demanding, or exceedingly jealous.

What if instead you prepared yourself to let go of this belief, and instead replace it with this more empowering belief: *I have learned from each of my past relationships. I do not know what the future holds and I am open to the possibility that this relationship will last.* Now your subconscious mind will be working towards helping you to continue to learn as you go, be open to change, and will allow for the possibility to emerge that you may be in a lasting relationship. It also can help to alleviate and release some of the emotional fear of abandonment that comes with the limiting belief it replaced.

EXERCISE: Limiting Beliefs that Create Fear

Identify the Regions of the Physical and Energetic Body Storing Fear

This is the part of the releasing fear journey that often takes the help of an experienced and trained bodywork coach. Just as an athlete who is injured will visit medical doctors and trained physical therapists, emotional healing in the body is complex work that does require expertise and attentiveness to issues of safety that can arise as we begin the journey of facing fears which have become stored in the body.

Remember: Your Journey Is Unique

Please avoid comparing yourself to others or your partner. Sharing about your experiences, journey, and emotion, is encouraged with people you can trust/feel safe with and your partner. But try not to compare yourself to others in the process. We all have our own experiences, conditioning, desires, upbringing, and uniqueness, and we also have our own energies, sensitivities, and subtleties, thus making our Path of Amplified Orgasm unique.

Desire, Fear, and Orgasm

Desire and fear are interrelated concepts that are part of our spiritual body, regardless of which religion, faith, or practice we individually ascribe to in our spiritual journeys. Desire is the body's way of telling us what we need to do to fulfil our life's purpose. However, unless we learn how to connect with our true desires, we can easily be distracted into putting energy into lesser (and sometimes even damaging) wants, cravings, compulsions, impulses, and compensatory desires.

As long as we are connected with our true desires, both in and out of the bedroom, then we can follow these desires without shame. We can learn to let them guide us on our life journey, where we can achieve our true purpose and experience the deepest levels of joy, satisfaction, spiritual enlightenment, and indeed, in the sexual realm, we may know amplified orgasm.

Symbols	Energy centre	Sanskrit Word	Colour Vibration	Location	Parts of the body	Emotional Aspects	Affirmations
	Crown energy centre	Sahasrara	Violet	Top of head	Upper skull, brain, pineal gland	Enlightenment, unity, wholeness (inner and outer beauty), connection with spirituality, pure bliss	I understand divinity of life I live in present moment I am one with the universe
	Third Eye energy centre	Ajna	Indigo	Between eye brows	Eyes, ears, base of skull, linked to pituitary gland, brain, pineal gland	Intuition, insight, realisation, understanding, wisdom, imagination	I see the world beyond myself I trust my intuition I see and experience greatness in my life
	Throat energy centre	Vishuddha	Blue	Throat	Throat, neck, nose, mouth, teeth, jaw	Self-expression, communication, inspiration, speaking truth	I speak my truth I express my feelings and emotions eloquently I express myself through creativity, art & other forms that inspire me
	Heart energy centre	Anahata	Green	Centre of chest	Heart, chest, arms, lungs, hands, shoulders, immune system	Love, compassion, forgiveness, inner joy	I love and accept myself I love everything around me I love my inner child
	Solar Plexus energy centre	Manipura	Yellow	Above navel	Small intestine, skin, digestive system (liver, stomach)	Self-respect, self-confidence, self-worth, personal identity, ego	I do what I love I choose healthy and positive relationships I devote myself for my personal growth
	Sacral energy centre	Svadhisthana	Orange	Below navel in pelvic area	Sexual organs, reproductive system, kidneys, bladder	Feelings, creativity, self-love, self-awareness, abundance, well-being, pleasure	I feel passionate I feel pleasure and abundance I feel nourished
	Root energy centre	Muladhara	Red	Base of Spine at the perineum	Legs, feet, spine, large intestine, rectum, prostrate	Trust, grounded, survival instincts (financial, food, shelter, fear etc), security, achievement	I am grounded I am safe and secure I am able to trust myself

Table: Types of desires and fears at different energy centres.

224

Fear can become a major hurdle to pursuing our true and deepest desires. Manifesting in many forms, and arising from many causes, fear must be identified, named, confronted, and released. If we try to avoid fear, while it may save us some pain in the short term, it will only lead to damaging patterns in our lives and relationships.

Fear is also stored in the body, creating energetic and emotional blockages that keep us from fully exploring intimacy, sexual pleasure, and indeed, orgasm. Although I have offered some starting points to begin to address fear in your life, as well as some practical exercises, I encourage you to find resources such as a certified bodyworker to address fear in the body, particularly for those who have experienced sexual trauma.

Now, at long last, it is time to turn our attention to the topic of orgasm directly. In the next chapter, we will explore this amazing experience of connection that has the capacity to energise all of our energy centres at once while aligning us completely with our partner across all layers of the body simultaneously. Yes, it has been a bit of a long road to get here, but next we turn to orgasm.

Chapter Six Summary:

- Desire arises from deep within us and guides us to our larger life's purpose. As such, desire is related to our spiritual body, regardless of which religion or faith we subscribe to on our spiritual journey.

- It is important to understand the difference between desire and other distractions from our life's purpose in the form of wants, wishes, impulses, compulsions, craving, and greed.

- The modern world is driven by encouraging compensatory desires through advertising and consumerism. Filling these desires only satisfies us for a short time, but ultimately leave us feeling empty and wanting more. Getting pulled by compensatory desires can derail us from putting energy into our true desires.

- Shame, often instilled by parents, cultural traditions, or societal norms, can get in the way of achieving our desires or even feeling deserving of having our desires fulfilled

- Repressing desire does not make them go away, it only damages our spirit by keeping us from our true life's purpose.

- The Principles of Desire can help act as a guide to make sure you are on track with identifying, connecting with, and being guided by your true desires.

- Fear can live in the emotional, mental, energetic, physical, and/or spiritual layers of the body.

- Fear often happens in direct relation to desire, and it operates to keep us from achieving our desires by blocking our path towards fulfilling them.

- Fear may be caused by past experiences, may be passed on through cultural norms, may arise from certain limiting beliefs, and it even has some genetic components.

- Fear may induce a flight, fight, or excitement response depending on the context and our individual life history.

- Avoiding dealing with or even naming fear is a common impulse because working through fear is a painful process. However, facing fear is the only way to address the root cause and release it from the body. Avoiding fear creates destructive patterns in our lives.

- There are many different kinds of fear relating to sex and orgasm because both require intimacy, exposing us to vulnerability where we can be deeply hurt if judged, betrayed, or abused.

- Fear is stored in the body and creates energetic and emotional blockages that must be released to fully experience amplified orgasm. Working with an experienced and certified bodyworker is a good way to approach this process.

ORGASM

Orgasm happens both from within us and from the connection between us. Your partner doesn't give you orgasm. He/She creates the space for it to happen.
Michael Charming

Men often believe they either know everything about female sexuality or they think it is a complete mystery. Women, on the other hand, may understand their own sexuality but often find it difficult to communicate, or have a hard time exploring their sexuality with male partners in the ways they would like to. As a result, female orgasms continue to remain a puzzle for many men and male orgasm remains confined to ejaculation.

In this chapter, I hope to change that. Now that we have the language to understand orgasm as a layered body experience, we can begin to get specific about how to cultivate sexual pleasure as a couple, grow passion and arousal during our sexual experiences, and come to know what it means to have amplified orgasm.

This chapter will explore several key ideas on the Path of Amplified Orgasm. First, we will ponder the orgasm gap, that is, the differential experiences of orgasm between women and men. Then, we will explore the concept of sexual polarity, and the role it plays in terms of both relationship and sexual dynamics in couples. And, we will look at the various models of the sexual response cycles that have been developed over the last 50 years among sex researchers.

Finally, we will open up the notion of orgasm, exploring several different kinds of orgasm that you may not be aware of. Suffice to say, this is quite an exciting chapter!

The Orgasm Gap

The orgasm gap refers to the gap that exists between women and men and their experience of orgasm. It refers to the fact that in heterosexual encounters, straight women have less orgasms than men, lower in fact than lesbian women, gay men, and bisexual women and men. Female orgasm isn't so elusive when women are alone or when women are together.

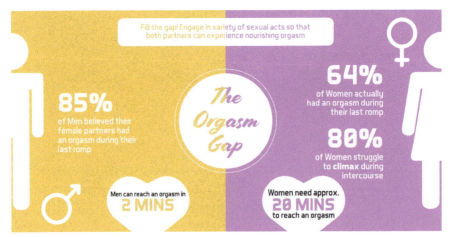

Figure 160: The Orgasm Gap

One study found that there was an orgasm gap of 52%, while another found that the orgasm gap tends to be higher in hook-up and casual sex than when sex happens in an intimate relationship.[77] One survey found that women tend to have orgasm 65% of the time while men experience orgasm 85% of the time, even though 95% of women reach orgasm easily and within minutes of sexual stimulation.[78] It was also found that women tend to have more orgasm when they masturbate than when they have sex with a partner. In the case of men, the orgasm rate doesn't tend to vary in relation to sexual orientation, but lesbian women report more orgasms (86% of the time) with their partners than straight women (65% of the time).[79,80]

What are the causes of this gap? One difference is that when men experience ejaculation, it is not a hidden experience. Both partners can witness the event. On the other hand, her orgasm is hidden as only the person who is experiencing it can feel whether she has had an orgasm or not. There is no physical, visible proof of female orgasm. This is further complicated by the fact that both women and men fake orgasm (although it is at least twice as common among women).[81]

Another difference between male and female stimulation that is often misunderstood is the role of the clitoris in female orgasm. Clitoral stimulation is often considered to be foreplay, something to get her in the mood, rather than central to the path to orgasm for women. In fact, one study found as many as 99% stimulate their clitoris when masturbating. A survey found that 78% of women find that their problems during heterosexual sex come down to inadequate clitoral stimulation.[78,82]

There is a lack of education around the female anatomy. Most men struggle to name and identify female genital parts, especially the clitoris. I have seen this over and over in coaching sessions. Men who have been in a relationship believe that they know

228

it all about their partner's anatomy, but the reactions that I see on their partner's faces tell me a different story!

In addition, the role of penetration in female orgasm is overemphasised across the board. Sex and intercourse are used interchangeably. Media, porn, and images create the false perception that women can have mind-blowing orgasms through intercourse only – actually a rare phenomenon.

Cultural expectations placed on women and men also play a role in the orgasm gap. For example, many women aren't comfortable about their own bodies or stay disconnected from their genitals after being shamed about masturbation or sexuality during adolescence. Many experience difficulty staying fully present during sex as a result. Some experience anxiety around orgasm due to past experiences of not being able to achieve it and fear of disappointing or hurting the feelings of their partner. These fears are then amplified by mainstream media and pornography, which often represent unrealistic images of female orgasm. In addition, since many men approach female orgasm as the same as male orgasm, it can create an interpersonal dimension to this pressure to orgasm with each and every sexual experience.

On the other hand, cultural stories about sex tend to reify male entitlement to sexual pleasure, the objectification of women's bodies for this purpose, and encourage us to see men as sexually aggressive and women as sexually passive. Even many women come to see their role in sex as being the "object" of the experience, rather than realising they are also a subject of the sexual encounter, entitled to their own experiences of pleasure and orgasm. These are not biological realities, they are simply cultural beliefs that we can sometimes manifest because of our belief in them as "natural." It truly demonstrates the power of the mind, culture, and belief, in the construction of our experience of sex!

Although the orgasm gap is often understood in terms of less orgasm for women in straight partnerships, we might also consider that men too have been negatively affected by cultural constructions of sexuality.

For example, how many men experience performance anxiety as a result of pressure put on them to be the sole creator of female orgasm? How many men have settled for climax (the mere act of ejaculation) as the be-all and end-all of the sexual experience? How many men have closed the sexual experience to just physical pleasure, rather than learning to experience the full depth of an emotional and energetic union between two people? We may never know the extent to which men have also been damaged by narrow cultural notions of sex because it can't simply be counted and compared with statistics. However, in my experience, it deserves mention as another aspect of the orgasm gap that is often overlooked.

EXERCISE: Exploring Your Own Orgasm Gap

Closing the Gap

To close the gap, we need to work towards resolving all of the above factors that cause the gap in the first place. This requires change at the individual levels, as well as a larger cultural shift in terms of our attitudes and knowledge of sexuality and orgasm.

For example, women may need to become aware of what gives them pleasure and then develop a practice of asking for what they want, how they want it, and when they want it. Men can learn more about the female anatomy, and the role the clitoris and G-spot play in female orgasm. Both women and men can work at their own emotional, psychological, and physiological issues to create room for sexual experiences that allow for exploration without judgement or the preconceived notions carried by harmful cultural misconceptions of sex and gender.

On a cultural level, sex education needs to include an emphasis on the pleasure of sex for both women and men, including its role in our mental and emotional well-being. Culturally supported sexism which condones the harsh treatment of women, or creates the context for a sense of male entitlement to pleasure at the cost of female shame surrounding sexual pleasure, needs to change. The media could do better at representing sexuality in ways that support women's entitlement to pleasure, and expanding male sexuality to include more emotional complexity, for example.

However, perhaps the most important thing we can do as individuals to close the orgasm gap is to learn more about what is happening during this experience. As we learn more, many of us will realise that it is not only women who can experience more orgasm and pleasure, but that many men have also been cut off from a deeper and more intense and fulfilling experience of orgasm through these same cultural filters. With that in mind, let's bring an open mind to learning more about what is happening during this wonderful experience.

Sexual Polarity: Masculine and Feminine Energies

Have you ever questioned why a relationship has become stale, lost its spark, became disharmonised, and the sexual connection died out over time? This can happen even if the lovers once experienced lots of spark, chemistry, and attraction in the beginning. Even an "over-the-moon" sexual connection can fade in time.

No matter how strong a love or friendship might be between the couple, the sexual connection often fades. In a lot of coaching with clients, the couple often say that their preferences have changed, that their relationships have grown up to emphasise friendship or companionship, and sex isn't really important anymore. When I hear this common story, I ask them individually if they would like to have more sex in life, and the typical answer is yes.

The magnetic field lines above the bar magnet

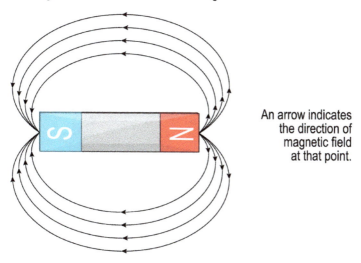

An arrow indicates
the direction of
magnetic field
at that point.

Bar magnet

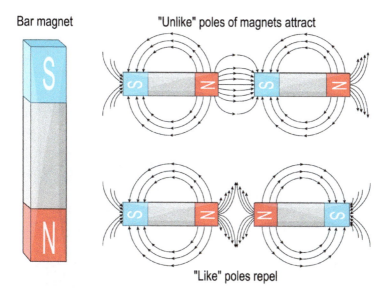

"Unlike" poles of magnets attract

"Like" poles repel

Figure 161: Magnetic fields showing energy polarities

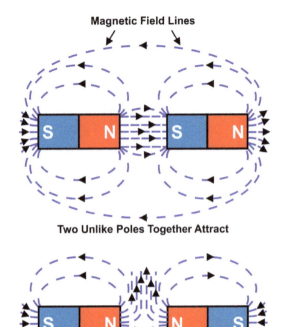

Magnetic Field Lines

S N S N

Two Unlike Poles Together Attract

S N N S

Two Like Poles Together Repel

Figure 162: Magnetic field lines: Opposites attract, the same pole repels (at the energetic level)

Figure 163: Energy field of the Earth

In my view, it is not that the desire for sex or the sexual energy itself gets diminished, but that couples often end up disconnecting themselves from sex because, deep down in their subconsciousness, they have decided they can't have engaging sex with their partner so there is no point in thinking about it. So, the question is, why does that spark, that sexual tension and attraction, that initial sexual chemistry, seem to die out? To answer this question, we must understand the principle of sexual polarity and depolarisation.

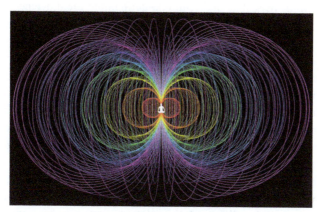

Figure 164: Energy fields of the human once the energy centres are fully awakened and connection with the subtle bodies is aligned

Sexual Polarity

Sexual polarity (a.k.a. sexual attraction) is a concept that comes from ancient Tantric principles and is often used to denote physical chemistry or the magnetic pull and the overwhelming response we feel at an energetic level when we meet someone with an energy that opposes our own. Tantra is a holistic approach to life and spirituality in which energy and consciousness are two sides of the same coin, unlike other spiritual traditions which pay little attention to, or even condemn, sexuality. This holistic view states that sexual energy flows between two opposite sexual poles, and the flow of this energy between two poles is called *polarity*.

Consider the north and south poles of the earth, which create huge dynamism and magnetism on our planet. Or, think of the positive and negative poles of an electrical outlet or a battery, which generate an electrical flow. Sexual polarity works in a similar way, creating the charge that stimulates the flow of sexual energy, arousal, and attraction.

The principle further states that the higher the difference in electric current, the stronger the intensity of the current. In addition, you can think of the power of opposing polarity that makes up the electrons and protons found in atoms, creating the extremely powerful bond at the heart of matter itself!

These two poles, which are key in transforming sexual energy, are also known as negative and positive, sun and moon, yin and yang, lunar and solar, masculine and feminine. (In Part II we will also explore other kinds of polarity that have emerged in role play and consensual kinky sex practices that go beyond sexual polarity, and the role they can play in fantasy, sexual attraction, arousal, and orgasm.) In terms of sexual polarity, the words masculine and feminine don't imply the difference in men and women due to biological sex differences, but are instead referring to different kinds of energies. Both biological men and biological women can be feminine or masculine. In fact, each human being has both masculine and feminine inside them.

Polarity is created in three main ways:

Biologically, which is based on anatomy, genetics, and hormone levels and categorised as male (men), female (women), and intersex (usually combinations of both male and female biological markers). This gender categorisation doesn't have to relate to energetic sexual polarity. Many researchers now understand biological sex as a spectrum, rather than a binary.[83]

Identity, which is based on beliefs, socially and culturally constructed concepts, and stereotypes which we often participate in to define and clarify our gender to others. For example, culturally we reinforce the notion that "real men don't cry" and, as a result, many men come to understand their own manhood as requiring emotional stoicism. While this may offer a social advantage in terms of being read by others as more "rational," it also comes at a cost: Many men are cut off from their full emotional life as a result.

On the other hand, gender stories about femininity encourage women to identify with putting other people's needs first. When it comes to sexual pleasure, she might be more willing to sacrifice her own experience of pleasure and prioritise his. This identity categorisation also doesn't have to relate to energetic sexual polarity, but the gender stories we choose to identify with and live out can influence our sexual polarity by making it feel more comfortable to embody either energy type.

Energetically, sexual polarity which is based on magnetic attraction created by two opposite polarising energies is categorised as masculine, feminine, or neutral. Both biological males and females have masculine and feminine energetic polarity within them. Moreover, this polarity can change and shift over time, through intentional changes or subconscious shifts as a result of sexual or other life experiences. The theory of energy polarity has been articulated in many traditions including tantra, yoga, and Chinese philosophy (where it is called Yin and Yang).

Figure 165-166: Yin and Yang polarity (left), the energy polarity between women and men (right)

Learning more about your own sexual polarity isn't about finding what is "right" or "wrong." It is simply about observing where you and your partner are right now, and learning that we all have the capacity to become aware of and influence our polarity to create the kind of intense and magnetic attraction we have lost. It is not about "recreating" the place where we were, either. Learning to be aware of and intentional about polarity offers infinite ways to explore new and exciting energy configurations that offer the opportunity to explore each other through deeply satisfying and, yes, richly orgasmic experiences.

What is important is to know which kind of energy you are exhibiting at a specific time, especially when you are connected with your partner, so that both of you can work on creating more polarity (opposing energies) between each other, which will help in amplifying the orgasm for the individuals and as a couple. Creating polarity will help you towards feeling as one, creating a whole, and will pave the way to profound orgasms.

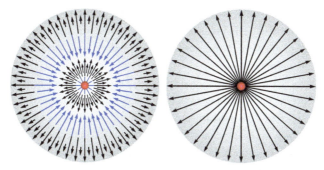

Figure 167: Electric flux around a point charge which shows the force that other charged particles would feel when placed near the particle that is creating the electric field. If the field charge is positive, field lines will point away from it and if the charge is positive, field lines will point towards it. The same concept applies to masculine and feminine energies and often we are not conscious about why we feel attracted or repelled by the other person. When our consciousness rises, we can change this attraction and repulsion consciously.

Masculine energy is like fire, and feminine energy is like water, so when masculine makes love to feminine, a profound orgasm emerges. When they meet, these two energies create something new and unique as a result of reuniting these great polar forces. The feeling of the physical body disappears, energy centres get activated and become harmonised, and both partners merge into one ball of massive energy release, resulting in profound orgasm at the auras and energy centres, including sublimation of the energy at the crown energy centre.

Sexual polarity can be felt but not seen, similar to magnetism. Sexual polarity gets dampened in long-term relationships primarily due to lack of awareness about this energetic polarity dynamic, how to cultivate it, how to switch it on and keep it turned on.

Figure 168-169: Sexual attraction between couples felt at the physical level

Are you having sex but it feels far from sexy?

Do you assume it is your fault or your partner's?

Do you try to have sex more often to remediate the other issues in relationship?

Do you feel that in spite of trying new positions, changing the frequency of sex, adjusting the intensity of sexual penetration, etc. that the sex still doesn't feel good?

Have you simply become buddies who rub genitals in bed, but miss the electricity and the spark between each other?

Has the sexual desire faded with your partner and started pushing you apart?

Have your ever experienced your relationship getting to a place where the teasing, smirks, and smiles that you used to find attractive in your partner have now started annoying you to such an extent that there are barely even any kisses offered?

If the answer to any of the above questions is yes, then by now you know that there are many subtle things playing under the radar which are not letting you have what you desire.

It is important to note that the principles of polarity exist in all relationships between people, not just those of a sexual nature. For example with friends, or in the workplace, we wouldn't want to be disrupted by lot of erotic energy moving back and forth among us, so we tend to naturally harmonise masculine and feminine energy for smooth relationships of all kinds. In fact, even when we are with our partner but outside of the bedroom, we seek to harmonise our energy rather than create polarity, and this is just fine.

However, if we spend too much time in harmony, and forget how to create polarity, we can see that a relationship can easily move in the direction of "companionship" and away from the dynamic play of polarity that we see among deeply passionate lovers.

It is interesting to notice too that there are situations outside of sexual experiences where creating energy polarity can be extremely helpful. High levels of polarity, for example, can be useful if we want to create something (sexual energy is creative energy), and not everything needs to end up in bed. So, strong polarity in such cases is great as it increases the energy flow and abundance of new ideas.

Masculine and Feminine Energy

In order to make the most of sexual polarity in our sexual encounters and in our relationships, it is important to be able to recognise this energy as it moves through our own bodies, as well as in our partner. Remember that no one person has just one or the other energy. Rather, different moments in our lives, different social contexts, and different triggers may cause one or the other type of energy to be our "go to." That being said, as we learn to identify the type of energy moving through us, we can become more intentional about choosing to find a balance which is healthy and conducive to strong connections and sexual resonance.

Figure 170: The Ardhanarishvara is form of Hindu dieties consisting of Shiva and Parvati which represents Masculine and Feminine energies of the Universe which is also present in each human being. It is shown as half-male and half-female with equal split in the middle.

Growing up in India, I often used to see this image of Lord Shiva and Goddess Parvati joined together, but I never understood what it actually meant. Sadly, there is no education and awareness around this topic in our country either. People often end up bowing and praying to them, considering themselves the devotee of Shiva and Parvati, but not really knowing what this image of them joined together means and signifies for each of us.

237

Characteristics of Masculine Energy (Yin)

Masculine energy is hot, strong, rigid, directional, linear, steady, focused, constant, dense, assertive, logical, decisive, and purpose-driven. Everyone has experienced this energy flowing through their bodies. Think back to a time when you were working on a project that had your complete attention. It may have been competing in a sports event, studying for a major exam in college, or pushing yourself to achieve something great. During this time you were driven by a clear sense of purpose, you knew exactly what to do next, you brought your strong will to push through obstacles in your path, and you successfully set goals and accomplished your ultimate achievement in the end. This is what masculine energy feels like, and as you can see, when properly harnessed, masculine energy is necessary and serves a great purpose in our lives.

Although it can help us accomplish great things, both as individuals and as a society, masculine energy can also become a destructive force. Sometimes characterised as "immature" masculine energy, in other places characterised as "out of balance," we can recognise this unhealthy force by its tell-tale signs: We become overly driven to the point of obsession, lose touch with our emotional reality and the feelings of those around us, selfish, addicted, stubborn, physically or sexually abusive, controlling, ego-centric, or too attached to material goods and status. On a social level, the constant war and environmental destruction that we see on a global scale are indications that our combined human energy field has lost balance towards this unhealthy masculine (Yin) energy.

Characteristics of Feminine Energy (Yang)

Feminine energy is cool, soft, flowing, fluid, yielding, surrounding, receptive, nurturing, wise, intuitive, emotional, supportive, and non-linear. Again, we have all felt feminine energy before. Think back to a time when you were learning something new and you could feel your perception of the world expanding as you became receptive to new ideas. Or, remember a time when you felt the emotion of love coursing through your body, and imagined wrapping that love around your partner. Likewise, that deep inner feeling of confidence that you have surely experienced at one time or another is that feeling of feminine energy coursing through your energy centres. Make no mistake! Feminine energy is just as powerful and critical to our experience as human beings.

However, like the Yin energy, Yang energy can become a destructive and unhealthy force if allowed to run rampant and out of balance. Immature feminine energy manifests when we are indecisive, overly-critical, manipulative, desperate, insecure, dependent in our relationships, needy, jealous, and verbally or emotionally abusive. On a social scale, we can see the development of lifestyle diseases such as obesity and heart disease as a manifestation of unbalanced feminine energy in our societies. Our modern way of living has focused on transactional relationships, leaving us constantly hungry and needy, a hole many people try to fill with unhealthy foods and addictive substances which abound in our world. These "fillers" never actually fill the hole which, at its root, is about the disconnection from each other at a fundamental energetic level.

EXERCISE: Identifying Masculine and Feminine Energy

Sexual Polarity in Relationships

Let's now take what we have learned about sexual energy (known as masculine/feminine, or Yin/Yang) and see how it manifests in our relationships. The feminine offers nurturing in both healthy and unhealthy ways (again, sometimes called mature/immature or balanced/imbalanced). Actions of love, affectionate kisses, soft touch, emotional support and guidance are all examples of the benefits that mature feminine energy bring to a relationship. However, immature feminine energy manifests in a negative way by questioning our partner's way of working or getting frustrated when they are lost, ridiculing their goals and dreams, or manipulating with deceit or seduction. Co-dependency is another example of how relationships can become toxic as a result of immature feminine energy running rampant.

Meanwhile, healthy masculine energy is also important to healthy relationships. It brings the kind of focus needed for problem-solving, the drive needed to secure the resources a couple needs to thrive, and the power to be analytical and strategic in times of crisis. Of course, if it becomes out of balance or if it is immature, this masculine energy can create a great deal of conflict, a loss of touch with the emotional and spiritual aspects of the partnership, and become obsessed with externals such as money, status, and accomplishment at the cost of the vital connection and intimacy of the partnership.

It is also important to understand that energy is dynamic in a relationship. The more stable, soft, relaxed, receptive, and centred masculine energy is, the more it will create trust for the feminine to come out and play together with the masculine. Hesitant, weak, passive, unclear, abusive or tensed masculine energy will cause the feminine to contract, shut down, and remain hidden.

Perhaps you are familiar with what this may look like in a relationship. For example, if a man is relaxed and is willing to listen to what his partner has to say, irrespective of whether what she is saying makes rational sense or not, it allows women to connect with her partner even more. But if the man starts quarrelling, trying to prove himself to be right, justifying himself, or becoming fixated on "fixing" the problem, then the woman may often either end up fighting back (conflict) or shut down completely (disconnection). Depending on the context of the communication, what she is desiring in her feminine energy is to be listened to and not fixed.

Many men might have also undergone this experience when all they are desiring is for their partner to listen and empathise, to be strong so that they can let their guard down and feel protected and safe, rather than to be focused on "fixing" him. When that happens, men are speaking from the place of their feminine energy, and at that time if a woman is able to switch to a healthy masculine energy, and hold the space for his feminine side to come out, it will foster a great connection between the two.

Depolarisation in Relationships and Sex

Remember the main question we asked at the beginning of this chapter? Why is it that so many relationships seem to experience a dampening effect on passion over time? Now we have the building blocks in place to answer this question!

As we have seen in Chapter Three, we as human beings have our own energetic bodies and when couples spend time together, the energetic bodies start mixing just like hot and cold water combine to create lukewarm water. For example, both people start picking up each other's behaviours, ways of talking, and habits. On an energetic level, their bodies start merging and becoming harmonised.

Let's think back to what we have learned in previous chapters about the brain, neural pathways, habits, sensitive spots, and emotional states. As couples learn to "get along" and have harmony in their daily lives, on an energetic level, they are practising energy harmony. Just like a well-formed habit, the more they exist in this energetic state, the easier it becomes to find it and the more powerful the neural superhighways associated with these energetic and emotional states. It may even become difficult to access a different way of engaging with each other, that is, with energetic polarity.

Depolarisation occurs when partners no longer have the play of masculine and feminine energies between them i.e. both partners are channelling the same type of energy, which causes the relationship to become stale or unbalanced. In other cases, depolarisation can occur when the opposing force of one pole doesn't match the similar force from another pole, as is often the case when high levels of conflict have caused both partners to "shut down" and avoid intimacy altogether. This is why the concept of polarity becomes all the more important in understanding how our masculine and feminine energies contribute towards orgasmic amplification or de-amplification.

Now, harmony is not necessarily a bad thing! After all, that is what we all want in a sustainable relationship. However, what works to keep the peace and build a beautiful friendship that is relaxed and easy going may work against the very tension we need to have a strong magnetic sexual attraction. From a sexual point of view, what we need is to be able to create opposing poles to be able to continue attracting each other. Luckily, we are not stuck choosing one or the other, harmony or polarity, we can have both! And, we can learn to become aware and intentional about adapting our energetic state to the situation so that we can have harmony during our daily routine, and passionate sex charged with intense polarity in the bedroom.

Figure 171: Women and men interacting with each other in their energy fields

In order to continue to create strong polarity forces, we need to develop awareness that it exists within each of us and between us, we need to cultivate less reactivity and more receptivity, and we must learn to intentionally navigate between the two forces.

What does this look like in practice? Imagine a man and a woman arguing about finances. He wants to buy a new car, and she wants to buy a new roof for their house. Both are using rational arguments to support their case, and both are goal-driven, fixed, and clear about their positions. As the argument progresses, neither will yield. They stop hearing the other, only making the same point from their side of the argument over and over. In this case, both the woman and the man are embodying their masculine energy, and the result, as we might expect, is conflict, as these two similar energy forces repel each other.

In order to come to a place of harmony and decrease the conflict, they will both need to come to a more balanced energy that allows them to see with empathy, compassion, and work towards a compromise (from their feminine energy). As their energy becomes less polarised and more balanced, they can find peace and harmony. So, depolarisation does have a time and a place, and when it comes to resolving conflict, it can be a very effective tool.

When couples get good at this kind of depolarised harmony, however, over time they can default to this more depolarised way of being. And, as you might imagine, since polarisation is needed for that sexual charge, it can lead to more of a companionship model of a relationship rather than one of passionate lovers.

The solution to this common problem of depolarisation is to become aware that embodying polarised (strongly feminine vs strongly masculine) types of energy is something we can become intentional about in terms of our sexual lives. In the case of mind blowing sex, polarisation is almost always necessary. The couple can learn to connect with polarised energy, which may even change between the partners as a sexual encounter unfolds, as a means to drive passion, arousal, and the amplification of sexual pleasure and orgasm.

The other alternative is that both operate from opposite energies on a day-to-day basis which brings turn-on, spark, and aliveness in the relationship. To do this, however, each partner needs awareness to see when this opposite polarisation is tending to result in conflict, and adjust accordingly. In order for this to be harmonious in a given situation, awareness of when one's partner's energy feels like it is coming strongly at them is the first step. They need to then voice this out and bring it to the attention of their partner in terms of the impact their energy is creating. In this way, both partners can dilate their energy enough so that it continues to keep the spark and attraction but doesn't result in conflict, and neither does it become harmonious enough that it ends up resulting in depolarisation.

In such a situation, the one with feminine energy can offer love, compassion, tenderness and support for the masculine, allowing the masculine partner to lead. Feminine energy stores wisdom, intuition, and creativity, and the person exhibiting this energy should use these traits to sense when her support would be beneficial. While masculine energy should sense when the feminine needs safety and courage and should exhibit such qualities to the feminine so that the feminine can feel safe and come out. The roles of each gender will change and both partners would need to be aware of when this is happening.

The more partners allow these roles to be changed automatically, offering less resistance to such change, the more fun, playful, sparkful, and turned-on the relationship will be. As we have seen, the nature of energy is to move. The more one partner tends to hold onto one particular type of energy, the less it will create a playground for the couple to explore the dance of sexual polarisation. Each will feel less invited to come and play at an energetic level. Over time, this will kill the spark in a relationship, because the partner who feels his/her energy is not allowed to be interchanged will start holding back.

When the masculine partner is leading, instead of questioning his ability to lead and to avoid the collapse of polarity, the feminine partner should be there to offer support. If she is offering love and tenderness, he should be able to be open to receiving this offering of love, rather than resisting it. This will create a much better flow between these two people.

On the other hand, our feminine energy also stores our wisdom and intuition. Therefore, she must sense that the masculine who is leading is trustworthy and capable enough to be able to lead. If not, she can either let him go, switch to a masculine energy, or stay in feminine energy and express how she is feeling, for example:

- *I'm feeling scared or anxious with the way you are leading.*
- *Let me know if you need help, love, and support.*
- *I feel confused as I am not sure if we are going the right way.*

As a masculine in the second instance, the best orientation would be to see whether the feminine is capable of giving love in the first place, because if she isn't then she would need to be able to get filled up first with love before giving love out further. The feminine, in this instance, can say:

- *I don't feel loved.*
- *I need more than what I am being offered to truly feel loved.*
- *I'm not open enough to be able to receive love at the moment.*

Our ability to either have a deeper understanding of where each partner is coming from and to be able to stay in balance will avoid collapse and conflict and will instead help in moving these energies upwards.

Energy Polarity and Orgasm

In order to amplify one's own orgasm and that of their partners, the three most important tasks that every individual needs to focus on are:

1. To become able to learn how to find a balance between one's masculine and feminine energies and knowing when each type of energy is most helpful in a given situation.

2. To become able to learn how to navigate within one's masculine and feminine so that, with profound awareness, one has the option to choose from either rather than being controlled by external or subconscious forces.

3. To become responsive to the energy of one's partner to create sexual polarity when it is helpful to do so, such as during sexual experiences.

In order to avoid collapse, it is important for us to be able to shift our attention and intention immediately. However, we can only do that when we have the awareness of what is happening in the moment. (Reminder: I have used male/female pronouns for the sake of making it easier to communicate these ideas, but this is not intended to imply that only men embody masculine energy, or vice versa.)

If a masculine finds that a feminine partner is not able to relax into her feminine due to insecurity, then instead of questioning her reasoning, the masculine can ask if there is anything he can do to make her feel relaxed. The feminine force can be wild, chaotic, and destructive. A masculine needs to be able to learn how to embrace this force and provide direction. The skill of a masculine here would be to be able to resonate with feminine energy first before sensing which direction they should be going together rather than coming up with a predetermined sense of direction. Only then will the feminine feel heard and supported. Only then will she be able to trust and surrender more into the masculine.

The feminine aspect needs to learn to not be able to shrink when faced with the strong and powerful presence of the masculine, but instead remember that he is there to offer support, protection, and help. She should allow the masculine force to come towards her rather than stopping the energy from entering altogether. The masculine skill here would be to sense the force with which he is coming at his partner and the feminine skill here would be to immediately ask for adjustment or offer adjustment if she feels the force is too much, or else it will result in the collapse of the feminine energy. However, what needs to be noted here is that it is masculine who would be holding the space for both feminine and masculine to grow together because for her to experience deeper states of orgasm, she will need to be able to let go of all control. In other words, the feminine orgasmic state is one of surrender. Note that both women and men can experience this type of orgasmic experience.

For higher states of orgasm at an energetic level, the greater the polarity, the stronger would be the energetic circulation. It is to be noted that at an energetic level, the reasoning of mind is not important because energy is felt through precognitive senses. Consider for a moment the taste of food. You do not need to analyse it with your mind or logic to know when it tastes good, and when it tastes "off." Sensing and tuning into energy flow is similar, particularly with practice.

I was once in a relationship with someone which, if I were to rationalise the reasons of being in the relationship, it would not make sense at all. We were completely opposite from each other in every aspect one can think of: age, life experiences, hobbies, behaviour, desires, life passions and goals, our personality (one was an introvert and the other an extrovert). But we still ended up being together and, for me, that was one of the best relationships I've had.

Did we have arguments? Yes indeed, plenty! Did we decide to break-up several times? Yes indeed, I even lost count. But we still continued to stay together because there was something between us that kept bringing us back. It was only when I started exploring the concept of polarity, that our relationship made sense. The energetic and opposing forces of polarity were so strong that we kept coming back and we both acknowledged that it was our desire to grow together and as individuals and that being in this relationship was the best way to do so.

I grew and expanded a great deal on the sexual level due to that relationship, even though our sexual desires, fantasies, and experiences were completely opposite to each other. The more I focused on the energetic interplay in our relationship, the more I allowed that felt sense to emerge from my body, the more my mind's rationalisation and chatter became quiet, and the more I cherished the beauty and teachings that our relationship had to offer.

Masculine and Feminine Orgasm

This is one of my favourite topics. Now that you have understood the masculine and feminine above, let's look at the masculine and feminine orgasm and how the masculine and feminine energies play in either amplifying the orgasm or in collapsing it. I often ask my students in workshops and classes: "What do masculine and feminine orgasms look like if you were to draw it on a piece of paper?" Some get stuck, some get confused, some look at me in bewilderment, some get shocked at my question, and many come up with a whole lot of answers.

In my view, this is what the masculine and feminine orgasm actually look like.

Diagram One

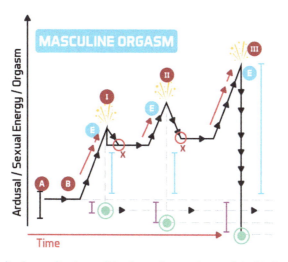

Figure 172: Masculine Orgasm denoting qualities of masculine sexual energy. Point A is the starting point. Point E is the point of no-return, i.e. ejaculation. Every time a point E is passed without climax, the next point E will result in more sexual arousal and feeling of orgasm which will also result in a higher level of consciousness. When they climax, men will often finish at the lower point (lower levels of consciousness and arousal) than what they started with as shown by dotted grey lines and green circular points.

This image shows what a masculine orgasm would look like if we were to draw this on paper. Because masculine orgasm works with masculine energy, it is linear, focused, aiming towards a direction (generally, always forward and seeking more pleasure or climax). For example, when a man portrays this masculine quality during sex, then he would generally be racing towards climax and if he has not learned the art of working with sexual energy, soon, he will end up climaxing (point A). After that, his energy will fall quickly (typically faster than a falling object from the sky). Normally, his presence, consciousness, attention, awareness and energy levels will finish lower than what he started with.

Because masculine energy is so focused, in his subconscious mind making her climax may be his only focus without even him being aware of it. If somehow he is able to hold his ejaculate and not climax at A, then he will be able to prolong his sexual experience until he reaches another peak (point B). And this process will continue.

Please note that, as mentioned above, even a female can show this masculine quality, in which case her orgasm is likely to be experienced more as a masculine orgasm.

Diagram Two

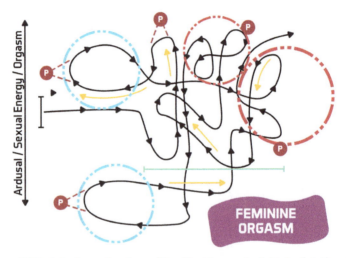

Figure 173: Feminine Orgasm denoting qualities of feminine energies. Points P reflects the spots where the orgasm has the capacity to peak and climax but instead of peaking, it carries on following further. The blue circle denotes that one can kind of sense where the orgasm is moving next while the path encircling red means it is difficult to tell which course it may move next. Hence, one will need to stay very attentive and present if one is to continue following the path travelled by this orgasm. This orgasm would feel like movement of weather in the atmosphere.

Here we see the feminine sexual energy, which operates like feminine energy which has no sense of direction, no purpose, and which just flows without knowing where it will land. During this flow, there can be peaks or there might not be peak at all. Feminine orgasm is not at all concerned with the number of peaks being there, and all that matters is the flow, whether it is up or down, left or right, or sideways, backwards, or forwards. As mentioned above, feminine orgasm is not restricted to females only, but to anyone who embodies the qualities of feminine energy.

Let's take a moment to notice some things from these diagrams. The masculine path to orgasm is directional, linear, focused on ejaculation, full of pressure and force, and goal-oriented. Meanwhile, the feminine path to orgasm is random, erratic, soft, goalless. It meanders on its own path and is emergent in the moment rather than fixed and predictable.

How can these different paths align? In short, they can't. Masculine sexual energy not only squashes the feminine orgasm at a certain moment, but it can also kill the feminine's desire and appetite for the experience. So those in masculine energy will need to learn how to fine-tune themselves to the extent that they can align with the sensitivity of feminine energy so that both can find resonance and be led by that energetic sexual charge created by sexual polarity.

Diagram Three

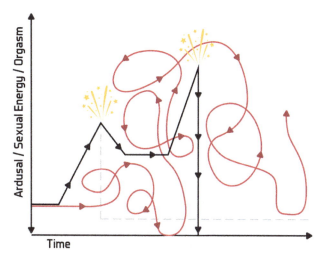

Figure 174: If masculine and feminine orgasm are to be put on the chart together, this is what it would look like in the beginning. There is so much mis-alignment and lack of connection. In a few places it might feel aligned, like the beginning and then somewhere in the middle and during the course of connection which could happen by chance.

If I am to put these pictures together, this is what it would look like. Diagram Three shows how much misalignment happens in terms of masculine and feminine orgasm when men have not learned the skill of becoming multi-orgasmic and when masculine and feminine are unable to find resonance between each other.

Diagram Four

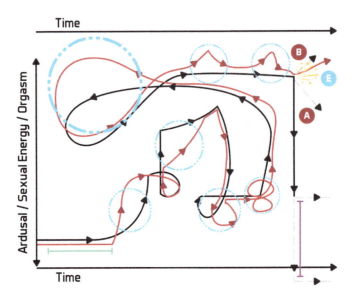

Figure 175: This is how the connection of masculine and feminine orgasm would feel like, if both the partners have been on the Path of Amplified Orgasm. The whole journey of physical intimacy and orgasm would feel connected, not only at physical level, but at other subtle body levels too. The area encircled by blue shows that there would be few divergences in connection every now and then, but both partners would have enough awareness, consciousness, presence, and attention to come back and connect again, hence the period of disconnections would be short lived. Once enough time has been spent, both partners would have the options to: climax as shown by point E, slow down as shown by point A, or keep continuing as shown by point B. When stopped, men would generally finish higher in terms of their arousal and consciousness than when the first started.

Diagram Four shows the orgasmic journey during any sexual connection of a completely aligned couple who have mastered the art of amplifying their orgasm and become multi-orgasmic. The section A and B in Diagram Four shows the misalignment happening during sex, but because the couple have a deep level of awareness, they are able to bring themselves back into alignment and carry on. The point C shows the point of ejaculation, at which point the man leaves the female. If the couple have consciousness and if the man doesn't desire to ejaculate, then the couple will carry on in this cycle further, as denoted by the dotted lines after point C.

In heterosexual relationships, women and men tend towards the complementary forces of dynamism and receptivity. What is receptive in women is dynamic within men and his psyche, and vice versa. The men who predominantly live in the masculine will portray receptivity near the heart area and dynamism and an emissive nature in the genitalia, whereas women who embody more feminine energy will portray receptivity at the genitalia and dynamism in the heart area. Hence, men tend to be more sex-driven, while women are more heart-driven.

Moreover, for the energy flow to happen at the receptive pole, the positive pole needs to be loaded first. That is why many men feel ready for love after sex when their sexual energy is met with fulfilment, while women tend to feel ready for sex when they feel a love connection first. This also explains why men tend to find it more difficult to become emotionally vulnerable, while women often find it more difficult to get sexually aroused.

It is because of this different polarisation occurring within each person that on meeting the partner that complements them at an energetic level, an electromagnetic circuit between them gets created. This circuit creates a nice loop resulting in the creation of an electromagnetic current that opens and expands the heart, magnetises sexual energy, and creates vitality, bliss, and profound happiness that nourishes the soul of each of the partners involved.

Before we move on, it is important to clarify that male=masculine and female=feminine is not always the case. Nor does it have to be. In fact, the extent that this kind of binary exists in couples is not determined by anatomy but, rather, by many factors including life experience, identity, and comfort embodying these sexual energies. While it is expedient to discuss examples where this binary tends to map as they represent a majority of heterosexual roles, this is not intended to imply that it is the only correct way for polarity to exist in couples.

For example, if a woman is predominantly masculine and the man feminine, then the roles would be reversed. However the underlying principle will remain the same i.e. such a woman would feel ready for love from her sexual energy while such a man would feel ready for sex through his heart.

Here is another important example. Consider that many couples are of the same sex. In the LGBTQ community, the terms butch and femme (or sometimes top/bottom) are often used to describe masculine and feminine energy within a couple, without confusing it with gender (male or female). This is sometimes applied to the sexual context (for example, a butch female may penetrate a femme female with a strap-on dildo). In the kinky community, where power dynamics are in play, this sexual polarity may be referred to as top/bottom or Dominant/submissive, again, not necessarily tied to biological sex. For example, a female top may embody masculine energy and a male bottom may experience something more in line with a feminine path to orgasm.

Furthermore, we are not "stuck" choosing between one or the other. Many people are able to embody both at different times. Known as "switches" in both the LGBTQ and kinky communities, these folks have figured out that they can become comfortable embodying both extremes of sexual polarity, as well as the places in between. In Part II, these and other types of polarity will be discussed in more detail.

Is a Partner Required to Explore Polarity?

One might ask a question: is a partner required to explore the bliss that can come from the interplay of sexual polarity as expressed between complementary partners? The answer to that is no. The majority of my adult life I have actually been single due to various reasons (moving cities, countries, exams, work pressure, lovers moving countries, etc), which has allowed me a lot of time to explore myself, within myself. When one doesn't have anyone to share the loving heart and sexual energy, what one can do is to work on themselves and merge these two energies together.

I had always thought that I needed to have a partner to feel really happy and to deal with my sexual energy in a positive way. But when I walked on the Path of Amplified Orgasm, I began to notice that my heart and genitals are actually connected, but there are different kinds of energetic currents happening at these centres which made them disconnected with each other.

When I started working on creating harmony between the two centres, it was very difficult at first as feelings and sensations of hurt, pain, and love associated with heart centre and erotic, strong sexual energy was at the sexual centre, creating a lot of discomfort, pain, anger, and even tears. But I stayed on the path and continued my daily and weekly practices. Then the day came where I noticed that these circuits had been sublimated. I felt so amazing, blissful, complete, and I felt whole, as if I had merged something inside me in a new way. It was a unique experience!

It felt so blissful that any kind of happiness felt so trivial in front of it. I had been running around in different relationships to feel myself complete and whole, and suddenly I found I was already complete and whole. Ever since that moment I have felt more bliss than happiness and it has made me realise that we shouldn't be running after happiness, but instead running after bliss. Happiness is a state of emotion just like sadness. Yes, it can be very beneficial for the heart, body, and mind, but it is actually bliss which provides benefits not only to heart, body, and mind but also to our overall well-being. Happiness is generally felt from a smaller portion of the body, while bliss generally is felt in the whole body, inside it, and around it.

I am not suggesting that we should all start living a solo and individual life, which I am not at all an advocate of. I love polarity. I love polarity between two people and I love to be in a relationship and see others in a relationship too. But what I am suggesting is that if you don't have someone to practise with, you can still make the best use of your time while being single. Because after this kind of experience, when you meet your opposing polarised individual, it will take the whole experience of loving another to a completely new level.

EXERCISE: Learning to Navigate Sexual Polarity

Orgasms and the Sexual Energetic Centre

As mentioned in Chapter Three, the second energy centre governs sexual energy, so if you want more sexual energy in your life, all you have to do is engage in activities, food, and lifestyles that will activate this centre. When this centre gets activated, you will automatically start feeling the sexual energy increasing, which over time, with enough discipline, observation, and practices, will start transcending into different parts of the body.

It's like this: if I turn on the switch relating to the bulb, the function of the bulb is to give light irrespective of whether it is day or night outside, irrespective of whether there is a requirement for the light or not in that space. In the same way, if you turn on the sexual energy centre, you will automatically start feeling the sexual energy irrespective of whether you want to have sex or not, irrespective of whether there is time for sex or not.

Figure 176: The function of the bulb is to give light irrespective of whether it is day or night.

Once you have learned the skill of activating it, you can then always alchemise this energy for many useful and creative purposes or for experiencing energetic orgasms alone or with your partner. If this centre is weak, your body will feel weak and your sexual potential will decrease and the sexual glands might not produce enough hormones. However, if this centre is excessively active, and if the energy is not channelled appropriately, it can result in sexual frustration, discomfort, sexual obsessions, restlessness, and can even result in unhealthy fantasies and addictions.

The more sexual desires and sexual arousals you experience, the more the energy gets directed to this centre, so if the arousal is full of affection and love, it will make this centre strong, expansive, and harmonious. But if the arousal is tight, aggressive, and selfish, it will make this centre weak, imbalanced, and it could even become closed.

Once you experience the energetic orgasm, then it will become so much easier, provided you are not holding onto the goal of wanting to achieve an orgasm or tied to any particular position or technique, and provided there are no blockages or stagnant and unwanted emotions and energies stuck in the energy channels to allow the free flow of sexual energy throughout the body. Every person's orgasm is unique and every person's Path of Amplified Orgasm is unique too.

EXERCISE: Activating the Sexual Energy Centre

The Sexual Response Cycle: Various Models

The sexual response cycle refers to a series of physical, emotional, and physiological phases that occur when an individual engages in physically intimate and sexually stimulating activities including masturbation, oral sex, mental sex, fantasies, etc. I will also refer to this cycle as the stages of orgasm in this book.

Different sex researchers have defined orgasms with various staged models of sexual response over the years. The aim of mentioning some of these here is to give you some insight into how complex it is to identify and map the body's sexual response cycle. Indeed, even those who study this process in the laboratory or clinical setting do not agree, particularly when it comes to female orgasm.

If the experts do not agree, then why investigate these models? The Path of Amplified Orgasm is unique to each individual and it is for each of us to define what kind of orgasm and pleasure we are experiencing, and to what degree and intensity. The focus is on what is rather than what *should be*. Perhaps one of these models will resonate more with your experience and give you a new tool to understand your own sexual response cycle. Helpful knowledge indeed!

A comprehensive knowledge and understanding of the physiological changes that our body goes through during sexual connection and orgasmic experiences can help to enhance those experiences further, deepen the relationship with the self and with our partner, and help to move us further on the path of orgasmic amplification.

These models are mentioned here just for guidance and are to be used as such. Every person is different and every path to orgasm is unique. You or your partner might experience some, all, or completely new stages during your orgasmic experiences. What is important is that you allow your body to progress or move from one stage to the other naturally without forcing it or becoming pre-occupied with achieving a specific milestone or checkpoint.

Many believe that orgasm is just 10 seconds of climax or, in the case of men, mere ejaculation. Orgasm is, in fact, much more expansive than what you may have come to believe. The Path of Amplified Orgasm is about exploring, experimenting, communicating, feeling, and staying with the sensations that arise during orgasmic connection and experience as much as possible. These stages can cross over, and some of the sexual response models mentioned below do not take into account the multi-orgasmic cycle where sex doesn't end in orgasm, or they assume that sex is necessary for orgasm, or they assume that achieving orgasm means the sex was amazing... none of which are necessarily true.

The sexual response cycle includes at least three phases:

- **Sexual Desire**: fantasies, thoughts, desire, increasing of libido
- **Sexual Arousal**: excitement and arousal experienced in the physical body, arousal of feelings, for example feeling turned-on
- **Sexual Orgasm**: peaking, explosion, increase in heart rate, breathing, discharge of fluids.

Both the partners experience these stages though the timing, intensity, and categories of these stages will vary with each sexual and orgasmic connection.

The Linear Models

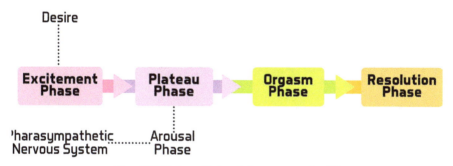

Figure 177: Master and Johnson's four stage sexual model

Masters and Johnson's – The Four-Phase Model (EPOR)

The first model of sexual function was described by Masters and Johnson in 1966, defined as the EPOR model.[84,85] They found that sexual response was divided into four phases and these happen in a linear way, each stage happening one after the other. This model has been widely used by various medical professionals, psychologists, psychiatrists, and pharmaceutical companies and has formed the basis of conceptualisations of sexual response in men and women despite the limitations in terms of defining sexual health and sexual problems or being very helpful in regards to understanding female orgasm.

(A) Male

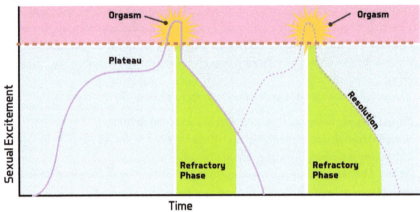

(B) Female

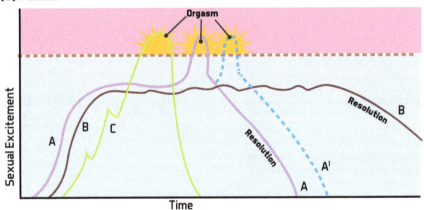

Figure 178: Master's and Johnson's four stage model: Arousal, Plateau, Orgasm and Resolution. A, B, C and the dotted lines denote different sexual cyclical responses.

According to this model, the sexual response cycle isn't complete until all four stages have occurred. These four stages are:

- **Excitement** (also known as turned-on, arousal, or initial excitement phase): This occurs as a result of physical or mental stimuli such as touching, caressing, kissing, or viewing erotic images, which leads to sexual arousal. Physical or psychological stimulation results in various body responses i.e. the penis or vagina expands, heart breath rates increase, blood vessels dilate, neck and chest flushes, nipples become erect and hard, etc. This phase can last from several minutes to several hours.

- **Plateau** (repetitive pleasurable movements): This phase occurs when the partners experience powerful surges of sexual excitement or pleasure and may begin to groan, vocalise, or make other sounds involuntarily
- **Orgasm** (burst of pleasure and release): This is considered to be the climactic, shortest phase of the sexual response cycle and typically lasts for only a few seconds in men, a bit longer in women, although the sensations are similar for both
- **Resolution** (followed by a refractory period in men): This is the final stage in which muscles relax, pulse and breathing slows down, swelling reduces, and the body gradually returns to its original state.

While it is important to understand that this model has since been widely critiqued, it was also responsible for debunking many myths about sexuality, female sexuality in particular, that were commonly held by medical professionals in this time. For example, Masters and Johnson's work provided focus on the role of the clitoris in sexual response and debunked the idea that vaginal lubrication originated in the cervix.

However, their model has been criticised as research continues to refine our understanding of sexuality and orgasm. A major critique is that the EPOR model assumes a linear progression of increasing sexual excitement from the onset of stimulation to orgasm, which is hardly the case, and it ignores the sexual desires and cycles of multi-orgasm in which orgasm might not happen at the end. It doesn't take into consideration other factors that impact orgasm such as subjective, psychological, or interpersonal aspects of sexual response (relationship intimacy, cultural, religious, and other social factors).

Inaccuracies have also been found in the years since. For example, the EPOR model states that only the vagina is lubricated during the arousal stage, but it has been shown that the labia produce their own lubricant. Another example is that they argued that it was the volume of ejaculate that determined the intensity of male pleasure during orgasm, when in fact, we have come to know that it is more related to the strength of ejaculation. The model also assumes that a sexually functional woman is always responsive to sexual initiation or stimulation, a rather offensive idea to modern sensibilities. Clearly we now know that things like consent, trust, hormones, libido, and individual sexual desires also play key roles in female (and male) arousal.

Kaplan – The Three-Stage Model (DEOR)
In response to criticisms of Johnson's model, noted sex therapist and researcher, Helen Singer Kaplan, proposed the Triphasic Concept in 1979.[86] One of her main critiques was that the Masters and Johnson model looked only at physiological aspects of the

sexual cycle, completely ignoring important aspects of psychology, including cognitive and subjective. Her model was also linear, and it suggested that both women and men follow this basic linear progression: desire, excitement, orgasm.

The Kaplan model was criticised because it was still a linear model (which might be more appropriate for men than women) and because it had put desire before arousal, which is not necessarily the case, especially for women. Also, the phases of sexual response can overlap and are not always sequential, which both the above models fail to address.

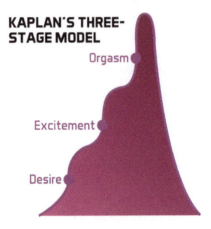

Figure 179: Kaplan's three stage model in which desire is identified as a separate phase of sexual response and each of these stages are independent with sequence being variable too.

The Circular Models

Whipple and Brash

In 1997, Whipple and Brash-McGreer created the first circular model of the sexual response cycle.[87] This new way of understanding the stages was specific to women. It was novel in that it included the notion that a woman's subjective experience of pleasure was directly relevant to whether or not she would feel inclined to initiate another sexual experience, which may include a seduction phase to initiate the next sexual encounter.

This model was important because it acknowledged the cyclical nature of women's sexual response, ignored by previous models. Their four stages include seduction (which includes the notion of desire), sensation (which includes both excitement and plateau), and surrender (which includes orgasm).

Despite having some value in noticing female agency in the sexual response cycle for women, the phase descriptions have not been widely accepted as independent phases of the female sexual response.

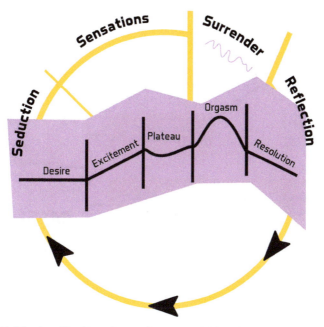

Figure 180: Whipple and Brash's circular sexual response model shows how pleasure in one sexual experience contributes to the seduction phase of the next sexual experience.

The Basson Model

In 2000, Rosemary Basson proposed an alternative model of sexual response, arguing that the linear model is good at explaining men's sexual response but fails to explain women's sexual responses.[88] Instead of focusing on spontaneous sexual desire, she focused on a responsive form of desire which was accessed once sexual arousal was experienced.

Her non-linear model incorporates a female need for intimacy. It describes how desire is responsive to intimacy and desire and arousal emerge in a non-linear way, particularly for women. It also offers us the insight that although orgasms may be part of how we experience sex, they are not the only path to feeling deep sexual satisfaction.

This model takes into consideration that a woman's ability to be aroused may be influenced by external factors like past sexual experiences, self-esteem, body insecurities, STIs, or abuse. The positive outcomes of the cycle will increase the subsequent motivation for the next cycle. This model also acknowledges the reciprocal relationship between arousal and desire and incorporates psychological, biological, and other contextual factors in a more comprehensive framework.

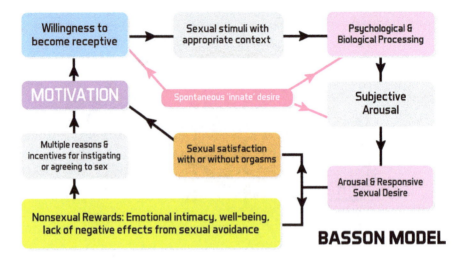

Figure 181: Basson's model of sexual response shows components of desires and the motivational factors that trigger such responses.

One of the biggest limitations of this model is it is largely intimacy based and doesn't really consider the sexual responses of women whose desires and arousal are not linked to intimacy. This model also ends up implying that women may be more sexually passive due to the emphasis put on sexual desire being response or receptive in nature. Still, the contribution to our understanding of female sexual response has been significant and lasting.

Multi-factor Models

Bancroft and Janssen – The Dual Control Model

In the last 10 years, many multi-factor models have been developed. One of which is the Dual Control Model credited to John Bancroft and Erick Janssen, which suggests that sexual response and associated arousal is ultimately determined by a balance between two systems in an individual's brain: the sexual activation or excitation system and the sexual inhibition system, each of which has a neurobiological substrate.[89]

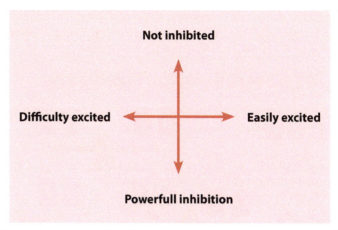

Figure 182: The Dual Control model explains sexual behaviour and response through sexual excitation and sexual inhibition.

Perelman – The Sexual Tipping Point Model (STP)

The Multifaction Etiology Of Sexual Function And Dysfunction

Desire/arousal is normally balanced with a natural range, which is then influenced by numerous mental and physical factors, which may very within and between experiences

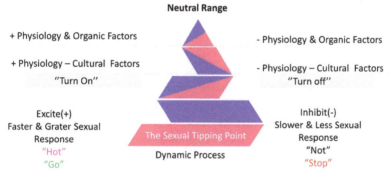

Figure 183: The Sexual Tipping Point model in which desire/arousal is generally balanced with a natural range, which is then influenced by numerous mental and physical factors, which may very within and between experiences.

The Sexual Tipping Point was created by Michael Perelman and suggests that a sexual response is determined by a balance between excitatory or inhibitory factors that may be psychological, organic, psychosocial, or cultural.[90] The sexual tipping point is highly variant from one individual to the next, as well as the context of the sexual encounter. When it is reached, a sexual response is expressed. Although we can understand the sexual tipping point as a pattern expressed as a normal distribution of aggregate data, it is complicated at the individual level by many factors, both mental and physical.

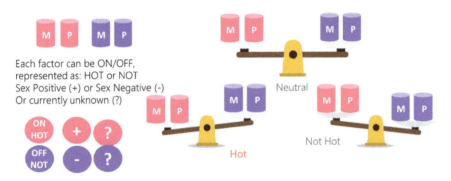

Figure 184: In the Sexual Tipping Point model, four containers hold all the known and unknown mental and physical factors that regulate sexual response. Sexual Tipping point is displayed on a scale which has a dynamic representation of the sexual response in any specific moment.

Metz and McCarthy – The Good Enough Sex Model

Michael Metz and Barry McCarthy introduced the 'Good Enough Sex Model'. It includes 12 core premises that are pre-requisites for couple satisfaction. Their approach emphasises a psycho-bio-social paradigm for sexual function and dysfunction.[91] The Good Enough Sex model encourages couples to integrate sex and intimacy into their relationship in ways that enhance the quality of their relationship. In this model, sex may have several purposes, not all of which are important all the time. For example, sometimes sex gives couples access to stress relief, while at other times, it may be more of a spiritual experience. In their model, emotional acceptance plays a key role in establishing the trust required for intimacy, and sex is seen as tied to relationship health overall, and vice versa.

One Taste – Eight Stages of Orgasm

The eight stage model was developed by One Taste, the organisation that developed the practice of Orgasmic Meditation. This model opens up the experience of orgasm well beyond that of the other sexual response cycles found in the previous models covered above. As such, it offers us a window to see that orgasm itself is much more than just a peak at the end of a sexual experience. Indeed, we can come to see it as having a life of its own and enough complexity and richness to deserve more attention and exploration. In this model there are eight sequential stages of orgasm, and each stage can be turned on or off. Although one can start this journey at any point, once initiated, the orgasmic cycle will follow a certain path. The below stages are listed with no ranking preference.

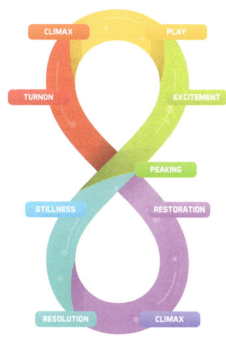

Figure 185: One Taste eight stages of Orgasm model in which orgasm is not stationary and one can start from any stage during this response cycle.

- **Turn-On (desire)**: sensation feels dynamic, sparky, desire and orgasm in subtle bodies begin to wake up
- **Excitement (purpose)**: Flushing, contraction, swelling, full engagement but presence is affected by overwhelming sensation
- **Plateau (play)**: a state where everything feels good possibly due to being extra sensitive or heightened sensation
- **Stillness (realisation)**: not moving and yet observing of all that has been experienced
- **Peaking (transition)**: Orgasm is moving throughout the body, starts to extend beyond the physical body, begin to feel groundless
- **Climax (possession)**: involuntary point of release, overflowing, bursting with orgasm, completely out of control
- **Resolution (recovery)**: empty after being cleared out at the climax stage
- **Restoration (pleasure)**: sensations, temptation, energy, excitement and everything else rising and building up.

I feel that this is one of the stronger models in terms of feminine orgasm, but it does not necessarily map to the more directional and linear masculine orgasmic energy. Nor does it adequately account for the effect of different energy centres and the energy field of the partner in terms of the impact this can have on the overall orgasmic experience.

What Exactly Is Orgasm?

So, based on what we have discussed so far in various chapters, if we are to define what an orgasm is, it would be defined in this way: movement of energies in our bodies, especially sexual energy, which triggers various spots creating emotion and feelings, felt as some form of sensation/s either in our layered body, our energy centres, or/and in any or a combination of our subtle bodies/auras. The extent of how deep, intense, and freely these energies will be able to move will depend on how activated and cleared these energy centres are, how aligned the auras are, and how much presence one's consciousness has on the layers of the body in any given moment.

As we can see from the definition of orgasm that I propose above, it expands the experience of orgasm well beyond what most people are used to including, or even conceiving of, as orgasm. And yet, these orgasmic experiences become available to us once we are open-minded and ready to explore them. And to that, we turn next to the many types of orgasm.

The list mentioned below is not exhaustive. However, I hope that it will enable you to start having a wider perspective of orgasm. You might have experienced some of these types of orgasm before, but may not have been aware of them. My invitation for you is to start to bring your awareness into the energy movement, your feelings, and the sensations happening in your body in each moment. Allow yourself to see what shifts with this kind of practice. For example, if a man has always been used to climax as the objective of a sexual encounter, then the state of becoming multi-orgasmic will require a lot of discipline, effort, and cooperation from his partner. Most importantly, both the partners would need to be open to the ideas of experiencing orgasms in new ways.

The list of orgasms mentioned below are just to give an idea of the kinds of orgasms that exist and can be felt. Our bodies are complex and unique and there is no limit to the number of orgasms one can experience, especially if we start becoming open to energies, feelings, and sensations. So, below is only scratching the surface when it comes to unique types of orgasms. People can also have orgasms through dancing, singing, hearing glass break, petting the cat, eating certain foods, etc.

Orgasms for Men

Although we have been taught to believe that there is only one type of orgasm for men, and that it can be equated to ejaculation (climax), this is not true. In fact, men are capable of experiencing several different types of orgasm, which we explore below.

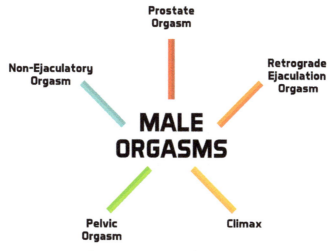

Figure 186: Various types of male orgasms

Climax (Ejaculation)

This is the type of orgasm most men are likely to be mostly familiar with as it is the type in which semen is ejaculated from the urethra. In this habitual pattern of orgasm, his efforts and resources are all focused on chasing this goal (whether consciously or subconsciously) for as long as he possibly can (and even as quickly as he possibly can, as he can find it difficult to experience the energetic discomfort he feels from delayed ejaculation). Feelings of happiness and bliss may follow this orgasm but so can feelings of disgust, shame, remorse, guilt, or unhappiness (often relating to cursing himself for ejaculating too fast).

Pelvic Orgasm (PC Muscles)

As the name suggests, this orgasm requires holding back the ejaculation and sending the energy back to the body and into the pelvic area. In order to achieve this orgasm, self-control of the genitals and pelvic floor muscles, movement of the pelvic area, relaxation of the mind, and long and deep breathing into the belly and genitals are required. This kind of orgasm is more intense, more pleasurable, and because there is no loss of semen, it is also very energising.

Prostate Orgasm (Direct Stimulation)

As we have seen in Chapter Three, prostate orgasm is achieved by stimulating the nerves of the prostate gland either with a finger or with an external object (such as a sex toy). Many men have never experienced this type of orgasm due to their own beliefs (such as discomfort with the idea of being penetrated, homophobia, fear of excreting, or negative associations with this area of the body) which can stop them from having this gland stimulated, or relaxing to enjoy it if they do.

Deeper relaxation of the mind and body, complete surrender, long and deep breathing, and relaxing anal muscles will be required to achieve this kind of orgasm. I am a very open person generally speaking, but it still took me a few months to be able to have my prostate gland stimulated by someone else. Even on the day when I was ready, my partner found it difficult to access the prostate because my sphincter and glutes were not relaxed, even though mentally I felt relaxed. It may take a few sessions before this area can be accessed and stimulated. When this gland is stimulated there is a possibility of a lot of emotions coming up, so both partners need to be practised at holding space, as discussed in Chapter Six. Although I have offered an introduction to prostate stimulation below, this is a topic that will be covered in more detail in Part II of this book.

> **EXERCISE: An Introduction to Prostate Stimulation**

Non-Ejaculatory (Retrograde Ejaculation) Orgasm

In this orgasm, the bladder's sphincter does not close off properly during ejaculation, so semen shoots backwards into the bladder. This orgasm is also known as a dry orgasm as no semen is released but he still experiences orgasm. This can cause fertility issues in men if practised incorrectly, especially if using too much pressure. See Chapter Five to learn more about the Million Dollar Point, which can create this orgasm in men with proper stimulation.

Non-Ejaculatory Orgasm

These kinds of orgasms are achieved when a man experiences the feeling of climax but without actually ejaculating. In order to become multi-orgasmic, men should aim for multi-non-ejaculatory orgasms. Note that when a man experiences this type of orgasm, there is no refractory period, which means his ability to experience additional orgasms is not diminished. In addition, each successive non-ejaculatory orgasm has the effect of adding to desire and attraction, amplifying and intensifying the sexual experience.

Orgasms for Women

Just like men, many women may only have experience with one or the other type of orgasm, when in fact, they are capable of many orgasmic experiences. Let's take a look at some of the more common types of orgasm that women can experience:

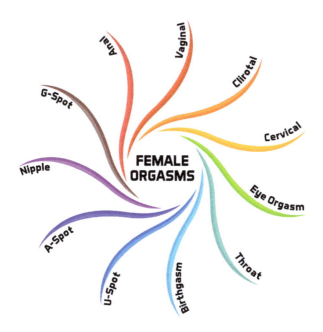

Figure 187: Various types of female orgasms

Clitoral Orgasm

As mentioned in Chapter Five, the clitoris has almost 8000 nerve endings, so stimulating this spot generates a great deal of sensation in her body. It is no wonder many girls from an early age use their fingers or sex toys to rub this spot, though I have had adult clients who have used pressure from toys to such an extent that it has made this spot numb. Through AOM coaching sessions, not only did these clients regain sensitivity, but they have also been able to feel orgasms in a way never felt before.

Men generally are not aware of the level of sensitivity involved to be able to give her deeply sensational clitoral orgasm. Most men view the clitoris as a whole, that is, if they are able to identify the clit in the first place. It is not just about sucking, nibbling, or using the tongue so that she can feel aroused. There is so much more to explore on this spot. There are many spots on clitoris, with each spot connected to different sets of nerve endings, and different kinds of strokes on these spots will give her different kinds of orgasmic feelings if done with the right amount of pressure, the right speed, and in the right direction from moment to moment.

EXERCISE: The Clitoral Principles

Vaginal Orgasm

This type of orgasm can be achieved through penetrative stimulation. This orgasm is not considered to be as intense as other orgasms, although it is felt deeper inside the vaginal canal. Depending on the state she is in, the intimacy of the connection, and whether the penetration is shallow or deep, this kind of orgasm can be very pleasurable on the physical level or it can result in much deeper, enriching, and expansive orgasms.

Clitoris and vaginal orgasm are considered to be the same by some people since vaginal orgasm is obtained through the stimulation of the vagina, which is an extended part of the clitoris. However, the author is of the view that these two are different types of orgasm because the spots being stimulated are different.

Clitoral orgasms are considered to be more physically intense and satisfying, but the sensations are generally limited to the pelvic region. Vaginal orgasms, on the other hand, are more psychologically intense and satisfying and are often experienced throughout the body.

> ### EXERCISE: The Difference Between G-Spot and Clitoral Orgasms

G-Spot Orgasm

G-spot orgasm requires the stimulation of the G-spot, discussed in more detail in Chapter Five. Sometimes G-spot orgasms can stimulate female ejaculation, or squirting. These orgasms are considered to be more intense than vaginal orgasms, but less intense than clitoral orgasms.

Anal Orgasm

Some women can feel stronger orgasms with anal sex due to the large number of nerve endings in this area. The anus is also an area that comes with some negative associations for some, and trauma for others. For some women this can be a very sensitive spot and for some they would need to have frequent anal stimulation to be satisfied, otherwise the energy would feel low, heavy, and stuck. Extra care needs to be taken during anal penetration as the thin tissue here is prone to being torn if not treated with care.

From an energetic point of view, the root energy centre is located within this area, so stimulation can help in activation of Kundalini energy, although this is not the only way to do so. We will be talking a lot about anal sex and how this can help in amplification of orgasm in Part II of this book.

Just like other parts of the genitalia, a lot of energy and trauma can be stored in this place, for both women and men, either due to bad past experiences or due to taboos which have made them keep this area tight and tensed. It is also possible that lot of dark energies and bad vibrations can be felt through the anal area (although this can be felt through various body parts) and it will depend on lot of factors as mentioned above i.e.

energy blockages, unreleased emotions, trauma, misdirecting the sexual and Kundalini energy, disharmonised energetic exchange from your partner, etc.

U-Spot Orgasm

The U-spot orgasm, also known as a urethra orgasm, occurs when the U-spot is triggered, especially during clitoral orgasm. This can also be experienced during urination and can feel tingling and light. The reason why women can experience urinary orgasms is because urinating is associated with letting go, so it can result in relaxation and may cause women to experience an orgasm or even a whole body orgasm.

Cervical Orgasm

These occur deep inside the body and can be achieved through penetrative sex or using a longer, girthier, sex toy. The cervix is considered by some to be women's inner core, and as such, it has the ability to create an orgasm that allows sexual energy to flow throughout the body with continuous waves of pleasure and vibrations which can continue for hours and can often lead to whole body orgasms. It is considered to be the most deep, profound, meaningful and most amazing orgasm a woman can have on the physical level as the cervix is related to a woman's feminine core which can energetically contain her creativity and sense of self.

Women can hold a lot of trauma from negative experiences of shame, abuse, and neglect in this part of the body. Hence learning to experience this type of orgasm can be an emotionally rich and healing experience. Just like the clitoris, there are many spots in the cervix area, and stimulating each of these will result in different sensations and orgasms. For example the spot right near the opening of the uterus is considered to relate to creating deeper intimacy and love. Some refer to these spots as the M-spot and X-spot.[53]

A-Spot Orgasm

As discussed in Chapter Five, there are many other sensitive spots in women's genitalia, and stimulating these spots will give her intense pleasure. The A-spot orgasm is achieved through stimulation of the anterior fornix erogenous zone (AFE zone), also known as A-spot, Deep Spot, or Double G Spot.

Most men are not aware of the kind of pleasure a woman can feel through an A-spot orgasm. Most women might not have experienced this themselves. Stimulating any of the unknown spots (A and other spots near the cervix) might feel strange to her in the beginning, but over time she might start enjoying this kind of pleasure immensely. Unlike the clit, which is a very sensitive spot, the A spot can take a significant amount of pressure, but make sure you are not rubbing against her cervix. Stimulation of the AFE zone results in vaginal lubrication and can make her feel aroused very quickly, but generally stimulation of this spot should happen when she is already warmed up.

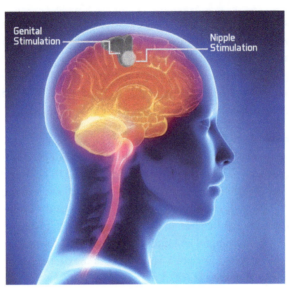

Figure 188: Nipples and genitals stimulate the same area of the brain as per one study. It showed that the area of the brain were affected like a 'cluster of grapes' for both women and men.

Nipplegasms (Nipple Orgasm)

Nipplegasms are orgasms attained through the stimulation of the nipples. fMRI scan research shows that the stimulation of nipples activates the same part of the brain (genital sensory cortex) that responds to genital stimulation; women's brains process nipple and genital stimulation in the same way.[92]

Eye Orgasm

Due to energetic transmission through the eyes, and the role this plays in the formation of trust, many women have felt orgasm through eyes. Trust is a felt sense that can be felt energetically, mentally, emotionally, and also physically. When we look into another person's eyes, an energetic transmission takes place which can make a person's body feel relaxed and create trust, especially for women. This relaxation and trust state can trigger hormones like oxytocin, which creates feelings of love, bonding, and empathy. When our eyes can create so much attraction for someone through just a look, just imagine what a prolonged eye contact and sexual intention can create in terms of orgasmic bliss between two lovers. This type of orgasm is categorised under women because they are often more sensitive and connected to deep feelings of trust and safety, although this type of orgasm can be experienced by men as well.

Birthgasm

Some women can experience ecstatic orgasms while giving birth due to the push and pressure involved during labour, which can stimulate the erogenous zones, resulting in an unexpected climax. It is, however, a very rare experience.

Orgasms for Both Women and Men

There are many types of orgasms that both men and women can enjoy! Here are a few to consider:

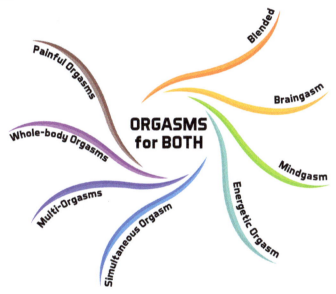

Figure 189: Types of orgasms which can be experienced by both women and men

Blended (Prostate + Ejaculatory or Vaginal + Clitoris) Orgasm

This kind of orgasm is when more than two erogenous zones are engaged at the same time. This type of orgasm can produce intense sensations, a burst of sexual energy, and in some cases, can stimulate the whole body, causing the whole body orgasm provided there are no energy blockages.

P-Spot Orgasm

Perineum orgasm refers to the orgasm experienced due to stimulation of the perineum, especially if someone finds this area to be one of the more sensitive areas. This area is sandwiched between two erogenous zones for both women and men, so it is often neglected but can be used for teasing or creating different kinds of orgasmic sensation.

This area can be stimulated alone or in conjunction with other areas (prostate or cock for men, clit or G-spot for women).

Braingasm

As discussed in Chapter Two, our brain is a powerful machine and orgasm is a whole brain experience. At a physical level, my experiences of brain orgasm included vibrating of my head, heat on and a few inches around the head, and tingling and pleasurable sensations inside the head. At an energetic level, especially after activation of the crown energy centre, I have felt tremendous bliss and energy moving from the top of my head downwards into my whole body and also outwards into space. There have been times when it has felt like I could experience neurons shooting from one end to the other in different parts of my brain. When this happened, it really felt like

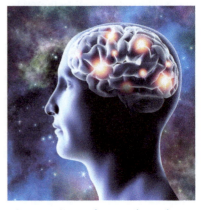

Figure 190: Neurons firing together producing tingles or sparkles or lightning like sensation in the brain; often referred to as braingasms.

a tingling sensation which was slightly uncomfortable but also very pleasurable at the same time. After these experiences, the brain can feel either activated, re-charged, and very alert, but a few times it has also included dizziness and headaches. Some of my partners have also experienced a tingling sensation inside their head.

Figure 191-192: ASMR provides a relaxing sensation or tingles in the brain and other sensitive parts of the body.

Recently, ASMR (Autonomous Sensory Meridian Response) has been gaining a lot of attention and is currently being researched.[93–95] ASMR has been considered to have longer term health benefits such as reducing stress and anxiety, and lifting mood for some. ASMR artists can include acts like whispering into a microphone, speaking softly, tapping, hand movements, loudly chewing or biting foods, scratching with the nails, or the crinkling and crumbling of a flexible material to produce the kind of repetitive sounds that can produce a lot of tingling and pleasurable sensations which can feel like a brain orgasm for those tuned in to this practice.

Mindgasm

The mindgasm, often referred to as fantasy orgasm, can be achieved by just thinking about an orgasm. Our subconscious mind is a powerful tool, and if we visualise and imagine, our subconscious mind can consider our thoughts real. Through regular practice, one can learn to experience mindgasm without any physical stimulation, and in some cases, these can be whole body orgasms.

Oral/Lips/Mouth Orgasm

As mentioned in the section relating to erogenous zones, the lips are made up of closely-set nerve endings classified as a mucocutaneous region of the body which is very similar to the nerve endings of the genitals. This kind of orgasm refers to the orgasm attained through kissing, especially when it is extended, passionate, and slow. The whole body is connected, so sensations felt in the lips, tongue and/or mouth can travel and be felt in the genitals and other parts of the body.

Throat or Deep Throat Orgasm

Women and gay or bisexual men can have orgasms when giving oral stimulation to men's penises. Deep-throat, or gagging, and rubbing one or two fingers at the back of the throat results in arousal of the pituitary centre which is situated at the back of the throat. Up until six years ago, I was not aware about the throat energy centre and how deep-throat by my partner, which stimulates that centre, can create such an amazing energetic and sensational orgasm. Of course, one needs to remember that this kind of orgasm would be unique, hence a need to remain open to experiencing pleasure and orgasm in a way which might not be at all related to one that you might have experienced before. And, of course, life experience and the stories and beliefs we have about oral sex are also going to play a major role in determining how much pleasure we associate with this act.

To enjoy a throat orgasm, one would need to bypass the gag reflex and build into it slowly. It will be very challenging in the beginning, as stimulating this reflex can make it feel like you are going to vomit, but over time it will get easier. One can also try this with thumbs and fingers, but it is more fun with a penis!

During the bodywork sessions, I often find that women who hold their breath often or who have suppressed their voice, can experience orgasm, convulsions, and spasms in different parts of the body when the tension and trauma is released, often accompanied by sounds. This is another type of throat orgasm. Throat orgasm can feel transcendental, pleasurable, and can lead to higher states of consciousness and trance states. The continuous stimulation of the throat, clearing of the throat chakra, regular communication, and experiencing orgasms can lead to better connection with intuition, deeper expression of needs and desires, opening up to more creativity and lead to higher potential.

Other Zonal Orgasms

These are the orgasms experienced through other erogenous areas of the body, as long as we are open to the possibility of exploring, observing, and receiving the sensations.

Energetic Orgasms

These types of orgasms are experienced in the body without necessarily involving any physical touch. Through regular practices of breath, muscle, body movement, and certain kinds of yoga postures, these kinds of orgasms can be made a part of daily living. Over time, these kinds of orgasms can provide a continuous state of bliss and happiness and keep the body energised, awake, and active. These kinds of orgasms have the ability to unclog blockages in the body, giving an overall sense of well-being to the individual.

Ejaculation or non-ejaculation is not necessary for these kinds of orgasms and even if ejaculation happens, unlike climax, the man would not feel energetically tired after the experience.

These are my favourite kinds of orgasms. As our bodies are made of hundreds of energy centres, so these orgasms can be felt from any part of the body i.e. the heart, lower back, bum, scalp, etc. The biggest skill a person needs to have to experience these kinds of orgasms would be to be able to channel the energy flow from one part of the body to another. We mentioned the seven main energy centres in Chapter Three, but there are hundreds of other small centres that exist in our body. So, it is natural that if those centres are activated, and if we allow ourselves to be able to develop the level of sensitivity required to feel that activation, then we can experience numerous kinds of energetic orgasms.

When I started experiencing energetic orgasms, I started feeling different kinds of sensations over different parts of the body at different times. Slowly, slowly, over time, those sensations started to unite with sensations felt in other parts of my body. Then there came a day when I experienced this kind of orgasm across my whole body.

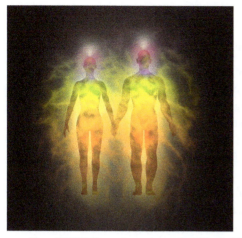

Figure 193-194: Energetic orgasms can be felt both within the body or around any part of the body. In order to experience such orgasms, one will need to develop sensitivity towards feeling of different kinds of energies. To experience these kinds of orgasms one will need to be patient, have practices that help them stay connected with themselves, and most importantly note that the energy levels and intensities will vary from moment to moment.

When one starts feeling energetic orgasms, one also starts experiencing different subtle bodies more easily. Strong relationships begin to develop between energetic centres, energetic orgasms, and subtle bodies. One feels complete, whole, and very connected with the universal energies around the body.

These kinds of orgasms can initially include some discomfort, as the body is working towards receiving and holding a large amount of energy, which often has been leaked out in the past in the form of ejaculation. However, over time, these become one of the most blissful orgasms to experience. Such orgasms result in implosion within the body rather than explosion outside the body. These orgasms can happen anywhere and anytime and originate from any part of the body.

EXERCISE: Getting Started with Energetic Orgasms

Multi-Orgasms

The waves of multiple orgasms over time can turn the experience of orgasms into full-body experiences as the sensations are felt in different parts of the body rather than concentrated on the genital area. Multi-orgasmic refers to the ability to be able to experience different kinds of orgasms in a short span of time, usually without ejaculation. In order to differentiate between the different kinds of orgasms being experienced, one will need a lot of awareness. We will be learning much more about becoming multi-orgasmic in Part II.

There are several benefits from learning to become multi-orgasmic. Here are a few:

- For a man, the fear of ejaculating too quickly disappears as now he has choice and control over whether to ejaculate or not. Many different types of orgasm also gives him the option to choose from several different experiences of orgasmic pleasure.
- The energetic exchange between partners can be felt and channelled in a more cyclic way, creating beautiful, energetic spirals.
- Becoming multi-orgasmic helps with further development on the path of spirituality and orgasmic amplification.
- It can create a change in the overall hormonal and chemical balance, creating a blissful and positive attitude towards life.
- It can be part of a change in mindfulness, creating an increase in attention, presence, consciousness, and awareness.
- Simultaneous orgasms become possible and the desire for sexual connection increases, which can also become a source of great nourishment and intimacy.
- Becoming multi-orgasmic builds one's capacity to hold different kinds of sensations and energies, which also provides benefits in dealing with overwhelming and intense situations in life.
- They enable the transfer of energy from one partner to the other, creating a nice energetic loop which will help in catalysing orgasm for both. As a result of this energetic loop, the energy will pass between each other several times, creating a huge energetic ball around the partners involved.

Implosive – Orgasms (Non-Depleting Multi-Orgasms)

As the name suggests, and unlike explosive orgasms where the partner climaxes and loses vital life-force, these are the orgasms which implode inside the body. Some of the orgasms which have been mentioned above would fall under this category in one form or the other, but an important point to note is that both partners can have implosive orgasms. In these kinds of orgasms, sexual energy is built up and channelled to move upwards through different energy centres (kind of imploding through each energy centre as it moves up), which creates extraordinary sensation and pleasure due to the mixing of energies with different energy centres and due to the imploding of the energy centres, which then release the energy stored in these centres to different parts of the body.

These are considered to be very healing in the sense that these orgasms have the ability to clear out any repressed emotions or blocked energy held within the energy pathways and bring energy centres into harmony and balance. To what extent the emotions will be cleared and energy released will depend on the intensity of the emotion and the energy itself. These kinds of orgasms are similar to energetic orgasms, with the exception that energetic orgasms might not follow a certain pathway and they might not have an imploding effect. These are also one of my favourite types of orgasms. Just like electric orgasms, these can be strong or subtle, lasting mini-seconds or for hours, and can be felt in single wave or multiple waves.

Whole body Orgasms

As mentioned above in energetic orgasms, once the sensations begin to join in different parts of the body, you will start experiencing whole body orgasms. The biggest difference between energetic and physical whole body orgasms is that the latter will result in ejaculation and not only is our energy depleted, but also our level of consciousness, awareness, and presence. On the other hand, with energetic whole body orgasms, we feel more energised and our level of consciousness, awareness, and presence actually increases. Our bodies are designed for enjoying pleasure, for enjoying wholesome orgasmic experiences, and not for just for climaxing and depleting ourselves.

Some of the benefits of energetic whole body orgasms are:

Figure 195: A glimpse of what an energetic whole-body orgasm can feel like. This can be felt as a slow experience of energy moving throughout the whole body and beyond or fast waves like ripples. One generally doesn't tend to have much control over their body when these kinds of orgasms are experienced or better put, one shouldn't put any force or control any part of the body and rather allow the energy to move through unless it is painful.

- All the benefits of multi-orgasms mentioned above
- Complete embodiment so we get to live and enjoy the full experience of being human rather than experiencing life by living in our head or our heart
- All the benefits of orgasms generally i.e. more oxytocin, more connection, more love, less stress, more confidence, etc
- Helps in creating balanced hormonal and energetic pathways that help to clear out various diseases in the body, which normal orgasms are not able to do
- Helps to feel more grounded so you are not impacted by the overwhelming situations of life so easily
- Helps in magnifying the inter-relationship between the various layers of the embodied experience (physical, energetic, emotional, mental, and spiritual).

Simultaneous Orgasms

Simultaneous orgasm refers to the state when both partners are experiencing orgasms at the same time. Most of the time you might have heard of simultaneous orgasm as climaxing together, but for me, and as you would probably expect by now, orgasm is much more than climax. So, simultaneous orgasm refers to when two partners are experiencing different states of orgasm within a shared space at a specific time, which can happen by individually stimulating oneself or each other.

Orgasm happens at so many levels, so in order to experience deeper states of simultaneous orgasm, a regular check-in with one one's own layered body experience and communicating these states with each other will allow both partners to stay present with each other. For instance, if one is feeling a lot of emotions coming up, while on the other hand their partner is feeling a lot of sexual energy, then there is a big mismatch. So, the person who is feeling emotions will need to convey those emotions, while the person who is feeling a lot of sexual energy will need to dilate the energy down so that both the partners can continue to stay connected throughout the course of love-making at as many levels as possible.

In order to experience deeper states of simultaneous orgasm, one can explore different parts of erogenous zones at the same time, but what is important to note is that you are not getting overwhelmed, and if you are, then that needs to be communicated, especially for men, to avoid climaxing too soon. We will be discussing different aspects of communication like consent, boundaries, safe words, and techniques like edging, tickling, and other nuances of love making in Part II of the book.

Transcendental Orgasms

Transcendental orgasms refers to those orgasms which are full of unique experiences which sometimes feel paranormal (such as out-of-body experiences), or a state where there is no existence of time and space, where spiritual awakening happens at a level which generally cannot be achieved by other means, and which results in great transformation of the self while also providing healing. Therefore, love-making can be considered to be one of the highest forms of a spiritual experience, though transcendental orgasms can be experienced without a partner too.

I have had experiences with transcendental orgasms both individually and with a partner. Each time the experience has been so unique, eye-opening, and transformative. One thing is for sure; to experience these transcendental orgasmic experiences, one really needs to go beyond the physical body and focus on expanding consciousness of the entire layered body as outlined in this book. By now you would know that sex, if focused on the physical aspect alone, will be boring, limited, and often repetitive.

One time I had an experience where, after love-making, my body, especially the heart and third eye chakras, continued vibrating for three days, and the whole experience felt so serene, calm, and deeply nourishing that it felt that I was no longer in my physical body. In another experience, it felt like I was engaging in love-making with nature (or should I say, nature was making love to my subtle bodies) and some of the impact of that could be felt in my physical body too.

Figure 196: Transcendental orgasms can often give the experience of shift of time and space or paranormal experiences. This can be experienced as a one-off experience or regularly by following certain practices that helps to lift the energy through various energy centres.

In transcendental orgasms, one's identity of self goes away and one feels connected to something bigger and it leads to a completely different level of consciousness, presence, and awareness. The whole experience can feel mystical, with experiences that can include seeing vibrancy in earth's colours, hearing sounds which can't be produced generally by humans, or feeling sensations in the body that have never been felt before. It is like a state of total bliss.

When experiencing these orgasms with a partner, transcendental orgasms will generally be experienced when energy from each chakra is interacting, supporting, and uplifting to the energy centre above it so that it creates a kind of a zig-zag loop between each other while also creating implosive orgasms inside each energy centre.

Painful Orgasms

Quite often, you will not hear this kind of orgasm being spoken about, but this is a type of orgasm that many people will experience at least once in their lives. For women, doctors have described the experience of painful intercourse and painful orgasm with terms such as dyspareunia and dysorgasmia. In my view, painful orgasms are far more than just occurring at the physical body level, however. Quite often, people are looking at the physical body to find a cure when the real issue is stagnant or blocked energies and unreleased trauma. Just like water cleanses and nourishes when in free flow, so do sexual energy and orgasm when in flow, but they can become uncomfortable and painful when stuck or blocked.

Figure 197-198: Painful orgasms can be very normal phenomena in some women and men. Instead of taking it personally, one should have a curious mind and work together to identify the root cause of what is making them feel that way.

When someone begins the Path of Amplified Orgasm, experiences of shaking, trembling, and headaches are normal as the energies are getting activated. When this happens, there is resistance being offered by the part of the body, which can be seen as shaking or trembling. There could also be a possibility that when energy is able to make its way through that part of the body but is unable to move further, it gets blocked in that section as a result, so any further activation of the energy in that area can result in a traumatic experience, pain, or discomfort.

Extreme care and precautions should be taken when working with energies as a result. As we have seen above in the case of polarity, we often end up quarrelling, even though the real issue that led to the quarrel might have been very trivial. This is because of opposing energies at play. In the same way, during sexual activity, if we have opposing energies at play, it can result in clash and discomfort.

Have you ever had an experience where you felt extremely aroused and ended up having sex with your partner, but the overall sex actually felt bad and yucky? So, while the feeling of arousal is due to polarised energy, at the same time, that bad and discomforting experience could also be due to polarised energy. That is why consciousness, presence, and awareness are very important for love-making, because the same polarising energies can also have opposing effects.

When I started my journey of orgasm, I would often notice that some of my practice partners would be moaning and crying in pain during their experience of orgasm, and I couldn't understand why. But, a few years later, when I began to join the dots, it all made sense.

I have worked with so many clients in bodywork who have had experiences of painful orgasms but, after our sessions, the nature of their orgasmic sounds changed and the orgasms began to be more pleasurable and, at times, healing.

Orgasm Is an Experience, Not a Goal

Orgasm is an experience to be fully sensed and felt from moment to moment.
It is not an achievement to be aimed for.
Michael Charming

My hope in writing this chapter is to expand your ideas and beliefs about orgasm. It is an experience that can be multi-dimensional, well beyond the physical realm, and far beyond the simple notion of "climax."

As I discussed in Chapter Two, your beliefs can be limiting or empowering, and your beliefs about orgasm are also this way. If you believe that orgasm and climax or ejaculation are the same thing, and if you believe that what you have known is all you can know, what you have experienced is all you can experience, then you will be limited by these ideas. However, if you are able to open your mind, and become curious about other forms of orgasm, then you will be amazed at the new kinds of orgasmic experiences that await you on the Path of Amplified Orgasm.

In addition to different kinds of orgasm, this chapter introduced the notion of polarity, and how using your own awareness of and ability to become intentional about polarity is a means to amplify the sexual experience to create resonance to take the orgasmic experience well beyond the physical realm. While I discussed the notion of sexual polarity here, I will explore other kinds of polarity in more detail in Part II.

Finally, as I end this chapter on orgasm, dear reader, I would like to remind you of what I believe to be one of the most important aspects of amplified orgasm. That is this: remember to feel each moment of each sexual experience, learn to focus on the sensation and the movement of energy in your body, let go of the destination, and embrace the journey. If you do these things, amplified orgasm will find its way to you.

Chapter Seven Summary:

- There is an orgasm gap, with heterosexual women experiencing fewer orgasms with their partners then straight men, bisexual women and men, and gay women and men.

- The magnetic pull of sexual attraction is due to polarity, or the notion that opposite types of energy attract. Sexual polarity, or the difference between masculine and feminine energy, is one important way to create and maintain strong sexual attraction, both before and during sexual encounters.

- It is important not to confuse masculine and feminine energy with men and women, strictly speaking. All humans are capable of embodying either/both types of energy at a given time. As we learn to become aware of masculine and feminine energy, we can better meet our partner with a healthy balance of both.

- Depolarisation is often the reason behind the death of sexual chemistry in many relationships. It can happen if a couple try to match each other's energetic state to avoid conflict, thus diminishing the role of polarity in constructing sexual attraction and dynamism.

- Masculine and feminine orgasms are different. Men and women are capable of experiencing either type of orgasm, for example, when men learn to become multi-orgasmic.

- The amplification of orgasm requires the creation of sexual polarity during the experience, in ways that are emergent in the moment and adaptive to each other.

- There are several models of the sexual response cycle and each offers us a chance to think through our own individual sexual experiences in new ways

- In order to experience amplified orgasm, we must open our mind to the idea that orgasm is much more expansive than we may have previously thought. In fact, both women and men are capable of a wide range of intensely satisfying orgasms.

- Energetic orgasms are available to those who choose to devote themselves to learning to tune into their energy centres and expand their awareness, presence, and mindfulness to include attention to the energetic realm

- Orgasm is an experience to be fully sensed and felt from moment to moment. It is not an achievement to be aimed for.

CONCLUSION: PRINCIPLES ON THE PATH OF AMPLIFIED ORGASM

We started this book using the metaphor of a hike through the woods and the layers of information found on a map. Let's return to that image in our minds now. As we travel the Path of Amplified Orgasm, we can use as our guide the map for each of the aspects of the layered body: emotional, mental, energetic, physical, and spiritual. As we take each of these individual maps, and lay them on top of each other, we realize that these layers of the embodied experience are also interactive. Taken as a whole, this map offers us our own unique Path of Amplified Orgasm.

Just like if we were to hike same trail many times, the experience of each hike will be different, provided we are conscious enough to observe the path travelled with complete presence. Similarly, due to different energies and bodies playing, every orgasmic experience is going to be different, though we may have the tendency to hook ourselves to a certain kind of experience due to our deep core preferences and sensitive spots.

Every sexual experience is part of the orgasmic experience, whether it aligns with our preferences or not, with our expectations or not, with our purpose or not. Each state is temporary, each moment is temporary, no matter how pleasurable and deeply satisfying it might be. Do note that if you are experiencing something that you don't want to experience, then it is because the underlying forces creating those experiences do exist within the physical and other realms of orgasmic world. You will have a choice to either move away from them or to go deeper into those experiences to find other revelations that lay underneath.

On this path sometimes you will move slowly, sometimes quickly, and sometimes you will need to pause, which can feel like forever. Sometimes you can proceed as if there is no tomorrow. So, observe and stay present as much as possible throughout the course of this journey and always check-in with yourself and your partner.

You have now been given different tools that can help you make your Path of Amplified Orgasm much easier, interesting, and transformational. Throughout the course of this path you will come across different sensitive spots and triggers that will play a part in creating different kinds of emotions and feelings. While sensitive spots and triggers will always change with old ones dying and new ones emerging, emotions and feelings will always remain with you throughout the course of this path and even afterwards. The more you proceed on this path, the more access you will have to heightened levels of intensity and range of emotions and feelings. It can feel like a roller coaster ride. It is both thrilling and a little bit scary! Our general tendency would be to hide our emotions and stay away from our feelings, which is exactly what you do not want to do if you are to enhance your experiences on this journey.

Our conditioned emotional responses and behaviour will change over time which will impact our various belief systems, sometimes changing them in a way and to such an extent that they feel shattered. Gradually all of this will pave the way for new belief systems to emerge that continue to support your growth, both as a sexual being and beyond.

Our bodies, which had remained numb for so long without us even being aware of it, will begin to open up and create experiences with many new sensations in our body. Feeling these at times will be full of surprises, thrill, and pleasure but at other times will also lead to confusion, shock, and discomfort.

As you will carry on this path you will begin to realise that orgasm is a whole body and mind experience. It will activate the brain to a level not felt before which will also have an influence on intellect, sharpness, decision making, and how you relate with life in general. New neural superhighways will result in the formation of new habits, and new beliefs which will start giving rise to some new form of identity. You will soon begin to realise that you had always been carrying five keys (consciousness, awareness, attention, intention, and presence) with you since your birth but now you will have a much better insight of how to make use of them for increasing the quality of not only your orgasm but the rest of your life as well.

Whilst on this path, you will come to know your energy centres better. The feeling and awakening of these different energy centres will bring you in direct connection with different sources of energy. The realisations of subtle body experiences as you embark on different trails of the path will help you realise that you are more than just this physical body, which will pave the way to a completely new world. Many times you will often leave the physical trail in front of you to experience these different trails of energetic fields. The combination of each of these will make you realise that every trail has several hundred mini trails within it, and no matter which trail you take, it will always be right in the moment. Every trail has its purpose. No particular trail you take is right or wrong in itself. The more aligned you will be, the more your consciousness will know which trail to take.

Even a tiny bit of reflection and exploration into this world might help to explain things that you may have experienced but not understood until now. You will begin to find out about your own home channel and all the other channels that exist. Moving to and fro between these channels might be slightly discomforting at first, but you will realise that this will deeply expand the range with which you operate in this world especially in dealing with your partner in relation to sex and intimacy. It's like crossing that hanging bridge which might feel scary at first, but once you are on it, it's full of fun and adventure. Surely, it will be scary as hell to cross that bridge, but once you have crossed over, you will say: "Wow, this was fun. Let's do it again!"

The familiarity and understanding of different erogenous zones will help you to know about your and your partner's physical body at a much deeper level. This will not only increase the level of pleasure your partner can experience but your curiosity and openness could even lead you to discover new zones that are a great source of arousal for you and your partner. When the other areas seem blocked or become No-Go areas, you can always come back to these zones to receive pleasure and experience orgasm which is an essential nutrient for our overall well-being.

Just like having good boots is important for a good hiking experience, so is having a healthier attitude with your own genitals. In the self-reflection hut you will find on this path, you will get to connect with your own shadow self and past trauma which will help you see why you have been doing and experiencing things in a certain way. There, through the help of a Certified Orgasm Coach and Bodyworker, you can sharpen the tools that could be used to learn to embrace the shadow self, realize it is a protector, and find healthy ways to allow it to have a voice in my life that are not destructive.

Throughout this path you will come across various check-in stations which will give you the opportunity to check in with your desires and fears. The Principles of Desire will help you gain clarity with your small, big, and core desires and will help you distinguish them from wants, compulsions, impulses, and greed. You will also get to name and face your fears and have the tools to work through with them so that you can feel more free and empowered to dive deeper into the realms of orgasm.

Becoming aware and adept and navigating sexual polarity will allow you to easily surf through the different orgasmic waves without depolarising or becoming short-circuited. Walking through these poles will give you the skills you need to operate from your masculinity and your femininity, adjusting to make the most of each moment during your sexual experiences.

In Part I of *Amplify Your Orgasm*, we have covered a great deal of ground! Hopefully you now have a strong grasp of the concept of the layered body and can begin to sense how a map of each of these layers can offer value to you on your own unique Path of Amplified Orgasm.

In Part II of this book, we will build on these basic principles, adding depth to these ideas with advanced practices and techniques, a much deeper look at relationship dynamics, and further exploration of the spiritual body in particular.

Since we have come so far together, I thought it might be helpful to provide you with a review of some of the key ideas we have covered in the book, which I call The Principles of Amplified Orgasm.

Principles on the Path of Amplified Orgasm:

1. The Path of Amplified Orgasm includes understanding and expanding our consciousness of each the layers of the body as well as how they interact. These layers include the emotional, mental, energetic, physical, and spiritual.

2. Amplified orgasm includes activation, synchronization, resonance, and amplification at all of the layers of the body, whether experienced alone or with a partner.

3. Orgasm should not be the goal of our sexual encounters. Rather, when we approach our partner with the intention of exploration and deep connection across multiple layers of the body, and we embody the principles of energetic polarity, amplified orgasm will follow.

4. Emotions and feelings need to be fully felt and expressed in order to move through them and establish the kind of deep intimacy required for amplified orgasm. Learning to express in the language of sensation greatly facilitates this process.

5. The physical body stores negative emotions, memories, traumas, and energies at the cellular level. In order to clear the flow of energy, one must release these blockages at all layers: emotional, mental, physical, energetic, and spiritual.

6. The mind is our gateway to perception, meaning, and identity. On the Path of Amplified Orgasm, we must identify those limiting beliefs that keep us from growing and expanding, and instead, choose empowering beliefs that help us unlock our limitless potential.

7. The seven energy centres and subtle bodies map how energy is constantly in motion, both inside and outside our physical bodies. Tuning in to this energy allows us to better understand our inner self, how we impact those around us, and how to forge deeper and more satisfying connections with our partners.

8. The physical body offers infinite ways to experience sexual pleasure that go well beyond the genitals. Learning to be ever curious will allow us to develop a deep, positive, and orgasmic relationship with both our own body as well as that of our partner.

9. Our true desires are trying to lead us to our life's purpose and as such they should not be repressed or denied because of fear. We need to learn to connect with our true desires and allow them to be our compass.

10. The Path of Amplified Orgasm is a journey of personal growth that takes time, dedication, and practice. It is sometimes painful and sometimes difficult. However, the benefits include the awakening of all of the layers of the body, deep intimacy, and experiencing the bliss of amplified orgasm.

PLEASURE, SENSUALITY, AND THE VOICE

Authored by Cordelia Zafiropulo

My approach and how I work with voice isn't about elocution, nor is it about received pronunciation or communication skills for that matter!

The most common way people understand the voice is as an aspect of the physical body. That is, voice is the creation of vibration by the vocal folds in the larynx. However, the voice is not simply an isolated entity, it is not simply the vibration of the vocal folds caused by exhalation, and it is certainly not merely in the throat. On the contrary, voice involves the whole being, going from the most subtle realms of thought and feeling deeply into the physical dimensions. Primarily voice is a sophisticated interplay between various body systems such as the respiratory system, the digestive system, the nervous system, and the endocrine system.

Two Aspects of Voice: Inner World and the Physical Realm

When working with voice, I generally discern between two main aspects. One being the psychological aspect of voice which is about our inner world, our thoughts, and feelings. It's that with which we're consciously identified; the content of our words, the ideas and beliefs we hold, the meanings we create, the experiences we have, our reasoning, and the language we use. In short, it is the psychological makeup of our identity as a whole.

The other aspect is the physical voice. This is composed of tonal qualities, such as pitch, pace, and range, as well as intonation and emphasis. It also includes breath, volume, and resonance and how relaxed or strained our voice can sound. This physical aspect communicates and shares emotions not by using words but by direct transmission. Through the combination of audio cues transmitted through the unique colour and use of our voice, information is directly imparted, bypassing the cognitive analytical function. This is extremely powerful and influences us on far deeper levels than we are aware.

These two aspects of voice mutually determine one another in many ways. Hence, working on the physical voice will inevitably bring up the psychological, and working on the psychological will clearly be audible in the physical. In other words, the voice is woven into the depths of the psyche, into the fabric of being, and it is utterly entwined with physicality. So much so, that there is a voice that lives in the body, which in some cases can be completely split off from who we think we are, that is, the perception of self.

Embarking on a journey with your voice is about reconnecting this body-mind split and integrating forgotten aspects. Essentially, it's about enabling an experience of the self within the body, while forging deeper connections between the physical, emotional, mental, and spiritual dimensions of ourselves. Most importantly for this book, the voice is also deeply connected to our capacity to embody sensuality, and as such, it relates deeply to sex and orgasm.

The Primal Voice and How Needs Determine Expression

The primal voice is a cry for help, a scream from fear, a moan from pleasure, or a squeal of glee that escapes in the moment without engaging the cognitive centres of the reasoning brain. In other words, a primal voice is uttered before we have a chance to think, analyse, and consider the pros and cons of vocalisation.

On this most primal level our voice is about getting our needs met, expressing what we want, and rejecting what we don't like. Getting in touch with it is a way to tap into core needs and desires that may be hidden from our conscious awareness.

Being utterly infused with emotion is a property of the primal voice. So much so that instinctive reflexes kick in that enable the swift movement of energy through the whole body causing expression as a result. Emotion and the movement of energy through the body are deeply connected to instant vocalisation. Unfortunately, however, our emotional expression as well as the wholesome nourishment of our needs rarely mature together. More often than not, one or the other is shut down prematurely, leaving us disconnected from our feelings or draining the emotive colour from our voice.

A voice devoid of emotive essence is like a dried up riverbed, with a trickle of water hardly reminiscent of a bubbling brook that can suddenly turn into a gushing torrent. Our physical needs and desires are the water that fills this riverbed. They are the emotive essence of embodied expression, connected to the primal quality of sound and the powerful sense of selfhood.

Pleasure and Voice

How and Why the Physical Voice is Connected to Sensuality

The tongue, lips, teeth as well as our jaw and palate are involved both in vocalisation and in nourishing the body. And, the mouth with its taste-buds, lips, and tongue is not only associated with nourishing ourselves, but also with arousal and pleasure. Taking this into consideration, these organs have multiple functions and, as such, offer a chance to see the interplay between the physical realm of voice and the energetic, emotional, and spiritual realms of the sensual.

Used to kiss, organs of the mouth become organs of sensuality and passion which demonstrate affection and open our body to receive and give pleasure. Used to speak, they become the means to communicate, make ourselves understood, express our emotions, or on a more primal level (as previously mentioned to get our needs met), to signal threat or cry for help. Used to take nourishment, the mouth and throat become the gateway of that which enters our body for both sustenance on the physical level (nutrition) as well as the emotional and energetic level through the visceral pleasures of eating, taste, and libation.

When working with the voice, the sensual function of these organs should not be dismissed. By bringing awareness to these organs through the felt sense and what I call sensory enunciation, the voice becomes saturated with a deep, luscious, sensual quality that has the capacity to nourish us from the inside. Feeling the gentle enunciation fully and softening into it will change the tone of your voice while fostering deeper connections to your sense of self.

Sensuality cannot be forced or conjured up on demand. Similarly, the voice needs to be approached with care, cajoled, and tended like a flower which opens at its own pace when the environment is right. That said, working with voice can offer tremendous benefits in re-patterning the nervous system towards pleasure.

Through my singing practice I began to cultivate deeply listening to my body and surrendering to the rhythm and flow of my breath while mentally focusing on the phrase of music I was about to sing. Instead of controlling my breath I began to align with my body's organic ability to know and adjust to the preceding phrase of music as needed for its accomplishment. This enabled me to touch places inside of myself that had long been forgotten, places that had been shut down. As those places were touched, I felt my sensuality awaken through the release of energy coming back into gentle vibration and resonance. Gradually this practice enabled me to weld deeper and deeper connections with my body, while fine tuning my perception and awareness of myself and my needs.

The Soothing Quality of the Voice

We are hardwired to be soothed by certain frequencies.[96]
Deb Dana

Working with sound can be a gentle means to reconnect to the body and sense of self. Being soothed by sound is a primal instinct which calms the nervous system. Vocalising is not just something parents can do for young children, we too can vocalise to send signals of safety to our own bodies thereby soothing our own nervous systems.

When we vocalise we do so by extending exhales. These extended exhales downregulate the nervous system by sending gentle vibrations through the tenth cranial nerve. This nerve, also known as the vagus nerve, travels through the heart, lungs, and digestive tract. It is the longest nerve in the body. The Recurrent Laryngeal Nerve, an important branch of the vagus nerve for the voice, supplies all the intrinsic muscles of the larynx and innervates the muscles that open the vocal cords. In short, these nerves are directly impacted by the sounds we make. The focus on prolonged, smooth, and sustained exhales, provides a continuous flow of subtle vibrations that travel like ripples through the body, gently touching organs and body parts such as the pharynx, larynx, heart, lungs, and diaphragm —connecting right down to the pelvic bowl.

Not only does vocalisation calm and downregulate the nervous system, it also has the capacity to gently invigorate and enliven a nervous system that is in a state of shut down. Often after an hour or two of working with voice, people will remark leaving with a sense of refreshment, feeling at ease and energised. This is because making sounds activates the sympathetic nervous system without going into a mode of defense. It connects the social engagement system to the sympathetic nervous system in a form of play. This is where the voice is so unique in its ability to calm, soothe, and simultaneously invigorate where necessary.

Pleasurable Sounds and Sounds to Invoke Pleasure

If you've ever sung extensively, you will probably have experienced how expression can be fulfilling in and of itself, even a form of experienced self-actualisation, so to speak. This is because it is a powerful way of touching ourselves and others. And, that touch happens through the direct transmission of sound.

Shortly after moving to London, it so happened that I was involved in a production of the Vagina Monologues. Being the voice coach within this production, I was faced with the task of coaching the women performing the monologues on how to produce sounds imitating real orgasm. I introduced what I called orgasmic sound exercises during the rehearsals to give the women the space and permission to invoke feelings of pleasure through sound and expression. The results were amazing; not only did the women immediately make sounds of pleasure, but more importantly, they connected to feelings of pleasure from where the sounds arose. By emitting and receiving sounds of pleasure, women were sharing and teaching one another how and where physical pleasure was experienced in their bodies. A space of mutual encouragement and acceptance opened, where experiencing each other's differences (in the ability to feel pleasure) was seen and heard. The exercises connected sexual expression to the voice, enabling sensuality to be expressed without being sexualised, forming a gateway into pleasure while increasing the capacity to feel it and give it expression.

I'm sure you can imagine how such exercises demand a capacity for intimacy and overcoming inhibitions. Most people cringe at merely hearing the sound of their spoken voice let alone sounds infused with the intensity of sensual and emotional colouring. This shows the intimate, personal, and revealing nature of our voices, the reason why working with voice is so profound and liberating, and why it can be used to access places within us we barely know.

The Metaphysics of Voice

How Sound Waves Penetrate Matter

Nada is a Sanskrit word that means sound; Brahma is a Hindu word meaning God. The term Nada Brahma, therefore, means that Sound is God. Quantum physics tells us that everything is energy, everything is vibration. Sound produced by the voice has properties that we know from simple physics: it is an energy wave with a particular amplitude and wavelength, it penetrates matter (whether in liquid, solid, or gaseous form) as vibration, and it is directional, carrying energy from one place to another. Sound is a vibration that affects every aspect of the human being. It affects matter as well as the less dense aspects of the human including the mental, emotional, and spiritual layers of the body and human energy fields.

Consider for a moment how sound needs a material substance in order to travel; this implies that it is highly interactive. The denser and harder that matter is, the faster sound waves will travel through it. Through air, sound waves travel at a speed of approximately 340 meters per second. Traveling through denser water however, they cover 1500 m/s, more than four times as fast! Sound waves cannot travel through a vacuum; the inherent nature of sound is contact, and without molecules that touch each other, sound cannot travel.

Because sound waves travel through matter, they have a penetrating quality. Naturally, we're all familiar with the invasive quality of an unwelcome noise. This is because sound penetrates us physically, quite literally. Conversely, through voicework we can experience the power and pleasure of making sound that penetrates the environment. Doing this, we direct energy through sound on a physical level through our bodies and impact other bodies and matter itself. Transmitting and receiving sound happens within our own body simultaneously! The sounds we make transmit both out of our body in longitudinal waves and also go through our bodies and penetrate our being. Through this we come to experience ourselves in a new way, holistically, through vibrational frequency, from the inside out.

When working with voice, many people remark upon the profound experience of truly hearing the resonance of their voices for the very first time. Often there is a sense of amazement accompanied by trepidation and awe. This comes from comprehending the power that lies within them and within their own voice. And, as the mystical words Nada Brahma proclaim, "Sound is God." Expressing the true nature of vocal potential freely is an immensely empowering experience promoting a solid sense of confidence and the deep recognition of the self.

An experience I had which demonstrated the impact that sound can have happened with a Sufi boyfriend. It so happened that my boyfriend's Sufi order were visiting Turkey during our stay in Istanbul. They had come from Italy to visit their affiliate Sufi order for a Dhikr which is a significant Sufi ritual to achieve oneness with the Divine. I was fortunate enough to be able to attend the Dhikr and since Sufism is the mystical branch of Islam, I was separated from the men and seated upstairs on a balcony with the women. I peered down at the men through a decorative screen that hid us from their view. There were about 400 men seated below in circles. Slowly they began chanting prayers and swaying to the rhythm of a small drum to keep the beat.

Gradually the deep resonant voices of the men began to take over, increasing in volume until they engulfed the entire mosque, washing over us like waves and waves of sound. We women remained silent and immersed in the sound rising from below. The whole mosque reverberated with the deep resonance of those many masculine voices which combined to create mighty soundwaves that caused an unknown membrane around us to pop, releasing energy through us like concentric rings extending outward after a pebble is dropped into a pond. There was expansion on every level of my being. It was a metaphysical experience caused by the sheer power of sound travelling through material substance, through all of us at once. I do not know whether the others experienced this in the same way, but my guess is they might have, for the purpose of this ritual was to make intentional use of the power of sound that has a penetrating quality of piercing through matter.

How the Voice Can Impact the Endocrine and Nervous Systems

The endocrine system regulates a variety of hormones in the physical body which are deeply tied to the body's homeostasis (or balance) as well as our emotional bodies. Hormones deeply affect the tone of voice.

The thyroid gland (a butterfly-shaped gland that is situated between the larynx and the top of the sternum) plays an important role in our overall health. It is one of many glands that function as part of the endocrine system, producing and releasing hormones into our bloodstream. Research has shown that malfunctions in the thyroid can have a wide ranging effect on voice.[97]

Whether you are slightly irritated or impatient, bored, anxious, relaxed, or happy is expressed in the tone of voice sending subtle signals to the environment that can be heard by an exquisitely attuned ear. Whether you are aware of it or not, your voice reveals your emotional state. In fact, scientists have mapped at least 24 emotions regularly communicated through brief vocalizations and tone of voice.[98]

It is important, however, to understand that the relationship between the voice and the endocrine system also goes the other way. That is, voice and sound affect our hormonal system. For example, one study showed that the sound of a mother's voice triggers in her infant the production of the feel-good hormone oxytocin.[99]

The voice can also reveal physical and mental health, so much so that science has begun to pre-diagnose illness before it is physically manifest, simply by analysing tone of voice.[100] In fact, one company called Beyond Verbal uses bio-markers from vocal analyses to predict illness.[101]

Through my years of training, I can say that I have developed the ability to hear where tension is held in a body by listening to a voice. I'm also able to infer much about a person's ability to feel, their breath, how embodied the voice is, and how they move energy, all from listening to their tone of voice.

Voice in Mystical traditions and Ritual

It's common knowledge that hormones affect the voice. What's less commonly known is that the voice can change the chemistry in our body, alter our hormones, and induce spiritual states.

Consider for a moment how voice has been used for eons all over the world in various cultures and traditions from singing national anthems in order to create a sense of identity and belonging, to the rhythmic chants of football fans cheering for their teams. Then there's the use of voice in tribal rites of passage, religious or ritualistic ceremonies such as the powerful deep chants of Tibetan monks, the ceremonial dance or challenge in Maori culture named a Haka, and the devotional prayers of a Sufi Dhikr. All these traditions have understood the power of using the voice in ways that are, unfortunately, unknown to logically-biased westerners.

One of the most interesting ways to look at the power of the voice to engage our energetic bodies is through various traditional ceremonial practises that use voice to create energetic fields that transcend the individual, create a sense of belonging, and transmit experiential knowledge from one generation to the next. In these collective fields the voice is used to move energy through the body and pass through spiritual portals into different states.

Inducing these altered states of consciousness is no coincidence and they do not happen by chance. In order to induce altered states of consciousness, what is required first is the purposeful intention to consecrate a dedicated space. Secondly, the presence of three core principles that predictably induce trance, alter states of consciousness (chemistry of the body), and initiate the rising of life-force energy, is required. These three principles are: connecting to the body and the breath, the repetition of intoxicating rhythms, and the use of the voice in chanting.

Some of these traditional mystical collective ceremonies transmit to participants knowledge of how to move and transmute life-force energy as it rises from the base of the spine. Tantric as well as medical traditions depict the rising of life-force energy as a serpent. This same movement occurs during sexual activity and can result in orgasm. What's probably less well known is that the same movement of life-force energy is connected to and can be activated through the voice. Similar to the rising serpent, the voice rises through the chakras becoming more refined and distilled in the process. Put in a more familiar way, this is the raising of the kundalini through the activation of the throat chakra.

Whether we use voice collectively or as individuals, it can connect us to something much larger and more transcendental than ourselves. As such, it provides a vital bridge between the material world of the physical to the transcendent metaphysical. It connects us to our shared humanity that is simple, humble and true, and to our Divinity that is magnificent, infinite and eternal.

Why Voice is Connected to Orgasm

The human ability to create sound through the entire body has the mind-blowing capacity to send and transmute energy from the most subtle layers to the most dense, while healing us on multiple levels. It restores the connection to our Divinity, re-integrates and melts aspects that are numbed, and penetrates and transforms matter, in and through our physical being and beyond. When vocal expression is wholesome and connected to the entire body, it is fulfilling in and of itself, and deeply affects our ability to feel orgasmic.

By allowing more soul-essence and sensuality to flow through the body, endless resources of energy are untapped. Such vocal expression confers a massive sense of power when it is in alignment with all energy bodies and the soul. The soul then resonates through all aspects of the being and we become well-tuned instruments.

As we have seen throughout this book, orgasm is so much more than just the mere pleasure or sensation attached to the physical body. In the same way, voice too is more than we believe it to be. It holds the keys to:

- reclaim shut down energy that was not allowed to be expressed
- access subtle fields and dimensions
- learn to purify and move energy as well as experience energetic orgasm.

Dr. Peter Levine, one of today's most renowned specialists in the field of trauma, and founder of Somatic Experiencing, has begun to make use of the voice to enable healing from trauma. To my knowledge there have been no scientific studies proving the affects voice work can have on the chemistry of our brain and neuro-plasticity, although the positive effects of singing have certainly been documented. It is my belief, however, that such studies will soon be conducted and reveal staggering results. Results that many people already know to be true through their own lived experience.

About Cordelia Zafiropulo

Cordelia's passion for healing and metaphysics developed through her studies and training to become an opera singer in Vienna. After more than twenty years of experience working with voice and expression, she started her own business You & Your Voice. Currently she is developing an online course that is a fusion between the ancient techniques of Belcanto (the art of beautiful singing) and the applied knowledge from Dr. Stepehen Poerge's Polyvagal theory. Her aspiration is to impart ancient knowledge to enable vocal potential, heal from trauma* and access states of bliss and pleasure.

Contact details:
https://www.youandyourvoice.com
Voicepowertraining@gmail.com
https://www.linkedin.com/in/cordelia-zafiropulo-53a21a83
https://www.facebook.com/Youandyourvoice/

*A note on trauma-informed voice work:
Since trauma is often deeply embedded in our sexuality and the way life force energy moves through us, it is also a topic that inevitably emerges during voice work. Please refer to the website *youandyourvoice.com* to read more about trauma informed voice work and how voice can be a tool for healing.

WORKS CITED

1. Ekman P. Emotions revealed. *BMJ*. 2004;328(Suppl S5):0405184. doi:10.1136/sbmj.0405184

2. Smith FD, Scott JD. Signaling complexes: junctions on the intracellular information super highway. *Curr Biol*. 2002;12(1):R32-R40.

3. Kendall PC, Hollon SD. Cognitive-Behavioral Interventions: Theory, Research, and Procedures. *Academic Press*; 2013.

4. Krach S. The rewarding nature of social interactions. *Frontiers in Behavioral Neuroscience*. 2010. doi:10.3389/fnbeh.2010.00022

5. Trezza V, Campolongo P, Louk J M. Evaluating the rewarding nature of social interactions in laboratory animals. *Developmental Cognitive Neuroscience*. 2011;1(4):444-458. doi:10.1016/j.dcn.2011.05.007

6. Fone KCF, Porkess MV. Behavioural and neurochemical effects of post-weaning social isolation in rodents-relevance to developmental neuropsychiatric disorders. *Neurosci Biobehav Rev*. 2008;32(6):1087-1102.

7. Pan Y, Liu Y, Young KA, Zhang Z, Wang Z. Post-weaning social isolation alters anxiety-related behavior and neurochemical gene expression in the brain of male prairie voles. *Neurosci Lett*. 2009;454(1):67-71.

8. Hart S. The brain of motor systems and emotions: the diencephalon and the limbic system. *Brain, Attachment, Personality*. 2018:123-140. doi:10.4324/9780429472541-7

9. Hamilton T. The Pineal Gland. *Res Medica*. 2014;6(4). doi:10.2218/resmedica.v6i4.863

10. Welker HA, Semm P, Willig RP, Commentz JC, Wiltschko W, Vollrath L. Effects of an artificial magnetic field on serotonin N-acetyltransferase activity and melatonin content of the rat pineal gland. *Exp Brain Res*. 1983;50(2-3):426-432.

11. Wilson BW, Wright CW, Morris JE, et al. Evidence for an effect of ELF electromagnetic fields on human pineal gland function. *J Pineal Res*. 1990;9(4):259-269.

12. Wise NJ, Frangos E, Komisaruk BR. Activation of sensory cortex by imagined genital stimulation: an fMRI analysis. *Socioaffect Neurosci Psychol*. 2016;6:31481.

13. The Mind-Blowing Science of Orgasms Explains Why We Get Performance Anxiety. Mic. https://www.mic.com/articles/126822/what-happens-to-your-brain-during-orgasm. Accessed August 25, 2019.

14. Komisaruk BR, Whipple B, Crawford A, Liu W-C, Kalnin A, Mosier K. Brain activation during vaginocervical self-stimulation and orgasm in women with complete spinal cord injury: fMRI evidence of mediation by the vagus nerves. *Brain Res.* 2004;1024(1-2):77-88.

15. Fried I. Human Lateral Temporal Cortical Single Neuron Activity during Language, Recent Memory, and Learning. *Single Neuron Studies of the Human Brain.* 2014:247-272. doi:10.7551/mitpress/9780262027205.003.0014

16. Silva GA. Neuroscience and artificial intelligence can help improve each other. Phys.org. https://phys.org/news/2019-07-neuroscience-artificial-intelligence.html. Published July 9, 2019. Accessed August 25, 2019.

17. Hebb DO. *The Organization of Behavior: A Neuropsychological Theory.* Psychology Press; 2005.

18. Doidge N. *The Brain That Changes Itself: Stories of Personal Triumph from the Frontiers of Brain Science.* Penguin Books; 2007.

19. Pace S. Acquiring Tastes through Online Activity: Neuroplasticity and the Flow Experiences of Web Users. *M/C Journal.* 2014;17(1). http://journal.media-culture.org.au/index.php/mcjournal/article/view/773. Accessed August 16, 2019.

20. WHO | Mental health: a state of well-being. August 2014. https://www.who.int/features/factfiles/mental_health/en/. Accessed August 16, 2019.

21. 7 Mental Health Benefits Of Orgasms That Will Rock Your Socks. Romper. https://www.romper.com/p/7-mental-health-benefits-of-orgasms-as-if-you-need-excuse-7952157. Accessed August 16, 2019.

22. Lakoff G, Johnson M. *Philosophy in the Flesh: The Embodied Mind and Its Challenge to Western Thought.* Basic Books (AZ); 1999.

23. Goffman E. *The Presentation of Self in Everyday Life.* Penguin Books, Limited (UK); 1990.

24. Freud S, Richards A. *The Standard Edition of the Complete Psychological Works of Sigmund Freud.*; 1953.

25. Kluger J. Why You're Pretty Much Unconscious Most of the Time. Time. https://time.com/3937351/consciousness-unconsciousness-brain/. Accessed August 24, 2019.

26. Morsella E, Godwin CA, Jantz TK, Krieger SC, Gazzaley A. Homing in on consciousness in the nervous system: An action-based synthesis. *Behav Brain Sci.* 2016;39:e168.

27. Dyer WW. *The Power of Intention: Learning to Co-Create Your World Your Way: Easyread Large Bold Edition.* ReadHowYouWant.com; 2009.

28. Judith A. *Wheels of Life: A User's Guide to the Chakra System.* Llewellyn Worldwide; 2012.

29. Judith A. *Eastern Body, Western Mind: Psychology and the Chakra System As a Path to the Self.* Celestial Arts; 2011.

30. Mercier P. *The Chakra Bible: The Definitive Guide to Working with Chakras.* Sterling Publishing Company; 2007.

31. Brennan BA. *Hands of Light: A Guide to Healing Through the Human Energy Field.* Bantam; 2011.

32. Oliver G, Detmar M. The rediscovery of the lymphatic system: old and new insights into the development and biological function of the lymphatic vasculature. *Genes Dev.* 2002;16(7):773-783.

33. Krüger THC, Haake P, Chereath D, et al. Specificity of the neuroendocrine response to orgasm during sexual arousal in men. *J Endocrinol.* 2003;177(1):57-64.

34. Van Kirk K. *The Married Sex Solution: A Realistic Guide to Saving Your Sex Life.* Dr. Kat Van Kirk PhD, MFT; 2013.

35. Kiernan J, Rajakumar R. *Barr's The Human Nervous System: An Anatomical Viewpoint.* Lippincott Williams & Wilkins; 2013.

36. George MS, Ward HE Jr, Ninan PT, et al. A pilot study of vagus nerve stimulation (VNS) for treatment-resistant anxiety disorders. *Brain Stimul.* 2008;1(2):112-121.

37. O'Keane V, Dinan TG, Scott L, Corcoran C. Changes in Hypothalamic-Pituitary-Adrenal Axis Measures After Vagus Nerve Stimulation Therapy in Chronic Depression. *Biological Psychiatry.* 2005;58(12):963-968. doi:10.1016/j.biopsych.2005.04.049

38. Mauskop A. Vagus nerve stimulation relieves chronic refractory migraine and cluster headaches. *Cephalalgia.* 2005;25(2):82-86.

39. Sackeim H. Vagus Nerve Stimulation (VNSTM) for Treatment-Resistant Depression Efficacy, Side Effects, and Predictors of Outcome. *Neuropsychopharmacology.* 2001;25(5):713-728. doi:10.1016/s0893-133x(01)00271-8

40. Carabotti M, Scirocco A, Maselli MA, Severi C. The gut-brain axis: interactions between enteric microbiota, central and enteric nervous systems. *Ann Gastroenterol Hepatol* . 2015;28(2):203-209.

41. Yoo BB, Mazmanian SK. The Enteric Network: Interactions between the Immune and Nervous Systems of the Gut. *Immunity.* 2017;46(6):910-926.

42. Mungovan K, Ratcliffe EM. Influence of the Microbiota on the Development and Function of the "Second Brain" – The Enteric Nervous System. *The Gut-Brain Axis.* 2016:403-421. doi:10.1016/b978-0-12-802304-4.00019-0

43. Auteri M, Zizzo MG, Serio R. GABA and GABA receptors in the gastrointestinal tract: from motility to inflammation. *Pharmacol Res.* 2015;93:11-21.

44. Neuroscientists show how brain responds to sensual caress. ScienceDaily. https://www.sciencedaily.com/releases/2012/06/120604155709.htm. Accessed August 16, 2019.

45. Science X staff. The neuroscience of erogenous zones. Medical Xpress. https://medicalxpress.com/news/2013-09-neuroscience-erogenous-zones.html. Published September 11, 2013. Accessed August 16, 2019.

46. Chia M. *Healing Love through the Tao: Cultivating Female Sexual Energy.* Simon and Schuster; 2005.

47. Lousada M, Mazanti L. *Real Sex: Why Everything You Learnt About Sex Is Wrong.* Hay House, Inc; 2017.

48. Rothemund Y, Qi H-X, Collins CE, Kaas JH. The genitals and gluteal skin are represented lateral to the foot in anterior parietal somatosensory cortex of macaques. *Somatosensory & Motor Research.* 2002;19(4):302-315. doi:10.1080/0899022021000037773

49. Chia M, Wei WU. *Sexual Reflexology: Activating the Taoist Points of Love.* Simon and Schuster; 2003.

50. Michaels M. *Partners In Passion: A Guide to Great Sex, Emotional Intimacy and Long-Term Love.* Simon and Schuster; 2014.

51. Science X staff. Touch and movement neurons shape the brain's internal image of the body. Medical Xpress. https://medicalxpress.com/news/2013-08-movement-neurons-brain-internal-image.html. Published August 26, 2013. Accessed August 16, 2019.

52. Foldes P, Buisson O. The clitoral complex: a dynamic sonographic study. *J Sex Med.* 2009;6(5):1223-1231.

53. Weeraratne M. *Emotional Detox Through Bodywork: A Woman's Guide to Healing and Awakening.* Authorhouse UK; 2016.

54. Hegarty PK. Male circumcision decreases penile sensitivity as measured in a large cohort. *BJU International.* 2013;111(5):695-696. doi:10.1111/j.1464-410x.2013.11794.x

55. Reiter E, Hennuy B, Bruyninx M, et al. Effects of pituitary hormones on the prostate. *The Prostate.* 1999;38(2):159-165. doi:3.0.co;2-5">10.1002/(sici)1097-0045(19990201)38:2<159::aid-pros10>3.0.co;2-5

56. Litwin MS, Lubeck DP, Spitalny GM, Henning JM, Carroll PR. Mental health in men treated for early stage prostate carcinoma: a posttreatment, longitudinal quality of life analysis from the Cancer of the Prostate Strategic Urologic Research Endeavor. *Cancer.* 2002;95(1):54-60.

57. Davidson J. The Multi-Orgasmic Couple: Sexual Secrets Every Couple Should Know. By Mantak Chia, Maneewan Chia, Douglas Abrams, and Rachel Carlton Abrams. New York: HarperCollins, 2000. xvi 204 pp., illustrations, notes, resources. Hardback, ISBN 0-06-251613-2, $24.00. *Journal of Sex Education and Therapy.* 2001;26(4):370-371. doi:10.1080/01614576.2001.11074451

58. Mantak Chia And. *Taoist Secrets of Love: Cultivating Male Sexual Energy.* Aurora Press, Inc.; 2016.

59. Jr. HGP, Pope HG Jr, Olivardia R, Borowiecki JJ III, Cohane GH. The Growing Commercial Value of the Male Body: A Longitudinal Survey of Advertising in Women's Magazines. *Psychotherapy and Psychosomatics.* 2001;70(4):189-192. doi:10.1159/000056252

60. Blond A. Impacts of exposure to images of ideal bodies on male body dissatisfaction: a review. *Body Image.* 2008;5(3):244-250.

61. Glasser M, Kolvin I, Campbell D, Glasser A, Leitch I, Farrelly S. Cycle of child sexual abuse: links between being a victim and becoming a perpetrator. *Br J Psychiatry.* 2001;179:482-494; discussion 495-497.

62. Gómez AM. Testing the Cycle of Violence Hypothesis: Child Abuse and Adolescent Dating Violence as Predictors of Intimate Partner Violence in Young Adulthood. *Youth & Society.* 2011;43(1):171-192. doi:10.1177/0044118x09358313

63. Thomas TA, Fremouw W. Moderating variables of the sexual "victim to offender cycle" in males. *Aggression and Violent Behavior.* 2009;14(5):382-387. doi:10.1016/j.avb.2009.06.006

64. Ullman SE, Najdowski CJ, Filipas HH. Child sexual abuse, post-traumatic stress disorder, and substance use: predictors of revictimization in adult sexual assault survivors. *J Child Sex Abus*. 2009;18(4):367-385.

65. Maslow AH. A theory of human motivation. *Psychological Review*. 1943;50(4):370-396. doi:10.1037/h0054346

66. Hill, Napoleon. Think and grow rich; how to sell your way through life. Cleveland: The Ralston Society, 1946. 381; 371 p. $2.00 each. *Science Education*. 1946;30(5):321-322. doi:10.1002/sce.3730300572

67. Steimer T. The biology of fear- and anxiety-related behaviors. *Dialogues Clin Neurosci*. 2002;4(3):231.

68. Michael T, Blechert J, Vriends N, Margraf J, Wilhelm FH. Fear conditioning in panic disorder: Enhanced resistance to extinction. *Journal of Abnormal Psychology*. 2007;116(3):612-617. doi:10.1037/0021-843x.116.3.612

69. Boissy A, Fisher AD, Bouix J, Hinch GN, Le Neindre P. Genetics of fear in ruminant livestock. *Livestock Production Science*. 2005;93(1):23-32. doi:10.1016/j.livprodsci.2004.11.003

70. Ishwar P. Neurochemical basis of fear. *Frontiers in Cellular Neuroscience*. 2016;10. doi:10.3389/conf.fncel.2016.36.00001

71. Morris JS, Ohman A, Dolan RJ. A subcortical pathway to the right amygdala mediating "unseen" fear. *Proc Natl Acad Sci U S A*. 1999;96(4):1680-1685.

72. Davis M. Neural systems involved in fear and anxiety measured with fear-potentiated startle. *Am Psychol*. 2006;61(8):741-756.

73. BBC News. Ancestral fear "causes brain changes." BBC News. https://www.bbc.com/news/av/science-environment-25182162/rat-study-shows-ancestral-fear-causes-brain-changes. Published December 2, 2013. Accessed August 23, 2019.

74. Understanding the Dynamics of a Fear Response. Verywell Mind. https://www.verywellmind.com/the-psychology-of-fear-2671696. Accessed August 23, 2019.

75. Volynets S, Glerean E, Hietanen JK, Hari R, Nummenmaa L. Bodily maps of emotions are culturally universal. *Emotion*. July 2019. doi:10.1037/emo0000624

76. Sunderwirth S, Milkman H, Jenks N. Neurochemistry and sexual addiction. *Sexual Addiction & Compulsivity*. 1996;3(1):22-32. doi:10.1080/10720169608400097

77. The Orgasm Gap: Simple Truth & Sexual Solutions. Psychology Today. https://www.psychologytoday.com/blog/stress-and-sex/201510/the-orgasm-gap-simple-truth-sexual-solutions. Accessed August 24, 2019.

78. Hite S. *The Hite Report: A Nationwide Study of Female Sexuality.* Seven Stories Press; 2004.

79. Parkinson HJ. Do lesbians have better sex than straight women? the Guardian. http://www.theguardian.com/lifeandstyle/2018/jul/09/do-lesbians-have-better-sex-than-straight-women. Published July 9, 2018. Accessed August 24, 2019.

80. Frederick DA, John HKS, Garcia JR, Lloyd EA. Differences in Orgasm Frequency Among Gay, Lesbian, Bisexual, and Heterosexual Men and Women in a U.S. National Sample. *Arch Sex Behav.* 2018;47(1):273-288.

81. Muehlenhard CL, Shippee SK. Men's and Women's Reports of Pretending Orgasm. *Journal of Sex Research.* 2010;47(6):552-567. doi:10.1080/00224490903171794

82. Cosmo Survey: Straight Single Women Have the Fewest Orgasms. Cosmopolitan. https://www.cosmopolitan.com/sex-love/news/a37812/cosmo-orgasm-survey/. Published March 16, 2015. Accessed August 24, 2019.

83. Montañez A. Visualizing Sex as a Spectrum. Scientific American Blog Network. https://blogs.scientificamerican.com/sa-visual/visualizing-sex-as-a-spectrum/. Accessed August 16, 2019.

84. Masters WH. *Human Sexual Response.* Springhouse Corporation; 1966.

85. Levin RJ. Critically revisiting aspects of the human sexual response cycle of Masters and Johnson: correcting errors and suggesting modifications. *Sexual and Relationship Therapy.* 2008;23(4):393-399. doi:10.1080/14681990802488816

86. Kaplan HS. *Disorders of Sexual Desire and Other New Concepts and Techniques in Sex Therapy.* Brunner/Mazel Publisher; 1979.

87. Whipple B B-MK. Management of female sexual dysfunction. In: Sipski ML ACJ, ed. *Sexual Function in People with Disability and Chronic Illness. A Health Professional's Guide.* Gaithersburg, MD: Aspen Publishers, Inc.; 1997:509-534.

88. Basson R. The Female Sexual Response: A Different Model. *Journal of Sex & Marital Therapy.* 2000;26(1):51-65. doi:10.1080/009262300278641

89. Bancroft J, Graham CA, Janssen E, Sanders SA. The dual control model: current status and future directions. *J Sex Res.* 2009;46(2-3):121-142.

90. Perelman MA. The Sexual Tipping Point®: A Mind/Body Model for Sexual Medicine. *The Journal of Sexual Medicine.* 2009;6(3):629-632. doi:10.1111/j.1743-6109.2008.01177.x

91. Metz ME, McCarthy BW. *Enduring Desire: Your Guide to Lifelong Intimacy.*; 2015.

92. Komisaruk BR, Wise N, Frangos E, Liu W-C, Allen K, Brody S. Women's clitoris, vagina, and cervix mapped on the sensory cortex: fMRI evidence. *J Sex Med.* 2011;8(10):2822-2830.

93. Lochte BC, Guillory SA, Richard CAH, Kelley WM. An fMRI investigation of the neural correlates underlying the autonomous sensory meridian response (ASMR). *Bioimpacts.* 2018;8(4):295-304.

94. Poerio GL, Blakey E, Hostler TJ, Veltri T. More than a feeling: Autonomous sensory meridian response (ASMR) is characterized by reliable changes in affect and physiology. *PLoS One.* 2018;13(6):e0196645.

95. Barratt EL, Davis NJ. Autonomous Sensory Meridian Response (ASMR): a flow-like mental state. *PeerJ.* 2015;3:e851.

96. Dana DA, Porges SW. *The Polyvagal Theory in Therapy: Engaging the Rhythm of Regulation.* W. W. Norton; 2018.

97. Junuzović-Žunić L, Ibrahimagić A, Altumbabić S. Voice Characteristics in Patients with Thyroid Disorders. *Eurasian J Med.* 2019;51(2):101-105.

98. Cowen AS, Elfenbein HA, Laukka P, Keltner D. Mapping 24 emotions conveyed by brief human vocalization. *Am Psychol.* December 2018. doi:10.1037/amp0000399

99. Seltzer LJ, Ziegler TE, Pollak SD. Social vocalizations can release oxytocin in humans. *Proc Biol Sci.* 2010;277(1694):2661-2666.

100. Robbins R. The Sound of Your Voice May Diagnose Disease. Scientific American. https://www.scientificamerican.com/article/the-sound-of-your-voice-may-diagnose-disease/. Accessed September 7, 2019.

101. http://beyondverbal.com/. Accessed September 18, 2019.

Conscious Dreams
PUBLISHING

Be the author of your own destiny

Find out about our authors, events, services
and how you too can get your book journey started.

f Conscious Dreams Publishing

🐦 @DreamsConscious

📷 @consciousdreamspublishing

in Daniella Blechner

www www.consciousdreamspublishing.com

✉ info@consciousdreamspublishing.com

Let's connect

Lightning Source UK Ltd.
Milton Keynes UK
UKHW051859181119
353787UK00005B/45/P